Remastering Morals with Aristotle and Confucius

Aristotle and Confucius are pivotal figures in world history; nevertheless, Western and Eastern cultures have in modern times largely abandoned the insights of these masters. *Remastering Morals with Aristotle and Confucius* is the first book-length scholarly comparison of the ethics of Aristotle and Confucius. May Sim's comparisons of the ethics of Aristotle and Confucius offer fresh interpretations of the central teachings of both men. More than a catalog of similarities and differences, her study brings two great traditions into dialogue so that each is able to learn from the other. This is essential reading for anyone interested in virtue-oriented ethics.

May Sim is associate professor of philosophy at The College of the Holy Cross. She is contributing editor of *The Crossroads of Norm and Nature: Essays on Aristotle's* Ethics *and* Metaphysics and *From Puzzles to Principles? Essays on Aristotle's Dialectic.* She has also contributed to *International Philosophical Quarterly, Journal of Chinese Philosophy, History of Philosophy Quarterly,* and *Dao: A Journal of Comparative Philosophy.*

Remastering Morals with Aristotle and Confucius

MAY SIM

The College of the Holy Cross

CAMBRIDGE
UNIVERSITY PRESS

CAMBRIDGE UNIVERSITY PRESS
Cambridge, New York, Melbourne, Madrid, Cape Town, Singapore, São Paulo

Cambridge University Press
32 Avenue of the Americas, New York, NY 10013-2473, USA

www.cambridge.org
Information on this title: www.cambridge.org/9780521870931

First published 2007

Printed in the United States of America

A catalog record for this publication is available from the British Library.

Library of Congress Cataloging in Publication Data

Sim, May, 1962–
Remastering morals with Aristotle and Confucius / May Sim.
p. cm.
Includes bibliographical references and index.
ISBN-13: 978-0-521-87093-1 (hardback)
ISBN-10: 0-521-87093-3 (hardback)
1. Ethics, Ancient.   2. Aristotle.   3. Confucius.   I. Title.
BJ101.S56   2007
170.92′2–dc22   2006025890

ISBN 978-0-521-87093-1 hardback

For
Aris Ezra Sim Chieun Liang DeMarco
and
Ambrose Yosha Sim Chieun Siang DeMarco

Contents

Acknowledgments

This book would not have been possible were it not for the generosity and encouragement from so many colleagues and friends over the past eight years. The research for several chapters in this book was conducted during a semester-long sabbatical from Oklahoma State University in 1999. For that sabbatical, I am grateful. I am indebted to Professor Tu Weiming for the enlightening conversations on the *Zhongyong* and for the use of the Harvard–Yenching Library during my sabbatical. My gratitude also goes to Professor Kurt Pritzl for enabling me to use the Mullen Library at The Catholic University of America when I was in Maryland during that same sabbatical. Thanks are due to the College of Arts and Sciences at Oklahoma State University for an Arts & Sciences Summer Research Grant in 2003 that supported my research on "A Confucian Approach to Human Rights," *History of Philosophy Quarterly* 21(4) (October 2004): 337–56. I retain this view of human rights in Chapter 6. For Chapter 6 I am heavily indebted to the National Endowment for the Humanities for a Summer Stipend Award in 2004. For a Research and Publication Grant from The College of the Holy Cross that supported the preparation of my index, I am deeply grateful.

My gratitude goes to the participants of the Society for Asian and Comparative Philosophy and the International Institute for Field Being for their helpful comments and encouragement when I presented the materials from many of these chapters before them.

David Jones, Robin Wang, Ronnie Littlejohn, and Lik Kuen Tong are friends from these societies who inspired me to develop a number of chapters into their present shape. For their inspiration and encouragement, I am most thankful.

A number of the chapters have been published in journals and anthologies, and I am grateful to their editors for permission to reprint them with slight modifications. "Aristotle in the Reconstruction of Confucian Ethics" and "The Moral Self in Confucius and Aristotle" were published in the *International Philosophical Quarterly* 41 (2001) and 43 (2003), respectively. "Ritual and Realism in Early Chinese Science," *Journal of Chinese Philosophy* 29(4) (December 2002): 501–23; "Harmony and the Mean in the *Nicomachean Ethics* and the *Zhongyong*," *Dao: A Journal of Comparative Philosophy* 3(2) (2004): 253–80; "Categories and Commensurability in Confucius and Aristotle: A Response to MacIntyre" in *Categories: Historical and Systematic Essays*, ed. M. Gorman and J. Sanford (Washington, DC: Catholic University of America Press, 2004), 58–77; and "Virtue-Oriented Politics: Confucius and Aristotle," in *Aristotle's Politics Today*, ed. Lenn E. Goodman and Robert Talisse (Albany: State University of New York Press, 2007), are publications for which I am indebted to the editors and anonymous reviewers for helpful comments during their preparation.

In spite of the fact that the topics in this volume are extremely fascinating, making work on them a pleasure, I very much appreciated the beachfront condo in Ocean City that my parents-in-law, Charles and Doris DeMarco, so generously offered during my sabbatical. By the same token, I am grateful to The College of the Holy Cross for welcoming my move to campus in the early summer of 2004.

As in my past projects, my husband, C. Wesley DeMarco, has been most supportive in this one and has played a key role in shaping my thoughts on many of these chapters. He may not always succeed in persuading me on certain issues, but our conversations always lead me to a better position. I am deeply indebted to Wes for his tempering effect on this whole project. Professors Alasdair C. MacIntyre and Roger T. Ames have also been extremely influential and inspiring in my attempts to compare Aristotle and Confucius. Both of them read many of these chapters while they were still drafts, and

I have benefited tremendously from my discussions with them. I know that I have grown since the first time I read Confucius' *Analects* eight years ago because he no longer reads like Aristotle. Similarly, Aristotle also speaks quite differently after my seven years of dialoguing with Confucius. I am truly grateful to Wes, Alasdair, and Roger for helping me find the voices of these two masters.

Abbreviations

APo	Aristotle, *Posterior Analytics*
Cat.	Aristotle, *Categories*
CC	Tu Weiming, *Centrality and Commonality*
DA	Aristotle, *De Anima*
DM	Confucius, *The Doctrine of the Mean*
FF	Roger Ames and David Hall, *Focusing the Familiar*
Met.	Aristotle, *Metaphysics*
NE	Aristotle, *Nicomachean Ethics*
Pol.	Aristotle, *Politics*
RR&R	Mary I. Bockover (ed.), *Rules, Rituals and Responsibility*
TFFS	Roger Ames, "The Focus-Field Self in Classical Confucianism"
TTC	David Hall and Roger Ames, *Thinking through Confucius*
Zy	Confucius, *Zhongyong*

Introduction

Melodrama is difficult to avoid when discussing the impact of Aristotle upon Western thought and practice and Confucius upon Asian thought and practice. Chinese culture is the single stem from which most East Asian cultures branch, and Master Kong is a taproot of these branches. Western cultures owe much to the Greek and Latin civilizations that styled Aristotle as the "master of those who know." Each thinker's prescription for life has influenced his traditions for millennia. Even in their rejection of the ancient masters, modern movements in both cultures have been shaped by their rejection, right down to their interpretation of the sciences and society. When I speak of "remastering" in this connection, I mean both to recommend that moral study return to a focus on these masters and that we try to recapture their sense that morality is above all a craft with demands and rewards of the utmost consequence for human life. Moral mastery is what both these estimable masters exact. Without it, we wander in the childhood of morality despite all our clever theories.

My project is a close comparison of the ethics of Aristotle and Confucius, with attention to their views of the cosmos, the self, and human relationships. Dialogue between Asian and European cultures is so important, and Aristotle and Confucius are so pivotal to these cultures, that I hope this study will not be the last. It does, however, seem to be the first monograph-length study of these two figures. An inventory of similarities and differences would hardly suffice. My aim is to involve these authors in each other's problems and to engage both in reconsidering the contemporary difficulties to which they speak with surprising frequency in one voice, or at least in genuine harmony. For instance, both men recognize the central place of virtues, enjoin us to get our practical bearings by modeling the behavior of exemplary individuals (rather than learning to apply rules), and emphasize social roles and pragmatic contexts. However, the situation is not simple: just where it seems the two might be most easily compatible, small divergences make for an unexpected rift; just where they seem most alien, some unforeseen subtlety makes for a surprising reconciliation.

The field of this study is stretched between problems of ethics and problems of "first philosophy" (i.e., the thoughtful consideration of our most basic presuppositions and beliefs about the most basic realities). I compare the central ethical concepts of the two figures and ask to what extent these concepts and their associated practices are bound by their respective cultures. I examine each author's most primitive assumptions about human beings and our natural and social environments and wonder to what extent each author's ethics requires or would be aided by a theoretical "first philosophy." The conclusion that emerges is that these two towering figures can help each other, reaching out to each other across the miles and to us across the centuries.

The questions I raise about culture are important because both Aristotle and Confucius admit that ethical practice and thought about ethical practice are context sensitive – so much so that critics have charged that their ethics are relevant only to a limited set of circumstances and offer no general prescriptions for life. I shall contest this. It is crucial to gain clarity about cultural context because of the titanic difficulties of translation and comparison this sort of study must face. My claim is that evaluative comparison is difficult but not impossible, and I aim to bring Aristotle and Confucius head-to-head, where the strengths and weaknesses of their ethics are revealed and each can suggest remedies for the other's deficiencies. In particular, I shall make the case that while Aristotle's ethics makes social training central and leaves room for cultural variation within the perimeters of shared natural function, Aristotelians can learn much from Confucians about the nature and ethical pertinence of ceremony and decorum. In other words, Confucian aestheticism provides resources for Aristotelian theoreticism. Reciprocally, Confucian traditions can learn from Aristotle a form of first philosophy that grounds talk of our common humanity without neglecting cultural or individual differences and roots ethics in a practical rationality that does not claim mathematical exactness or exceptionless legislation. Aristotelian metaphysics provides resources for Confucian parochialism.

The questions about first philosophy are important in part because prominent Aristotelian thinkers (e.g., Alasdair MacIntyre in his *After Virtue*) have argued that a teleological metaphysics is not a prerequisite to Aristotelian ethics. Confucian commentators such as Roger Ames and the late David Hall judge that first philosophy is tantamount to "foundationalism" and is wed to a view of "transcendence" that is avoided by Confucianism, to its credit. To many thinkers, metaphysics is the bane of Western thinking, is best avoided in ethical theory, and is not only unnecessary but quite possibly destructive of a humane ethical life that is tolerant and situated. I shall argue, to the contrary, that it is the dependence of Aristotle's ethics on his first philosophy that underwrites its claim to cross-cultural relevance and shall suggest that certain features of Aristotle's view of human nature (in relation to nature generally) provide needed supplements to Confucian ways.

In the end – I say it now in full cognizance that the point will really make sense only after a number of detailed analyses – it turns out that though Aristotle refers to practices and manners and what we might think of as "aesthetic" dimensions in the pursuit of a fine (*kalon*) life, he says too little about them and what he says is far from useful. Confucius can help here. On the other hand, Confucius leans so hard on proprieties and decorum that his own appeals to something beyond authoritative manners (e.g., as his appeals to nature or to the mandate of heaven) are thin and inexplicable. Here, Aristotle can help. But again, we shall find the situation far more complex and interesting. Moreover, Aristotle takes human relations far more seriously in his ethics and politics than he does in his teaching about the soul and first principles of being. Confucius can help here with perceptive reminders about the centrality of human relationships. My argument will be, finally, not merely that each man's teaching has assets that make good the liabilities of the other man's teaching but that each already has an opening in his teaching by which the other might enter. Neither tradition will remain untransformed by this encounter – not in its ethics and not in its metaphysics.

It is true that within a broader historical purview, one can find Aristotelians who make more of the latent aesthetic dimension and matters of style and mode of comportment. There are also people who emphasize the imagination more than Aristotle the Stagirite did and who develop the connection between rehearsal for agency and theatrical preparation or between modern forms of identity and novels. One can find thinkers (e.g., Dewey, particularly in his later, Aristotle-inspired phase of growth) who press process and relationship more than Aristotle did in his theoretical, if not his ethical, works. If that is true, why should we not remain within the many departments of the Occident? Why go to an alien tradition – Chinese Confucianism – to make such points? Similarly, one can find later Confucians (e.g., Song neo-Confucianism, culminating in Zhu Xi) who bring out a latent but by no means elaborated metaphysical element in Master Kong. Why then turn to Aristotle to provide a metaphysical supplement, even supposing one is needed or useful?

The first and overriding reason is the one noted at the outset: it is simply interesting and important to compare two key figures from alien traditions, even if similar corrections and supplements were available in their own histories. Second, talk of similarity is notoriously vague. It is not the case that the same points about relationship and context will be pressed if we look to Dewey rather than to Confucius to help Aristotle. It is not true that the same points about aesthetic sense will be made if we direct Aristotle to modern Hegel- or Nietzsche-inspired thought. Nor will the same points about first philosophy appear if we direct Confucius forward to Zhu Xi rather than sideways (as it were) to Aristotle. Third, my juxtaposition provides useful test cases for the respective schools of thought. Think of it – so much thought and practice in the West and the Middle East have grown up under the tutelage of Aristotle that it is difficult to find a culture that might put to the test Aristotle's claim to a sort of universality. Chinese culture is sufficiently different and sufficiently removed to provide an attractive test case to see if Aristotle's ethics could be received, understood, and evaluated. Confucius repeatedly invoked the Zhou *li* as embodying the ways and means of cultivating a humane life with others, a guide that was far superior to the available alternatives. Two and a half millennia hence (if not before), these observances are no longer live options. How then might we guide our selection and enshrinement of authoritative observances? This is not something Confucians left to individual choice. It is not a matter of personal preference among transient patterns but a matter of the stabilization and standardization of ethical norms, norms that are precious and fragile treasures neither easily found nor readily retrieved. Aristotelian reflections on forms of ethical and political life can help to test and amend the Confucian reliance on *li*.

I focus on a couple of primary texts at the roots of these two traditions for several reasons. A focus on early primary texts is useful first because these are foundation documents that demand and deserve attention. They require, it must be said at once, quite delicate handling. It is easy to exploit vagaries and ambiguities, caving in to anachronism (at best) or ideological imperialism (at worst). Too often, the people who approach such a project with an open and curious mind lack adequate expertise, while the best-prepared specialists have their own projects to promote. Despite these temptations, the foundation documents are useful, frankly, just because of these uncertainties; that is, such texts contain elements in key teachings that are unspecified or underdetermined and that their later traditions specify. Those tantalizing moments of unstipulated inexactitude in the foundation documents make the project of comparison riskier but possible and, possibly, more fruitful.

Not everyone believes that such comparisons are feasible, given the distances – historical and cultural, linguistic and conceptual – separating Aristotle and Confucius. Concepts such as *li* (authoritative observances that are to guide the choreography of behavior), *shu* (reciprocation), *yi* (appropriateness), *xiao* (filial piety), *zhing* (deferential respect), *zhong* (the personal integrity and reliability that imply fidelity and loyalty to appropriate others), and *dao* (way) in Confucius do not have straightforward counterparts in Aristotle. By the same token, *dikaiosunê* (justice), *megalopsycheia* (magnanimity), *energeia* (being as enactment), and *entelecheia* (immanent finality as an attractor for process and development) are central notions in Aristotle that do not have counterparts in Confucius. Study must take great pains to try to achieve a negotiated response. Sometimes direct translation is possible and sometimes it is not. Where no translation is possible, this is itself a result significant for finding snares for intercultural communication and evaluative comparison.

This is a pivotal problem – perhaps *the* problem – for comparative studies. I provide no special treatment of translation problems here, in the conviction that because actuality implies possibility, the best way to argue for the possibility of fruitful comparison across cultural, linguistic, and conceptual divides is simply to accomplish it. However, I do try to suggest how the categories and concepts most pivotal for each thinker might be appropriated and assessed by the other.

For example, even the perfunctory reader of Aristotle and Confucius may notice that both thinkers stress personal qualities of moral excellence or "virtues" as opposed to geometrically pure duties or juridical "rights" in their ethical thought. But this may be a superficial and even possibly deceptive similarity. Readers socialized into Greco-Latin habits of thought will find it entirely natural to take *ren* or *yi* to be "virtues" and therefore to be candidates for a slot on Aristotle's list of *aretai*, understood as excellences of character. However, there is no term that corresponds to "virtue" in the Chinese original, no covering generic under which these particular qualities might be subsumed as types.

Part of this, but only part, is a problem with the translation of basic terms between Confucius' Chinese and Aristotle's Greek. It is good to appreciate that there is not even one adequate translation that will meet the strictest standards of translation. Recognition of this point cultivates carefulness and humility. On the one hand, paraphrase and supplement will often suffice to provide a rendering that will not count as a translation in the strict sense. On the other hand, once we adopt standards on which there is at least one rendering, there will be indefinitely many renderings that are no less adequate. In short, there is more than one way to translate Confucian sources in a target idiom (Aristotelian, Hegelian, Deweyan, or what have you), given enough compensating calibrations, even though none will prove *uniquely* faithful or *fully* adequate. Whether we find too many or too few adequate translations will depend on our standards of translational faithfulness – and they are no more fixed than the aims of translation. This simple point expresses a complex situation in a nutshell. Too often, philosophers defend either the thesis that there is not even one adequate translation of an idiom (e.g., Confucian) in an alien idiom (e.g., Aristotelian) or the thesis that there are many, perhaps indefinitely many, translations of the first in the second. But each is a partial truth that becomes fixated into what looks like an independent "position" only if we ignore the dependence of the claim on standards and norms that are variable in the nature of the case. There is a kernel of truth in both incommensurability and indeterminacy theses. Both points need to be held in view throughout. So there is cause to say both that there is no adequate translation of Confucian sources in an Aristotelian idiom (according to the strictest standards of faithfulness) and that (given suitable adjustments and marginally less unbending standards) there is at least one.

Of course, friends of incommensurability, such as MacIntyre, do not lean on problems of term–term translation alone. Two traditions are incommensurable when each has its own norms of interpretation, accepted patterns of explanation and justification, and standards of rationality. In the most radical situations, there are no shared standards and measures, and none that are – according to MacIntyre and others – neutral between them that might serve as an independent court of appeal. When dealing with rival claims, each tends to image the other in its own terms and according to its own norms. In such a situation, each side easily convinces itself of its superiority and ultimately fails to achieve a genuine understanding of the other.

For instance, a Confucian may notice that an act of giving fails to conform to *li* (authoritative observances or normative patterns of conduct). Perhaps the giver neglected to use both hands and bow in the act; omitting that element of the *li* would prevent the act from being truly generous and the agent from being *ren* (where *ren* is the highest Confucian virtue, sometimes translated as benevolence or humaneness). Such an omission would be necessarily "invisible" to the Aristotelian, according to MacIntyre. The Aristotelian, who lacks even the words to translate *li*, must fail to see the moral shortcoming, MacIntyre thinks. By the same token, an Aristotelian may notice that an act fails to conform to the proper function of the *psychê* for a citizen of a *polis*, where both *psychê* and *polis* are understood in very specific teleological ways. This shortcoming will be "invisible" to the Confucian because he lacks the pertinent concepts – the Confucian even lacks the words for *psychê* and *polis*, after all.

I shall argue that while Aristotle might well have been baffled by
the Confucian demand that one must use both hands and bow in
order for the giving of a gift to have moral worth, he would nevertheless recognize both the ethical importance of manners and the
fact that manners may vary. That granted, there is no bar in principle
to mutual understanding on this point. For instance, Aristotle knows
that a giver who flings a gift at his recipient with a sneer is not acting
generously and not exhibiting virtue, no matter what universal rule
his act embodies. Similarly, Confucius appeals to no entity that we
call the "self" (in several meanings of that term), much less a metaphysical *psychê*, and he neither knows nor invokes any political
arrangement sufficiently like the Greek *polis*. Nonetheless, Confucius
undeniably shares with Aristotle an appreciation of the importance of
what we call social and political institutions for the shaping of moral
thought and practice. He also appreciates that there is something in
us that is harmed by wrongdoing, a locus of relation and action (if not
of independence and preference) that is shaped by one's social
environment and in turn either upholds or undermines it. Hence
there are some grounds for dialogue about the moral self, even if
only some of the features Aristotle ascribes to the *psychê* are part of
the Confucian's conceptual lexicon.

Similarly, Confucius has no explicit list of categories corresponding to or even rivaling Aristotle's infamous inventory. But
I shall argue that Aristotle's categories have functional analogues
in Confucian thought. A close reading of the text will bring out these
functional analogues that I shall use to underwrite the claim that
Aristotle and Confucius share a basic set of categories.[1] To show how

---

[1] In line with my earlier remarks about translation, this is not to be taken as the claim
that Aristotle's categories are explicit in Confucius or as the claim that they are
there fully formed but implicitly, or even as the claim that Aristotle's categories
uniquely express Confucian intent. Rather, I shall show that Confucius recognizes
and appeals to distinctions between action and passion, quantity and quality,
situation and outfit, and even between people (as organic wholes) and their
relationships, and shall argue that these distinctions are central to his moral
teaching. Each of these items is comparable to its more explicit Aristotelian
counterpart in several specifiable respects. Although not identical in every way,
these Confucian "categories" are close enough kin (the "substance" category will
require special handling instructions) to underwrite the comparison and ground
dialogue.

these thinkers share a fundamental set of categories is also to show that there are grounds for a limited sort of commensurability and hence for the possibility of dialogue. Without these more generic categorial grounds of speech and thought, such dialogue would be impossible. That is because their principles, their standards of thought, and the weights and measures of their judgment differ in important ways. But without their sharing at least tacitly some basic categories, it would not be possible even to speak of such differences intelligently.

MacIntyre for some years has expressed reservations about the possibility of cross-cultural comparisons of the sort I wish to take up. A great tradition, according to him, is unable to understand another tradition in that other's own terms because each tradition's practices and concepts are organically intertwined, having grown up together in a shared history. Lacking a shared history ipso facto implies the impossibility of deep communication or shared understanding. Because concepts are creatures of context, there are no context- or history-neutral concepts and standards and no impartial perspective outside of all traditions from which one could assess one's portrait of the other or evaluate the other's rival claims. However, it is possible, according to MacIntyre – if difficult and rare – to learn a second tradition from the inside, acquiring a kind of "second first language" that allows one to begin to learn the history and to master the conceptual scheme of each. It is the lack of shared history that blocks understanding; this history can of course develop, and a person who learns both traditions from the inside in this way can act as a bridge person to help that shared history come to be.

In the MacIntyrean diagnosis and remedy, the unit of analysis is the tradition (as opposed to the text, the concept, the proposition, or what have you). A bridge person is better situated to assess the merits of each tradition as a whole. This assessment focuses on how and how far each is able to recognize its own limitations, how and how far each provides the resources for overcoming these limitations, and indeed how and how far each tradition lays itself open to possible correctives from other, quite alien traditions of thought and practice. In this study, I aspire to act as a bridge person in something like this mode. MacIntyre is surely an influence, and my argument as a whole exhibits something very like this pattern. However, while I accept his diagnosis of the problem, my sense of the remedy owes more to the *Topics* of Aristotle.

The means of comparison adopted in this book is grounded in my understanding of Aristotle's conversational dialectic. This "topical" approach to comparison is detailed in my *From Puzzles to Principles? Essays on Aristotle's Dialectic* (Lanham, MD: Lexington Books, 1999) and summarized in Chapter 2 of this volume. To be sure, aspects of conceptual and linguistic divergence are discussed in almost every chapter of this book. Nevertheless, I aim to focus resolutely upon points of interpretation and comparison, leaving methodological and metaphilosophical considerations for another venue.

Closely related to problems of term translation are issues about definition – the functions of definition, how sharp definitions must be to serve those functions, and whether definitions can be true or false. I tackle these issues in Chapter 3. Contemporary Confucian commentators too often suppose that Confucius is entirely unconcerned with definitions. I argue to the contrary that it is not a prejudice merely of Western thinking to suppose that learning and knowledge want definition and a due measure of objectivity. The Confucian practice of rightly ordering names (*zhengming*) can profitably be understood as a quest for true definitions – with caveats about essentialism – in the sense that the "right" name, like an Aristotelian definition, aligns language with nonhuman nature as well as with other human beings and human practices. Confucian names are neither rigid designators of individuals nor expressions of immutable essence, but they are also not mere tools of practice or linguistic convention. The notion of a "rectification of names" has its classical locus in the ancient emperors' calendar reforms; in such reforms, there are, to be sure, political and pragmatic elements, but also an endeavor to track the movement of the heavens and so align heaven and earth. The Confucian "rectification" of ethical names is like this. Not a matter of pure theory, it is not pure pragmatism or a matter of tidying mere conventions either. In some interesting ways, Confucius' attempts to define virtues in his discussions with others and in his criticisms of their understanding are quite like Aristotle's procedure of definition in the *Nicomachean Ethics* and the *Topics*, even while they are not really like Aristotle's stricter procedures of scientific definition in the *Prior Analytics*. Definitions are important to both Aristotle and Confucius because having good definitions of virtues and vices improves one's ability to identify and correct one's weaknesses and develop the pertinent qualities.

Still, Confucius gets almost all the content of his moral notions out of the *li* and therefore is limited both in his ability to justify his ordering of names and in his ability to criticize or rectify the *li*. Aristotle has more room for appeal and better grounds for criticizing existing institutions and practices because of his more developed metaphysics of nature. In Chatper 1, I argue for the very idea of using Aristotle in the service of a Western appreciation of Confucius. Here I introduce several issues discussed in more detail in other chapters and pave the way for the suggestion that something like Aristotle's teleological metaphysics can help sort out tensions internal to Confucian thought, such as the tension between leaning on the Zhou *li* while appealing to the mandate of heaven, between the goodness of human nature and the need for training and cultivation, and the unity of thought and action.

Both men teach that virtue is a cultivated disposition to choose a qualitative "mean" in action. It is crucial to see that there is a real agreement here even though there are important differences in what a "virtue" is (a difference that proves to be incidental) and what a "mean" is (a difference that proves to be significant). Chapter 4 is devoted to sorting out issues about harmony and the mean. I argue that the functional analogue of Aristotle's *meson* is Confucius' *he* (harmony), not *zhong* (the term most often translated as "mean"). Here is a case where Master Kong seems more "metaphysical" than the Stagirite. His "mean" is a natural equilibrium that grounds and pre-exists the tendency toward balance in things. This tendency toward balance and its antecedent equilibrium is exhibited in and referenced by harmonious human relationships and relation-enhancing actions. Moreover, while Aristotle plainly believes that human moral teleology is an instance of nature's ruling pattern, he does not believe that human moral action affects the fate of the cosmos at large. Confucius does seem to believe that ethical agency not only embodies the mandate of heaven but holds it up like a pillar. Somehow, moral agency not only reflects the nonhuman order but affects it. I discuss the assets and liabilities of both views.

Chapter 5 bears down on issues about the nature of the self and its best life. Part of the task of Chapter 5 is to elaborate the senses – outlined in Chapter 2 – in which one can speak of a "human being" in the sense of an organic whole with an integrity and being of its own. Aristotelian substances (I have in mind here "sublunary" substances such as animals and plants) are not insular or autonomous or final.[2] But Confucius seems to describe people in ways we would call more relational and processive. Because a process exhausts itself in its coming to be, a process cannot be a locus of responsibility or an origin of action over time. Similarly, a nexus of relations cannot act or even terminate relations. That is why interpreters (such as Fingarette) who claim that the Confucian "self" does not require or even permit the ascription of what we call "personal responsibility" or "choice" even if in error, are at least consistent. I argue with equal consistency, but I think with greater faithfulness to the text, that Confucius does require of people a kind of choice about filling their roles well or poorly and a definite sort of responsibility for being morally ample (*da ren*) rather than petty (*xiao ren*). For that reason, we must admit that Confucian teaching implies a self that is in a limited sense a "substance."

Neither Confucius nor Aristotle believes that knowledge of definitions and rules suffices for practical moral guidance. Both men appeal to paradigmatic persons or exemplary agents as living models whom agents should imitate both for character development and for guidance in particular situations. Chapter 5 elaborates some of my earlier claims about the centrality of exemplary agents and tries to indicate some of the implications for Confucian metaphysics of the roles and features Confucius ascribes to these exemplary individuals. Once again, an examination of the unstated metaphysical

---

[2] Aristotle uses criteria such as finality, independence, endurance, and so on to pick out an entity (*ousia*, standardly and misleadingly translated as "substance") from among other phenomena. However, these criteria fully apply only to his *nous*-god. Plants and animals and the like in the sublunary world are not, according to Aristotle, fully final or self-sufficient, entirely self-centering or self-involved. Although criteria such as self-sufficiency and finality do mark the trajectory of Aristotle's line of thought, his application of them shows precisely that he does not take human beings to be fully independent or to be essentially "autonomous" individuals in the modern sense of this term.

implications of Confucian ethics helps both to point up its strengths and weaknesses and to make openings for dialogue with Aristotle.

Because ethics for both authors centers on character and its qualities and relations, getting clear about the self that is formed in character will help clarify the nature of ethics in each case. I argue that Aristotle's insistently individualistic metaphysics cannot account for the thick relations required by his own ethics of character and politics of virtue. The Confucian self, on the other hand, is so relationalistic that it is difficult to see how it could function as a source of agency or locus of responsibility as Confucian ethics demands. Furthermore, Confucian agency is so embedded in ritual that there seems to be no more solid source of moral norms that might help assess existing proprieties and manners.

A comparison regarding the nature of persons – their capacities and qualities and their relationships – will need to avoid both the presumption that the agent is ultimately an insular individual and the presumption that the agent is a nexus of relationships and processes with no interiority or integrity of its own. This discussion is fraught with conceptual pitfalls – perhaps more than any other topic in the book. It is nonetheless pivotal for several reasons. When Aristotle asks about human well-being, he quickly turns to questions about human *being*. The focus and source of this being is the *psychê* – even more precisely the rational "part" of the *psychê* that marks what is distinctive to humankind. The well-functioning of this part of ourselves is the best thing in us and most to be prized, Aristotle argues. Although it is formally identical in every member of the species and thus what underwrites our talk of shared human nature and common basic virtues (and, according to later Aristotelians, the moral equality of persons), an actual *psychê* is always this-*psychê* and hence individual. This individual principle of individuality is the core of each whole living human being (body and "soul," with rational and irrational aspects).

Aristotle sustains this focus on the individual even when he tries to give an account of human relationships in justice and friendship. On the one hand, Aristotle constantly keeps in view the point that moral virtue and practical wisdom are good for human relations and communities at the same time that they are good for individuals. There is no tension for Aristotle, as there is for so many contemporary ethicians, between the good of individuals and that of communities: a set of basic moral excellences defines the moral health of both. That is good. On the other hand, it is sometimes difficult to see how Aristotle's soul doctrine and his metaphysics of substance can fully accommodate this ethical insight. The problem becomes even more acute when we broaden the issue to include that supramoral intellectual virtue of *theôria*; that is, the meditative enjoyment of achieved knowledge of the first principles and causes of being. It is difficult to see how one's enjoyment of knowledge of ultimate things morally benefits others or even involves real relationships with them.

In spite of Confucius' insight into the essentially relational fabric of ethical life, he also is in a bind. On the one hand, his view of filial piety puts priority on reverence to parents and siblings regardless of their vices, and that demonstrably dents society.[3] So the very loyalties that had been taken to enrich society may, we think, wound it. Moreover, if one becomes genuinely and sincerely humane by extending familial care to all others, this would seem to come at the expense of thinning out the emotional and behavioral energies that one can direct to one's own family. It seems then that Confucius could benefit from a more developed account of the human person who is the bearer of roles, the source of the choice to fill roles well or poorly, and the locus of the responsibility to do so well. I shall also argue that he needs a better account of what is common to persons to underwrite his striking claim that all people have (or should have – I discuss this extensively) the opportunity to pursue the way of virtue. He also needs a better account of the good of persons that would not require us to lean so much on a fabric of interrelated roles and norms that we cannot adequately criticize. A metaphysical account that yokes principles of human nature with principles of nature generally helps us to understand that there is an objective basis for the human good above and beyond custom or ritual. Confucius, I shall argue, had gestured toward such a basis in several texts; Aristotle can help make it useful and intelligible.

---

[3] That is, we believe today that what appears to us to be Confucius' recommendation of a blind obedience and loyalty to abusive parents or tyrannical rulers impairs the recipients of such blind loyalty no less than its performers.

Part of this discussion refers to Chapter 4, on harmony and the mean, a doctrine that is commonly disdained – even derided – by modern rule-obsessed ethicians in the West. The more practical ramifications are discussed in Chapters 6 and Chapter 7, on politics and friendship. In Chapter 6, I explain how the family is sufficient for the habituation of virtue for Confucius, whereas Aristotle requires not only a good family but also a decent political regime. Although Confucius has been accused by critics of being incredibly parochial, I show that there are definite ways in which Confucius makes the mean or harmonious action more accessible to more people than does Aristotle, for whom only a select few can attain the moral and intellectual excellence at the essence of well-being. On the other hand, there are ways in which the Confucian mean is even more elusive than Aristotle's because while the way is open to all, no one ever seems fully to achieve it. While Aristotle insists on more and more definite preconditions for virtue, the Aristotelian life of the mean would have been available to barely a quarter of the Athenian population who were citizens and actually achieved by only a few individuals. This complex issue about moral opportunities and achievement is made more complex – and richer – when we consider moral relationships with nonhuman beings. I argue that for Confucius the development of the self requires harmonizing not only with other human beings but also with nonhuman animals and other living and nonliving things in the natural environment. This would extend Aristotle's view of the things that fall within a human being's power and responsibility considerably. Confucian "virtue ethics" (the term is not entirely applicable) is hence a resource for Western virtue ethicians with respect to questions about good relations with nature in the large, without a doubt urgent questions of today.

Aristotle's insistence that there are political preconditions for virtue invites a closer look at the place of politics and moral education in both thinkers. I noted earlier that nothing in Confucius answers directly and without qualification to Aristotle's *polis*. Moreover, neither thinker has a conception that might be translated directly and unproblematically by the modern notion of "state" or "civil society." These absences do not argue for the irrelevance of Aristotle and Confucius to each other or to contemporary troubles. Both thinkers make broad enough claims that they can be understood to address recognizable features of social life and the large-scale institutional management of that life. Moreover, both thinkers speak with one voice – and against members of their own milieus – in taking moral education to be the prime point of political life and the inculcation of moral virtue the main task of leaders. In this they also stand united against all modern forms of liberal individualism where the main task of states is taken to be the protection of individual liberties and the permission (if not promotion) of individual acquisitiveness.

Both men are attuned to a wider range of societal functions, even in their assertion of a prime purpose. However, Aristotle recognizes many other varieties of constitutions and different forms of regimes with their own tasks and primary purposes (such as economic gain or empire), and he argues that a number of these are legitimate forms of rule. Confucius, however, seemed to champion one sort of feudal system exclusively. Many commentators believe that Confucius thought that the best sort of society had already been realized in the Zhou dynasty. Other commentators, who do not find Confucius so Romantic, recognize that the master thought that at least the germ of the right way of rule was present in the Zhou *li* so that his aim was to recapture this ideal element and develop it further, perhaps extending the possibility of the best life to a wider class of people. In either case, Confucius spends most of his time extolling the ideal and enjoining people to pursue it. Aristotle, unlike Confucius, distinguishes between a best or ideal regime (a monarchy of moral excellence closest of all his options to Master Kong's) and a more practicable regime (the Aristotelian *polity*, which is a mixed regime) that is a sort of mean between idealism and pragmatism.

For the same reasons, Aristotle and Confucius also differ in their attitude toward the multitude. Aristotle's ideal monarchy and his mixed regime both leave the majority of people to perform service functions in order to help a small citizenry attain self-sufficiency and self-rule. As a consequence, so far as moral virtue needs political action, either the life of moral virtue is limited to those few citizens or at least a full participation in that life is limited to them. Confucius encourages everyone to cultivate him or herself; his ranking of moral achievement does not track political differences. He, like Aristotle, thinks a depth of virtue is rare, but he does not exclude people in service functions from a full participation in the life of virtue. Still, there is a sense in which both thinkers require all human beings to cultivate the virtues in the ways they can to the extent they can, so that they may contribute to the whole community by being good in their social roles and good as human beings. It is this emphasis on the cultivation of virtues by both thinkers that will provide a resource for our contemporary discourse on human rights.

Family life is centrally important for both Aristotle and Confucius. However, Confucius sees the state as an extension of the family; the relation between ruler and ruled is the relation between father and child painted on a bigger canvas. Here there is essentially no division at all between familial rule and political rule or between public and private life in general. Aristotle, on the other hand, does distinguish private from public life – though he does not separate them nearly as sharply as do thinkers in modern liberal political cultures. And while he admits that family structure and regime form do influence each other, for Aristotle political institutions are not merely outcroppings of biological family life. The life of virtue gets its important beginnings in family relations that are geared to the necessities of life, but it grows and flourishes in a public life of important decisions about how people might live well together. For the Stagirite, political life and social institutions grow out of the family but develop a sphere of their own that answers to a distinctive set of human purposes.

In Chapter 6, I show that Confucius and Aristotle have very different attitudes toward the rule of law. Confucius so completely embeds moral principle in customary norms and the model persons embodying and exhibiting them that he hangs all his political hopes on rule by an exemplary individual who inspires others to virtue. Aristotle agrees that if a community could find such an exemplary leader they should all acquiesce and follow this person. Certainly he argues that a good regime must have good rulers; virtue is indispensable to good government because no political machine runs unaccompanied. But the Stagirite believes that the appearance of a person who combines exemplary moral and leadership qualities – one who could serve as moral monarch or ethical emperor – is an extraordinary event and we should not build our regimes around the expectation of finding such a person. Moreover, while Aristotle certainly does not trust impersonal mechanisms and does not put such full faith in "political process" as we moderns do, he does argue at length for the rule of law. In this, too, he is un-Confucian. He praises the lack of passion in law and thinks law can rule because law can embody a common human reasonability. This goes hand in glove with Aristotle's recognition that moral principle has grounds above and beyond personal qualities and social customs. Nevertheless, Aristotle's unwritten laws, which are embedded in *ethos*, are comparable to Confucian *li*. Such comparability offers the opportunity for each to learn from the other the significance of laws, written and unwritten, for politics.

This discussion of law, a topic explicit in only one of the masters, leads to a discussion of human rights, a topic explicit in neither. It is pertinent not only to modern concerns but also to my discussion of virtue-based politics. That is because my suggestion is that there is a virtue-oriented approach to human rights that draws on the resources of both traditions – indeed it is made more fruitful with both for reasons made plain in this chapter – and ought to be acceptable to both. The core idea is that the life of virtue has practical prerequisites that we ought to claim as our due. When we claim we are due these prerequisites, we are claiming them as moral rights. This virtue-oriented approach leaves us with a somewhat different list of basic moral rights than we find in the books of liberal individualists. That is good because it holds out the promise of a critique of the dominant traditions of our day, because it brings a fresh voice into the conversation about rights, and because it gives these virtue-oriented traditions something more to say to rights theorists beyond the assertion that they are believing in fictions.

To be sure, nothing in the original texts of Aristotle and Confucius addresses the rights issue; I am drawing implications of the dialogue that it is my purpose in this volume to promote. It is merely one example of the fruitfulness of this dialogue. Nothing in Confucius answers to the rule of law or quite answers even to the justice (*dikaiosunê*) that is the crown of Aristotelian moral virtue and the highest other-regarding excellence. Master Kong emphasizes personal relationships – and especially familial relationships and their extensions – over any more impersonal idea of justice or law. However, readers of the *Nicomachean Ethics* who look exclusively to the function argument and the doctrine of the mean may be surprised to notice that Aristotle devotes more pages to issues about human relationships than any other topic. In Chapter 7, I compare these two thinkers' views on friendship – understood broadly to include all centrally important modes of human bonding. Topics include the kinds of friendship and their preconditions as well as the reasons each author adduces for befriending others (for instance, whether one ultimately always loves another out of self-love). Friendship for both authors is significant not only for its pivotal role in the cultivation of virtue but also for the cohesion of societies. Amity is the glue of community. Both authors hold that the society in which one lives, and the people with whom one associates, significantly affect the kind of person one becomes. Both agree that friendship in the intended sense is a central moral issue, not peripheral to the formulation of rules or the setting of limits that are taken by most moderns to be the main tasks of ethics.

Nevertheless, despite many similarities between the two authors, there are many more differences of note. Once again, we find that Confucius derives all forms of friendship from familial relationships and all legitimate forms of political rule from the father–son relation. Aristotle, on the other hand, more carefully distinguishes among spousal, sibling, and parental relations and argues that there are important differences between all these family relations and "friendships" (in the broad sense Aristotle invokes and I wish to echo) among a citizenry of equals.

Again and again we find a Confucian point hinging on a direct analogy with a paradigmatic example, while Aristotle's central points almost always hinge on a batch of options adumbrating a focal purpose. Both modes of thought are, arguably, analogical. Aristotle's mode of thinking is *pros hen*; that is, "toward one" in a way that includes reasonable alternatives even as it prioritizes them. Take the case of friendship. Aristotle distinguishes between a few kinds of friendship worthy (more or less) of the name, but he also strives to locate a primary and central sense of friendship. This is the sense of friendship where friends wish above all for each other's well-being and know that the essence of well-being is found in the life of moral and intellectual excellence. The other kinds of friendship (relationships based on the pleasure or utility of one or both partners), while genuinely friendships, are less than ideal in various ways and degrees. Moreover, Aristotle claims that the less than ideal forms of relationships point forward toward the one best form that is the definitive purpose at issue. Confucius does not share this quasidialectical mode of thought. He seems to look for a direct analogy with a concrete, paradigmatic case. Confucius' correlational style of thought seems to move in the orbit of relationships, while Aristotle's *"pros hen"* style of thought moves in the ambit also of relations of relations. When we attend to the Confucian tendency to think in terms of simple, resonant analogies, it will be less surprising that all relationships are modeled more or less directly on family relationships and all legitimate forms of rule will embody the pattern of the father–son relation. Aristotle instead will argue that there are various legitimate forms of friendship and political rule even though all these forms point forward toward a primary and central case that involves the pursuit of virtue.

Confucius and Aristotle both present an alternative to modern egoistic understandings of ethics and friendship. Both thinkers – in distinctive ways – manage to direct us to a kind of moral content where self-interest and other-directedness cross. This is the life of virtue. The cultivation of virtue is good for me – indeed it is the essence of my happiness if not the whole of it, according to Aristotle. At the same time, it is good for my friends and for my culture. It develops my character and develops my community in the right ways. This double aspect of the life of virtue seems to confuse many modern readers.[4] Confucius and Aristotle both sometimes write as if the point of good action were primarily the improvement of the agent's own excellence, and some commentators use these passages to argue that Aristotle or Confucius is, in the end, an egoist, and virtue ethics is an ethics ultimately concerned primarily with self-development or one's own happiness. But both authors also declare that other-regarding virtues are the highest moral excellences. Other commentators use these passages to argue the case of altruism. But both sorts of commentator miss the fundamental point about the life of virtue, a point upon which Aristotle and Confucius concur despite

---

[4] I say "double aspect," discerning between, on the one hand, my good and, on the other hand, the good of others. If we distinguish between my relationships and my community or society, then we could speak of the triple aspect of virtue, which benefits at the same time myself, my relationships, and my community.

a wealth of other differences: what we call virtue is good for me and good for others. Genuine friendship occurs between good people who are concerned with doing good for each other for the other's own sake, even as they are concerned with their self-cultivation as well. In a life of virtue, these projects intersect.

Finally, though I aim in this modest volume to address a wide range of pertinent secondary literature, again and again the thread of argument leads me to return to a handful of figures, most notably Alasdair MacIntyre, Tu Weiming, Roger Ames, and the late David Hall.

MacIntyre asserts that Aristotelianism provides the only real alternative to a postmodernity that clings, directly or indirectly, to Nietzsche. (That is the most significant contest in large part because the Nietzscheans have provided such an effective critique of the Enlightenment experiment with autonomy. MacIntyre knows of course of the continuing influence of Kant, John Stuart Mill, and others, but he sees what the progeny of these Enlightenment figures do not – that their views have been effectively refuted.) MacIntyre's assertion, however – at least in its most familiar form – presumes a set of options limited to canonical Western figures.

Hall and Ames, on the contrary, find the roots of Enlightenment rationalism and universalism in Greek philosophical pretensions to rational transcendence of their customs and cultural ways. Mentioning but not discussing in any detail the complicity of Aristotle, they imply that when postmodernism demolishes the pretension to rational transcendence of custom, it eliminates Aristotle as well. To their great credit, Hall and Ames find a timely alternative in Confucian ways of thought and action, though they believe the genuine Confucian alternative must be rescued from the historical sediment of medieval neo-Confucianism and interpreted in something like a neopragmatic mode. Confucius speaks a "deconstructed" language, they claim, eschews metaphysics, avoids invoking any sort of transcendence (which they believe is illusory in any event), and neither argues for nor supposes a "self" that is either autonomous or substantial. Their Confucian alternative agrees in these and other ways with the new pragmatism that emerges from the postmodern critique. At the same time, however, Confucian ways based on family and tradition do not succumb to the fragmentation and dispersion that postmodernism affords us. For Hall and Ames, therefore, Confucius offers us a pragmatic aestheticism that accords with the virtues of postmodernism while avoiding its vices.

Comfortably or uncomfortably, my argument in this volume settles between these authors. I argue with MacIntyre that immanent critique of Western traditions directs us backward to Aristotle's case for the virtues, though I find tensions internal to the Aristotelian case that prevent us from simply accepting Aristotle. On the other hand, with Hall and Ames I sense that Confucius holds out real promise on just the points at issue, though if we cling to a Confucius who remains closed to rational critique and validation through an appeal to first principles, we shall be stuck with a figure who is so parochial that he will have nothing useful to say to our age with its quite different manners and rituals. In other words, just to the extent that Hall and Ames succeed in showing that Confucius depends entirely on inherited patterns of practice, however "focused," they will have shown – contrary to their intent – the irrelevance of Confucian ways to the important project of the critique and reconstitution of contemporary modes of thought and practice. At this juncture, Tu Weiming's reading of Confucius, which is more open to a metaphysics of nature, will serve my argument considerably.

I concur with MacIntyre that the Aristotelian tradition is superior to its rivals among Western alternatives. It is superior not only because it can diagnose the failures of its rivals in ways they cannot and can offer remedies for those failures that they lack the resources to provide, but also because the Aristotelian approach can diagnose its own shortcomings and open itself to the possibility that only a quite alien tradition can provide the correctives it requires. My claim is that the Confucian approach provides many of these correctives and does so better than any Western option I know. I shall also argue that it is perhaps more difficult but by all means possible for a Confucian approach to find within itself the resources to become open to rectification from a distinct and even quite alien tradition. By dint of a host of fascinating consonances and dissonances, the Aristotelian tradition is the best candidate for this job. It is my sincere hope that the volume in hand will contribute to a further understanding of these two masters of morals and to a fruitful exchange between two great traditions.

1

Aristotle in the Reconstruction
of Confucian Ethics

In almost two decades of renewed interest in Confucianism, scholars such as Hall and Ames, Heiner Roetz, and Cheng Chung-ying have appealed to Western figures to help reconstruct Confucian thinking.[1] Following this well-traveled way, I wish to argue in this book that the alliance of Confucius with Aristotle is particularly fruitful.

To talk of the good life is to talk about the kind of person one should become. Aristotle and Confucius both pursue the question of the good life, and both recognize that the question of what kind of person is happy is a question that admits a fairly definite sort of answer. Moreover, the answer of these two quite disparate masters is strikingly similar: the happy life is the life of exemplary

---

[1] Hall and Ames attempt to reconstruct Confucius' thinking by appealing to the process philosophy of John Dewey; Heiner Roetz reconstructs Confucian ethics by using Karl Jasper's "Axial Age" theory along with Lawrence Kohlberg's cognitive-development theory; and Cheng Chung-ying uses Martin Heidegger for a hermeneutic investigation into the Confucian framework and Alfred North Whitehead for a reconstruction of the conditions of creativity in Confucian thought. These are just a few that have succeeded in illuminating Confucius' thinking. See David Hall and Roger Ames, *Thinking through Confucius* (Albany: State University of New York Press, 1987) (hereafter *TTC*); Heiner Roetz, *Confucian Ethics of the Axial Age: A Reconstruction under the Aspect of the Breakthrough toward Postconventional Thinking* (Albany: State University of New York Press, 1993); and Cheng Chung-ying, *New Dimensions of Confucian and Neo-Confucian Philosophy* (Albany: State University of New York Press, 1991).

virtue.[2] Both thinkers emphasize virtue and the significance of exemplary individuals for training in virtue and the dependence of such training on the right sort of social-political context. Aristotle calls the person of exemplary moral virtue the *phronimos*; Confucius calls him the *junzi*. Of course, Aristotle and Confucius hardly agree on every point, and Aristotle's *phronimos* and Confucius' *junzi* present different portraits of the living moral paradigm. It is important to notice the similarities and differences and to ask which claims are genuinely normative and which are due to cultural bias.[3] My task in all this is normatively moral as well as scholarly and comparative: I wish to ask who is right about significant ethical issues and what resources each tradition can provide where no answer is extant.

A dialogue between these two great ethical traditions is more helpful on this score than is an examination of either tradition in isolation. In this chapter, I shall discuss pertinent features of Aristotle's *phronimos* and Confucius' *junzi*. Because both philosophers' ethical views are inseparable from their discussions of political and social life, I shall also say just a bit about social relations and political institutions, though these topics are taken up in more detail only in my final chapters. This chapter ends by asking whether either the Aristotelian or the Confucian tradition has the resources to justify their norms of virtue in the absence of the contexts that gave birth to them.[4] I argue that though Confucius'

---

[2] For Confucius, the good life or happy life *is* the life of the morally ample person (the *da ren*), modeled on the *junzi*; for Aristotle, happiness is *essentially* the life of virtue modeled on the *phronimos*, though happiness as a whole involves various incidentals as well, such as wealth, good birth, and friendship, in addition to this essence.

[3] Such a comparison is also significant because while there may be scholars who recognize the centrality of the exemplary individual to moral education, they may not be aware that both Confucius and Aristotle share such a view. For example, Herbert Fingarette, in his "How the *Analects* Portrays the Ideal of Efficacious Authority," claims that Confucius alone, in Fingarette's survey of the history of Eastern and Western theories of ideal authority, recognizes that "the exercise of authority will rest crucially on an authoritative person's acting as a model." See Herbert Fingarette, "How the *Analects* Portrays the Ideal of Efficacious Authority," *Journal of Chinese Philosophy* 8 (1981): 29–49.

[4] Alasdair MacIntyre, in his *After Virtue* (Notre Dame, IN: University of Notre Dame Press, 1981), elaborates the idea that such norms have a meaning and point only when embedded in the pertinent social contexts and the idea that shared contexts (whether historically given or constructed in real dialogue and exchange) are a

family-focused and *li*-bound ethics fails to provide such resources, Aristotle's metaphysical view of human virtue allows him to arrive successfully at an outline account of moral virtue even in the absence of the proper political context.[5]

An exhaustive account of the similarities and differences in Confucius' and Aristotle's lists of virtues is beyond the scope of this chapter.[6] However, by focusing on their respective views on exemplary individuals and on certain key virtues possessed by these individuals, we can get clearer about the similarities and differences as we assess the significance both of exemplary individuals and of these select moral virtues.

Both the *junzi* and *phronimos* possess all the moral virtues according to Confucius and Aristotle, respectively, and both are said to be effective in accomplishing moral actions in a social-political realm. When Confucius was asked about the authoritative person, or the one who embodies all the virtues here, *ren*[7] (oftentimes the same as the *junzi*), one of his responses was as follows:

---

prerequisite to cross-tradition understanding. My qualified agreement with MacIntyre's thesis will become plain enough in due course.

[5] I am not alone in this positive endorsement of metaphysics – for example, Tu Weiming and Benjamin Schwartz agree that Confucianism is not at odds with metaphysics. I say more about Tu and Schwartz later in this chapter.

[6] For an interesting defense of comparing moral concepts across cultures that takes into account the ties of these concepts to concrete practices in different cultures, see Antonio Cua's discussion of the notion of "functionally equivalent moral concepts" in his *Dimensions of Moral Creativity* (State College: Pennsylvania State University Press, 1979), 76–78, and his "Tasks of Confucian Ethics," *Journal of Chinese Philosophy* 6 (1979): 55–67.

[7] I find three senses of *ren* in the *Analects*. First, *ren* seems to be a particular virtue that is intimately bound up with knowledge (*zhi*), deference, ritual propriety (*li*), learning (*xue*), and other qualities that make one virtuous. See 6.23, 12.1, 15.31, 15.33, and 17.8. All references and translations, unless otherwise stated, refer to *The Analects of Confucius: A Philosophical Translation*, trans. Roger T. Ames and Henry Rosemont, Jr. (New York: Ballantine Books, 1998). As Tu Weiming, in *Confucian Thought: Selfhood as Creative Transformation* (Albany: State University of New York Press, 1985), puts it, "It may not be far-fetched to suggest that *ren* is in a subtle way linked up with virtually all other basic Confucian concepts" (Tu, 87).

Second, *ren* is also a more general term referring to the embodiment of all the virtues in the two passages I quote here and also in 4.3, 4.4, and 15.10. (See Tu's *Confucian Thought*, 87, where he says, "*Ren* symbolizes a holistic manifestation of humanity in its commonest and highest state of perfection.")

Finally, there is a sense in which *ren* is a general virtue that conditions other virtues and perfects them. See 14.4, "Those who are *ren* must necessarily be bold

A person who is able to carry into practice five attitudes in the world can be considered authoritative. . . . Deference, tolerance, making good on one's word (*xin*), diligence, and generosity. If you are deferential, you will not suffer insult; if tolerant, you will win over the many; if you make good on your word, others will rely upon you; if diligent, you will get results; if generous, you will have the status to employ others effectively. (17.6)

At another time, Confucius speaks of four characteristics of a *junzi* while talking about Zichan, the most able and upright politician of his time. He said:

He was gracious in deporting himself, he was deferential in serving his superiors, he was generous in attending to the needs of the common people, and he was appropriate (*yi*) in employing their services. (5.16)

Confucius' *junzi* is thus one who possesses the appropriate self and other-regarding virtues and the skill to accomplish the moral ends he sets out before him. Conducting himself in a way that wins the trust and cooperation of others, by truly promoting the good of others (12.16, 12.22, 17.4) rather than promoting his own gain at the expense of others, is the way of the *junzi*. So the *junzi* is not one who, like Thrasymachus in Plato's *Republic*, is only acting "justly" to secure his own gain. He is one who recognizes the evanescence of such self-promotion. Accordingly, Confucius said, "Wealth and position gained through inappropriate means – these are to me like floating clouds" (7.16).

For Aristotle, similarly, the *phronimos* is one whose full possession of the moral virtues gives him the right ends or moral universals that govern his actions and allow him to act as a courageous, temperate, generous, mild, truthful, and just person. In a situation that calls for action, he will always choose the right action (means) to attain the one or more appropriate moral goals. The *phronimos*, like the *junzi*, is

(*yong*), those who are bold need not necessarily be *ren*" (my translation; see 4.3 and also Tu's *Confucian Thought*, 85, where he also seems to recognize this sense when he says: "Through the general virtue of *ren*, such values as bravery and intelligence are being transvalued. Bravery and intelligence as contributing elements in the symbolic structure of *ren* must now be understood as courage and wisdom.")

   I do not think it is unfair to use Western terminology and call these senses of *ren* the particular, universal, and intermediate senses. How these senses or aspects of *ren* function when we act well toward others and oneself I shall discuss later in this chapter.

acting for the good of others around him rather than merely for his own good at the others' expense. For example, when he rescues someone, such an act of bravery is for the sake of helping the one who is endangered rather than for his own honor or material gain. As such, Aristotle's *phronimos* is also not simply a clever one (*deinos*) who always knows the best means to attain any arbitrary goal – Aristotle does not share the view that morality is indifferent to ends. Rather, the goal is always the actualization of some morally virtuous act by choosing the best means.

From the preceding discussion about how the exemplary individual in Aristotle and Confucius pursues the good of others (rather than his own gain at the others' expense), one might think that to be exemplary all one needs is to be self-effacing. Rather, Confucius and Aristotle hold that such moral actions build one's own character. As Confucius puts it:

> ... the one of *ren*, desiring to establish oneself, establishes others (*ren*); desiring to promote oneself, promotes others. (6.30, my trans.)[8]

Confucius holds that it is through our social relationships, governed by *li*,[9] that we become who we are (see 5.26). Hence, by improving those around us, we are also improving ourselves. By constantly acting morally toward others, one is making oneself into, or maintaining oneself as, one with *ren*. This is because one with *ren* is one who is disciplined and does the right thing because it is right rather

---

[8] This interdependence of self and other cultivation is also shown in 4.15, where Confucius tells one of his closest disciples – Zeng – that his "way (*dao*) is bound together with one continuous strand," which Zeng then explains to the other disciples: "The way of the Master is doing one's utmost (*zhong*) and putting oneself in the other's place (*shu*), nothing more." *Zhong* and *Shu*, as Wing-tsit Chan, in *A Sourcebook in Chinese Philosophy* (Princeton, NJ: Princeton University Press, 1963), puts it, are best explained by Zhu Xi, where "*zhong* means the full development of one's ... mind and *shu* means the extension of that mind to others" (Chan, 27).

[9] Following Fingarette, *li* for Confucius does not simply refer to the "historically persistent forms of actual conduct" because historical forms often reflect the "moral degeneration" of actual behaviors. Rather, *li* refers to the "authenticated norms for conduct" that the Zhou dynasty had handed down. Only the wise and virtuous still adhere to these social norms or rules for conduct. These rules govern the proper ways to conduct oneself toward one's family members and others in society, be they one's friends, superiors, or subordinates. See Herbert Fingarette, "The Music of Humanity in the Conversation of Confucius," *Journal of Chinese Philosophy* 10 (1983): 331–56.

than for his own selfish gain (see 4.12, 4.16). For example, Confucius remarked that "Through self-discipline and observing ritual propriety (*li*) one becomes authoritative in one's conduct. If for the space of a day one were able to accomplish this, the whole empire would defer to this authoritative model" (12.1). The significance of cultivating this disposition of being concerned with the good of others, rather than being selfish and egoistic, is most obvious when Confucius replies to a question about *ren* by saying that *ren* is to love others (*ren*, 12.22). When one loves another, one is, as Hall and Ames point out, taking "someone into one's sphere of concern, and in so doing, ma[king] her an integral aspect of one's own person."[10] Because to love is to will the good, to love others is to extend one's interests and concerns to what is good for people in general. To do what is good for others entails that one knows what is good for others (*ren*) in general. For example, to know that bird meat is healthy for human beings enables one to encourage others to eat bird meat. This explains why the response that *ren* is to love others (*ren*) is coupled with Confucius' response that knowledge is to know others (*zhi ren*). This knowledge of what is good for human beings will also benefit oneself because one can apply this knowledge to oneself and achieve one's own good. For example, to know that bird meat is good for human beings and including bird meat in one's own diet (for one is human, too) will lead to one's own good. Hence, for Confucius, loving others is intimately bound up with loving oneself. This is confirmed by Confucius' remark that *ren* is not simply one who makes others love him, nor one who loves others only, but is one who also loves himself.[11] Such a view of self-love also shows itself in Confucius' view of friendship – that friendship helps one develop his *ren*.[12]

Aristotle, too, holds that repeated virtuous actions will lead one to have the appropriate virtues (*Nicomachean Ethics* [*NE*] II, 1103a15–1103b25). Because the moral virtues are the perfections of the appetitive part of our soul while *phronêsis* (or practical wisdom) is the perfection of the practical part of our rational soul, we are fulfilling the function of both parts of our soul by living virtuously. For

[10] *TTC*, 121.   [11] *TTC*, 121, quoting from the *Hsün Tzu*.
[12] See 12.24: "Master Zeng said, 'The *junzi* have friends through refinement (*wen*) and through friendship promotes *ren*'" (my trans.).

Aristotle, acting virtuously realizes what is appropriate to our nature, and doing so is a good that also makes us happy (1144a1–10).[13] Like Confucius, Aristotle holds that the *phronimos'* knowledge does not consist simply in knowing what is good for an egoistic self but rather in "what promotes living well in general" (1140a27).[14] Thus, for both thinkers, by knowing and doing what is good for others in general, one is also doing what is good for oneself. While Confucius asserts that *ren* is to love others, there does not seem to be such an injunction in Aristotle. Nevertheless, if Confucius' claim about loving others means that one is to do what is good for others, Aristotle agrees when

[13] Aristotle dismisses the nutritive and perceptive parts of the soul as uniquely human because they are shared with plants and animals, respectively (*Nicomachean Ethics* [*NE* hereafter], 1098a3–5). He holds that the substance or essence of a human being lies in his rational soul. More specifically, Aristotle maintains that the human form/soul (*psychê*) is divided into the rational and nonrational parts. The rational part is further divided into the contemplative and deliberative parts, where the contemplative part has as its objects eternal objects, whereas the deliberative part has as its objects changeable objects. The nonrational part of the soul is divided into the controllable nonrational desires (*orexeis*), which include appetites (*epithumiai*) and emotions (*thumoi*), and the uncontrollable vegetative parts. The rational soul is perfected when it performs its functions of contemplation and deliberation well. When perfected, the rational part has the corresponding intellectual virtues of *theôria* and *phronêsis*, respectively. The nonrational part of the soul is perfected when we are disposed to function well in our appetites and emotions by obeying the rational part, which tells us what is appropriate for each of these faculties. When this occurs, we are said to have the moral virtues. The vegetative part is beyond our control. Our human nature or rational soul, for Aristotle, dictates how we function well. And functioning well is part of what makes us happy. See *NE* 1102a15–1103a10 and also 1097b35–1098a16. For a contemporary discussion of how the proper function of the rational soul includes the control of the nonrational parts, see Terence Irwin's *Aristotle's First Principles* (New York: Oxford Clarendon Press, 1988), in which he says: "In confining the human function to a life of action of the rational part, Aristotle does not exclude all animal or vegetative activities. He assumes only that rational activity is the distinctive and essential feature of the human soul, and that this organizes the human being's other activities in the way perception organizes a nonrational animal's other activities. The life of action will include other activities besides the activity of reasoning; but in a human being they are essentially guided by reasoning" (Irwin, 364).

   Also see Ed Halper's *Form and Reason: Essays in Metaphysics* (Albany: State University of New York Press, 1993), in which he says, "Practical reason serves as a kind of bridge between theoretical reason and the emotions, and following its dictates imparts a kind of rationality to the nonrational portion of the soul" (Halper, 72).

[14] All quotations are from the *Nicomachean Ethics*, trans. Terence Irwin (Indianapolis, IN: Hackett Publishing, 1985), unless otherwise stated.

he claims that the *phronimos* necessarily acts correctly with correct knowledge in the right situation and that this achieves what is good for human beings in general (*NE* VI, 1140a27, 1142b20–30). To assert as Yu Jiyuan[15] has that Aristotle cannot explain "why a rational person needs to cultivate other-regarding virtues" because a good person only does good for others to perfect his or her own nature is to misunderstand what a moral virtue is and ultimately to misunderstand what justice is for Aristotle. Yu's interpretation of Aristotle, that one only does good for others to perfect one's own character, will fail to perfect an agent's own character (i.e., achieve the moral virtues) because this action and intention fail to satisfy Aristotle's condition that the agent must decide on a virtuous act for the act itself and not for the agent himself (1105a33). Likewise, Yu's view will also fail to win one justice because justice, as the crown of moral virtues for Aristotle, is strictly other regarding – to achieve another's good rather than one's own good (1129b31–35, 1130a4–6).[16] Similarly,

---

[15] Yu Jiyuan, "Virtue: Confucius and Aristotle," *Philosophy East and West* 48 (1998): 323–47.

[16] General justice, as the crown of moral virtues for Aristotle, is strictly other-regarding. As Aristotle puts it, "Justice is the only virtue that seems to be another person's good, because it is related to another; for it does what benefits another, either the ruler or the fellow member of the community" (1130a4–6). For a discussion of the contrast between particular and general justice, see C. David C. Reeve's *Practices of Reason* (New York: Oxford Clarendon Press, 1992), in which he says: "Special justice is concerned with *pleonexia*, with wanting more and more without limit of the external goods of competition (1129b1–4). General justice is 'complete virtue, not unconditionally complete virtue, but complete virtue in relation to another' (1129b5–7), so it is concerned with external goods just as the other virtues of character are" (Reeve, 168). See also Sarah Broadie's discussion of a "broad" sense of justice in *Ethics with Aristotle* (New York: Oxford University Press, 1991), 111–12.

Concerning the charge of egoism against Aristotle, see Chapter 7 and also Richard Kraut's *Aristotle on the Human Good* (Princeton, NJ: Princeton University Press, 1989), 9–11, where he defends Aristotle against charges of egoism discussed by commentators such as W. F. R. Hardie, Terence Irwin, Harold A. Prichard, W. D. Ross, and Henry Sidgwick. Kraut says that even though the philosophical life is the best for Aristotle, nothing that he says prevents one from choosing the political life, which aims at attaining the happiness of others, for Aristotle never insisted that one must maximize the life of contemplation.

Terence Irwin, in his *Plato's Moral Theory* (New York: Oxford University Press, 1977), acknowledges that charges of egoism against Aristotle stem from his "claims that the final good for each man is his own happiness, and that a virtue must contribute to the virtuous man's happiness (*NE* 1106a15–24)" (Irwin, 255). However, Irwin goes on to defend Aristotle against psychological or ethical egoism

that the *phronimos* loves himself and others is also evident in Aristotle's discussion of friendship (*NE* IX, 1169b2–1170b19), where friends who share our moral virtues give us pleasure because they enable us to observe better actions in which we take pleasure (i.e., our own actions) (1169b30ff).[17] Agreeing with Confucius, Aristotle quotes Theognis, who says that "good people's life together allows the cultivation of virtue" (1170a11).

We have seen how the exemplary individuals of Aristotle and Confucius possess moral virtues. While such an individual acts for the good of others, he is also furthering his own good because the good for human beings in general applies to himself. Furthermore, the practice of virtuous actions also cultivates one's own character. Having seen that these exemplary figures act on a knowledge of general truths about what is good for others, let us look at the knowledge of particulars that they possess because it is knowledge of particulars that makes them effective agents in particular situations.

Aristotle observes that the *phronimos* does not know only universals (e.g., that courageous acts are to be pursued) but also particulars because he is concerned with action, and it is particulars that can be acted upon (1141b15–20, 1142a13–15). Aristotle's exemplary individual also knows that a particular situation calls for acting bravely, temperately, or justly and he knows the appropriate action that brings about the end of bravery, temperance, or justice. For example, while discussing the *phronimos'* deliberation, Aristotle claims that:

Good deliberation is correctness that reflects what is beneficial, about the right thing, in the right way and at the right time. (1142b27–29)

by saying that such charges rest on the false assumption that "there are no genuinely other-regarding virtues, contrary to what we and most Greeks suppose about justice" (Irwin, *Plato's Moral Theory*, 255). Irwin goes on to show that Aristotle's self-love does not imply solipsism and hence is compatible with the pursuit of virtue. As he puts it, "for the virtuous man will love the rational part of his soul, and will care about its aims, which require the pursuit of virtuous and admirable action (1168b23–1169a18)" (Irwin, *Plato's Moral Theory*, 259). See also Irwin's "The Metaphysical and Psychological Basis of Aristotle's Ethics," in *Essays on Aristotle's Ethics*, ed. Amélie O. Rorty (Berkeley: University of California Press, 1980), 48.

[17] I say more about friendship in Confucius and Aristotle in Chapter 7.

Aristotle also tells us that justice is our highest and most complete virtue in our relation to others. He says:

Justice is the only virtue that seems to be another person's good, because it is related to another; for it does what benefits another, either the ruler or the fellow member of the community. (1130a4–6)

The *phronimos*, then, is one who possesses justice because he is always acting at the right time, in the right way, and about the right thing, and accomplishes what is good for another.

Similarly, for Confucius, the *junzi* is also one who can see what is appropriate (right) for a situation and does it. An examination of some of the passages in which Confucius uses "*yi*" will reveal that it is used in three senses. The three senses of "*yi*" refer to (1) the disposition or virtue that leads the *junzi* to act justly in particular situations; (2) the individual act actualizing his disposition of *yi* in a particular situation; and (3) the *kind* of action that is just (i.e., a universal standard shared by the community conversant with *li*).[18]

---

[18] More elaborately, the first of three views of "*yi*" is the dispositional sense, which is evident in the following passages: "The Master said, 'Exemplary persons [*junzi*] understand what is appropriate [*yi*]; petty persons understand what is of personal advantage [*li*]'" (4.16; see also 4.11: "Exemplary persons [*junzi*] cherish their excellence; petty persons cherish their land. Exemplary persons cherish fairness; petty persons cherish the thought of gain"). These passages show that *yi* refers to the tendencies or inclinations toward equity as opposed to greed. Thus, even prior to a given action, the *junzi* is already disposed to act according to such a virtue of justice. This interpretation sees *yi* as a disposition that makes one's action express justice no matter what the situation. It even seems to be a virtue that conditions other virtues so that they cannot be put to bad use in whatever situation. This is seen in the following passage in Confucius' response to Zilu's question about whether the *junzi* esteems boldness (*yong*). Confucius replied: "The exemplary person gives first priority to appropriate conduct (*yi*). An exemplary person who is bold yet is lacking a sense of appropriateness will be unruly, while a petty person of the same cut will be a thief" (17.23).

The second sense of *yi* refers to the act that exemplifies *yi*. The *junzi*'s act exemplifies *yi* because, like Aristotle's analysis, it is the right thing to do, at the right time, and done toward the right person. Part of the rightness of his act comes from its accordance with *li*, while the other part comes from his style of humility and sincerity in performing it. This seems to be the intersection of the universal and the particular, doing the right *kind* of action in a particular situation, made right by the agent's actualization of his dispositions in this particular situation. Examples of this second sense are: "Having a sense of appropriate conduct (*yi*) as one's basic disposition (*zhi*), developing it in observing ritual propriety (*li*), expressing it with modesty, and consummating it in making good on one's word (*xin*): this then is an exemplary person" (15.18); and "Exemplary persons in

All three senses, exemplifying the agent's disposition, the concrete just action, and the *kind* of action that is just, are "focally related," to use a term from Aristotle. This is because they all relate to justice, be it the agent's disposition, the concrete instance of an agent's just act, or the *kind* of action it is. But all three senses of *yi* allow Confucius to stress the justice of the *junzi* and his actions in much the same way that the *phronimos'* justice consistently lets him do the right thing at the right time.[19]

Just as justice for Aristotle is the crown of our other-regarding virtues, *yi* for Confucius sums up the abilities that allow one to act correctly toward others. The *phronimos* with the fullness of virtue necessarily possesses justice and self-regarding virtues such as courage, temperance, and self-love. Similarly, the one with *ren*, for Confucius, is disposed to *yi* and so extends himself to doing what is good for human beings in general and is so cultivated that he loves himself.

A notable difference between the *junzi* and the *phronimos* is that whereas the *junzi* is capable of error, the *phronimos* is perfect in his practical wisdom. Whereas the *junzi* is constantly learning to better himself, the *phronimos* has attained the completion or end of man's practical wisdom.[20] Confucius said, "To transgress and not correct such transgressions is what is called transgression" (15.30, my trans.). For Confucius, then, to transgress *li* seems normal and is not blameworthy; it is only when one does not rectify one's transgression

making their way in the world are neither bent on nor against anything; rather, they go with what is appropriate" (4.10). Hall and Ames stress this second sense at the expense of the two others based on their allegiance to process philosophy.

The third sense of *yi* refers to the *kinds* of just actions or universal standards of justice shared by those in the community conversant with *li*. Let us look at some passages that make this also a plausible interpretation of *yi* for Confucius. At 2.24 he says, "To see what is appropriate and not act is to lack courage" (my trans.); and at another point, "But wealth and position gained through inappropriate (*buyi*) means – these are to me like floating clouds" (7.16). This sense of *yi* is an abstraction of the second sense of *yi* (i.e., concrete actions expressing *yi*, when generalized, become the third sense). So, for instance, one can say that equitable actions are just and stealing is unjust even apart from considering any dispositions to justice or considering any just action in particular.

[19] As for Aristotle, the three senses involved in justice require knowledge of the universal, particular, and concrete universal that the *phronimos* embodies.

[20] He will never act incorrectly, otherwise he will not be a *phronimos*. See 1140b20, b23–25.

and hence correct one's character that one is culpable. The natur-
alness of transgressions to Confucius reveals itself when he compares
them to eclipses of the sun and moon, which are rare but visible to all,
but once rectified, everyone will look up to him again (19.21; see also
9.24). Confucius' view is that continuous learning (*xue*) is needed to
sustain the virtues. Because the *junzi* is committed to an endless
prospect of learning and improvement, he takes his transgressions as
opportunities for learning and hence for bettering a self that already
possesses the relevant virtues.

One basis for the difference between the perfection of Aristotle's
phronimos and the fallibility of Confucius' *junzi* is Aristotle's teleological metaphysics and the lack of such a metaphysical basis in
Confucius. By saying that Aristotle has a teleological metaphysics,
I mean that he has a view of human nature that determines the
human end or goal. Aristotle holds that the substance or form of
something is its nature (see *Metaphysics* [hereafter *Met.*] 1015a6,
1014b36, 1022a24–28; see also 1031b19–23, 1041b29–32) and its
cause (see *Met.* 1041a27–30, 1041b7–9 and 25–28). Aristotle
maintains that the soul is the form of the human body (*De Anima*
[hereafter *DA*] 412a22) because the uniquely human function is the
activity of the rational soul rather than the function of the nutritive
or perceptive parts (*NE* I, chs. 7 and 13). It follows that the human
nature, or cause of the "what it is" of a human being, is the activity
of the rational part of the soul. It is the rational soul as form rather
than the matter, or the combination of form and matter, that is the
primary substance for Aristotle because it satisfies the criteria
of being primary in definition, knowledge, and time and being
capable of existing separately or independently (*Met.* 1028a32–36).[21]

---

[21] That "substance," "form" (*eidos*), and "essence" have among their many senses one
that denotes the primary substance or formal cause of something in Aristotle's
Metaphysics (e.g., soul in the case of man) has been argued by commentators such
as David Balme, "The Snub," *Ancient Philosophy* 4 (1984): 1–8; Michael Loux,
"Form, Species and Predication in *Metaphysics* Z, H, Θ," *Mind* 88 (1979): 1–23;
John A. Driscoll, "EIΔH in Aristotle's Earlier and Later Theories of Substance," in
volume 9 of *Studies in Aristotle*, ed. Dominic J. O'Meara (Washington, DC: Catholic
University of America Press, 1981), 129–59; and Alan Code, "Aristotle: Essence
and Accident," in *Philosophical Grounds of Rationality*, ed. Richard E. Grandy and
Richard Warner (Oxford: Clarendon Press, 1986), 411–39. See also note 13 of this
chapter for how Aristotle's ethics is metaphysical.

Aristotle also demonstrates that God is the ultimate cause of such primary substances.[22] God, for Aristotle, satisfies the criteria for primary substance and also the conditions of being complete and self-sufficient. Because human beings are most like God in being self-sufficient (*autarkês*) and complete (*teleios*) when they are using their rational soul, the activity of the rational soul is also the human goal.[23] Notice that the *telos* of a human being is determined by the kind of substance he is and thus is metaphysically determined for Aristotle. In short, it is our nature that dictates our good. Fulfilling the functions of these parts of our nature (i.e., the rational and nonrational parts of the soul) is our end and defines our perfection. Confucius' *junzi*, on the other hand, is fallible because Confucius does not elaborate an explicit teleology and metaphysics and so is under no demand to define the state of completed human perfection.

Whereas Aristotle defines our good from our rational soul, Confucius defines our good from the Zhou *li* and his own innovations on *ren*.[24] Whereas Aristotle's starting point is from a nature that all human beings possess, Confucius' starting point is from a person in context, where she plays certain roles that are prescribed by the *li*. Aristotle's view has the quality of universality and stability, whereas Confucius' view has the quality of adaptability and uniqueness. Aristotle's view of the end has the support of metaphysics, whereas

---

[22] For a good discussion of the relation between primary substance and God as the principle and cause of primary substances, see Ed Halper, *One and Many in Aristotle's Metaphysics: The Central Books* (Columbus: Ohio State University Press, 1989). Halper says: "There are indications in the central books that these other beings as well as form depend on a principle that is still higher, the *ousia* that has no matter (H6, 1045b21–23) and is pure actuality (1050b19). Because it exists apart from matter, such an actuality is more one than any of the beings examined in the central books. . . . Since unity is a key criterion of *ousia*, something that is one in the highest way ought to be an *ousia* in the highest way" (Halper, *One and Many in Aristotle's Metaphysics*, 229).

[23] See *NE* X, ch. 7, for Aristotle's arguments on how the life of *theôria* is the highest and God-like life because of its self-sufficiency, continuity, completeness, and pleasure.

[24] Ames and Rosemont, in *The Analects of Confucius*, 50, note the liberty Confucius has taken with the term "*ren*" given its sparse occurrence in the earlier classics and the frequency with which questions were raised about it in the *Analects*. As they say: "*Ren* does not occur in the earliest portions of the ancient classics, and only three times in the later parts. This unexceptional usage compares with 105 occurrences in the *Analects* in 58 of the 499 sections."

Confucius' view has the support of a tradition. However, the contrast between metaphysics and tradition is not as straightforward as it seems. In spite of Aristotle's fixed metaphysics of human nature, there is enough room for individual variations and adaptations to particular situations in his account of the *phronimos* that this contrast between metaphysics and tradition does not yield the result it is supposed to yield, namely inflexibility on Aristotle's account as opposed to flexibility and adaptability on Confucius' account.[25] Rather, the contrast lies in the presence as opposed to the absence of a metaphysics, and hence the presence as opposed to the absence of a standard of justification for adhering to a certain tradition.

The contrast is not between metaphysics and tradition because Aristotle works out of a tradition, too – one he had inherited from Homer and Hesiod and the Presocratics. This is evident in his works, which often begin with an account of his predecessors' views and then, through arguments, he shows how his rectified accounts are better than theirs.[26] Confucius' views, on the other hand, though often beginning with what his interlocutors say, end up with his own assertions regarding the virtues, often supported by appeals to a tradition, at times combined with his own intuitions and innovations, but not going much further. Confucian commentators are aware of the lack of justification in Confucius' adherence to the Zhou *li*. For instance, Philip Ivanhoe says with respect to the *li* that:

The primary difficulty is providing a convincing justification for the traditional rituals which Confucius followed and advocated. Confucius' allegiance to tradition was largely unexamined, motivated by his belief in a past Golden Age which relied upon a cultural system sanctioned by Heaven.[27]

---

[25] Confucian commentators who resist a metaphysical reading of Confucius include Xinzhong Yao, "Self-Construction and Identity: The Confucian Self in Relation to some Western Perceptions," *Asian Philosophy* 6 (1996):186; and Roger Ames, "The Focus-Field Self in Classical Confucianism," (TFFS hereafter) in *Self as Person in Asian Theory and Practice*, ed. Roger Ames, Wimal Dissanayake, and Thomas Kasulis (Albany: State University of New York Press, 1994), 201. See Chapter 5 of this book for a detailed discussion of their positions.

[26] For accounts of Aristotle's dialectical method, see *From Puzzles to Principles? Essays on Aristotle's Dialectic*, ed. May Sim (Lanham, MD: Lexington Books, 1999).

[27] Philip J. Ivanhoe, "Reweaving the 'One Thread' of the *Analects*." *Philosophy East and West* 40 (1990): 17–33, especially 31.

Similarly, in response to the assertion that "The only moral and social necessity is to follow *li*," Michael Martin asks, "How are we ever to know that and on what grounds are we to convince others?"[28] That some kind of justification is required for the *li* stems from the fact that there can be blind spots in any tradition that could lead to the mistreatment of certain groups of people, such as women and children. A rebuttal could be made that Aristotle is just as guilty with his prejudices against women and in his acceptance of slavery, in spite of his metaphysics. Indeed, Aristotle was blinded by his tradition in these respects. Perhaps we should find Aristotle even more culpable because he should have recognized from his metaphysics of human nature that women and slaves have the same type of soul as his citizens and hence should not be discriminated against. Nevertheless, Aristotle's personal culpability is no reflection upon his metaphysics. This is because his own metaphysics acts as a neutral standard that can be used to check his own prejudices – in this case, to criticize his own prejudices against women and slaves. This tool of self-criticism is the reason for having a standard of justification for one's views – in Aristotle's case, for having a metaphysics.

Before elaborating on the difference between Confucius and Aristotle with respect to the absence or presence of a standard of justification for their respective moral virtues, let us examine their similarity with respect to the development of the exemplary individual. For Aristotle, we need the following conditions, apart from being a human being with the right material nature, in order to become a *phronimos*. We need to live in a *polis* where our external goods are satisfied. For instance, we need to be born free men rather than slaves, have our basic necessities supplied, and have political connections to help us accomplish our actions. Most of all, we need to have other *phronimoi* around so that we have models after whom to tailor our habituation of the moral virtues. Confucius, like Aristotle, relies heavily on the family and society for the

[28] See Michael R. Martin, "Ritual Action (*Li*) in Confucius and Hsun Tzu," *Australasian Journal of Philosophy* 73 (1995):18. See also Chad Hansen's "Freedom and Moral Responsibility in Confucian Ethics," *Philosophy East and West* 22 (1972): 169–86, in which he speaks of the lack of philosophical reflection on the normative aspects of *li*, hence making it descriptive rather than normative.

development of the exemplary individual. Confucius also stresses the need for such individuals to provide role models for the development of others.[29]

Let us now consider if one could arrive at the moral virtues for Confucius in the absence of the proper social and political contexts within which we have the exemplary individuals to show us what the virtues are. Because the *li* (ritual proprieties) are inherited from the past, one could imagine not only the ability of Confucians to arrive at an account of the moral virtues but also account for a *junzi*'s coming into being even if these models and contexts were absent.[30] Put otherwise, it seems that one could, in the absence of the prerequisite social context, still study *li* and appropriate these rituals for oneself and hence reconstruct the appropriate moral virtues.[31] Hall and Ames (*Thinking Through Confucius*, hereafter *TTC*), for instance, illustrate such an appropriation by showing how Confucius and his students appropriate the *Book of Songs* for themselves so that it acts as a source for their own personal transformations. Two critical points regarding such an appropriation are (1) that it relies on the authority of this work, so that if one rejects its authority along with "the authoritative structure of personal, social, and political experiences" (*TTC*, 64) that it constitutes, as one might do in a changing society, one would be left without any stuff for one's cultivation; and (2) that such an appropriation, if one stresses creativity in it as Hall and Ames do (*TTC*, 66–67), presupposes that one is already cultivated in such a way that one can select what to appropriate and what to leave out. In this case, the *Book of Songs* seems to be an accident for one's expression of his creativity rather than a prerequisite for one's becoming creative. Thus it becomes questionable if this book, as Chinese culture exemplified, really forms the "authority sine qua non for all knowledge and conduct," as Hall and Ames claimed for Confucius (*TTC*, 67; see also 62–68). If these criticisms against Hall and Ames' interpretations of the

---

[29] See 13.6, 13.13, and especially 5.3 for the necessity of having good models in order to become virtuous. See Chapter 6 for an extended discussion of the necessity of a good state for ethical development in both thinkers.

[30] See Confucius' complaint about the rarity of people with virtue (e.g., 4.6, 6.29, 7.26).

[31] For how *li* establishes one's character, see 8.8, 16.13, and 20.3.

appropriation of *li* textually (i.e., by studying the *Book of Songs*) are valid, they also suggest that such textual transmission of *li* does not allow Confucius to reconstruct an unquestioned set of moral virtues. Another reason why one is unlikely to appropriate the ritual proprieties textually is because of the inseparability of *li* from the society within which these proprieties are exercised. As Fingarette puts it, "There is no power of *li* if there is no learned and accepted convention, or if we utter the words and invoke the power of the convention in an inappropriate setting."[32] Hence, it seems that the reconstruction of the moral virtues, in the absence of a society that practices the *li* that Confucius values so much, becomes highly improbable, though possible in principle.

Aristotle, on the contrary, could still formulate a theory of the necessary virtues that a human being must achieve to become a *phronimos* in the absence of the necessary social and political conditions. This is because of his metaphysics. From Aristotle's metaphysics, a human substance has its essence or form, which dictates what he is and how he functions. Such a form already provides content for human virtues by elevating the rational function and by subordinating the nonrational functions (such as the emotions and appetites) to the rational soul. Thus, a general theory of human virtue can be derived intellectually even absent the relevant political background needed for the practical cultivation of virtue. That Aristotle's metaphysics determines his ethics was discussed in note 13 earlier in this chapter. Other commentators who have argued for the metaphysical basis of Aristotle's *Ethics* include Terence Irwin, who says that:

[Aristotle's] argument begins with his assumptions about happiness; and ... these are not arbitrary assumptions, and not merely common beliefs, but consequences of his general theory of the soul, form, and essence.... The argument of the *Ethics* depends on more than common sense. It depends on

---

[32] See Herbert Fingarette's "Human Community as Holy Rite: An Interpretation of Confucius' *Analects*," *Harvard Theological Review* 59 (1966): 53–67, where he says, "There is no power of *li* if there is no learned and accepted convention, or if we utter the words and invoke the power of the convention in an inappropriate setting, or if the ceremony is not fully carried out, or if the persons carrying out the ceremonial roles are not those properly authorized" (Fingarette, "Human Community as Holy Rite," 63).

the whole view of natural substances outlined in Aristotle's metaphysics and psychology. (Irwin, 51)[33]

Some interpreters wish to say that Confucius' reliance on the family for the inculcation of *li* is his saving grace.[34] The family, it is

---

[33] See Irwin's "The Metaphysical and Psychological Basis of Aristotle's Ethics," 51. For more essays defending metaphysical readings of Aristotle's ethics/politics, see *The Crossroads of Norm and Nature: Essays on Aristotle's Ethics and Metaphysics*, ed. May Sim (Lanham, MD: Rowman and Littlefield, 1995), especially chs. 1–3.

[34] Benjamin Schwartz, *The World of Thought in Ancient China* (Cambridge, MA: Harvard University Press, 1985), 97ff. Schwartz discusses how an individual for both Confucius and Aristotle might achieve "a high level of moral perfection" in a corrupt society where the past traditions are "distorted and fragmented." Schwartz thinks that Confucius has an edge over Plato in the realization of the exemplary individual because the good that Confucius is after was already realized in the past, whereas Plato relies on reason to construct "the good society," which is yet to be realized. Plato's republic is in turn required for the guardian's attainment of his perfection. Confucius' and Aristotle's man, on the other hand, Schwartz maintains, can "achieve a high level of moral perfection even when the [*d*]*ao* does not prevail in the world" (Schwartz, 97). Presumably this is because of Schwartz's view that they already know what the perfection is and Schwartz's interpretation that the realization of their exemplary individuals can come about privately (independently of society) either through direct, private teaching or through the family (Schwartz, 97, 101). See notes 31 and 32 in this chapter for my skepticism toward learning and appropriating the past *li* (in the absence of a social context in which *li* is exercised) to attain *ren* for Confucius.

That it is impossible for one to become a *phronimos* through teaching, independent of proper models and necessary external conditions for Aristotle is evident in his assertion that moral virtues are not teachable but habituated. For proper habituation, one needs the proper external goods and models – which are absent without a *polis*. For the necessity of a *polis* for habituation, see Anthony Kenny, *Aristotle on the Perfect Life* (New York: Oxford Clarendon Press, 1992), 43. For the necessity of models for the habituation of the young, see Nancy Sherman, *The Fabric of Character: Aristotle's Theory of Virtue* (New York: Oxford University Press, 1989), 179–80. For the unteachability of practical wisdom, see Sim, *The Crossroads of Norm and Nature*, 62.

With respect to becoming a *junzi* by relying on proper family life, Schwartz realizes that proper family life relies on a good political order. As Schwartz, in *The World of Thought in Ancient China*, says, Confucius "admits that in a society where the [*d*]*ao* is absent, the families of the masses who suffer deprivation and oppression cannot be expected to realize the moral potentialities of family life.... He would ... agree that the situation could only be remedied through the political order and that the task must be undertaken by the good and the wise" (Schwartz, 100). For Schwartz, these good and wise in turn rely on the family for their cultivation. It seems that Schwartz is caught up in a vicious circle here. Corrupt families rely on the society for their remedy. The society in turn relies on the family for its remedy (via the *junzi*). Such a circle is consistent with Confucius' thinking.

argued, is an effective vehicle for one's moral training because it rests on natural kinship and love. However, because Confucius models the society after the family, ailments of the society are reflected in ailments within the family, if they did not arise from the family in the first place.[35] Thus, the same absence of *li* that plagues a modern Chinese society may also plague a modern Chinese family.

One might argue that Confucius can determine moral actions independently of *li* and independently of a definite set of universally valid moral virtues because of his Golden Rule. Such a rule is exemplified by Confucius' concept of *shu*. As he puts it, "Do not impose upon others what you yourself do not want" (12.2; see 15.24, 6.30, 5.12; and also *Zhongyong* [hereafter *Zy*] 13[36]). This universal rule seems to help one determine moral action independently of

Yu Jiyuan, in "Virtue: Confucius and Aristotle," reiterates Schwartz's emphasis on Confucius' reliance on the family for our moral education. However, in contrasting Confucius and Aristotle, Yu seems to present an Aristotle who emphasizes legislation more than the family in our moral education when Aristotle's emphasis is on the necessity of both. Contrary to the tension Yu finds between the family and legislation, Aristotle unites the two in the purpose of habituation. Legislation is needed because correct laws provide an environment where one will be trained correctly: "Someone who is to be good must be finely brought up and habituated, and then must live in decent practices"(1179b32–36; see also 1180a15). Laws provide the context for such good upbringing for Aristotle. Legislative science provides the correct political context for good upbringing because it is the knowledge of the universal – what is good for all (1180b15–20). For Aristotle, such knowledge of the universal guards against the arbitrariness of individual rules in cities where legislators do not attend to upbringing (1180a25–28).

Legislation then, for Aristotle, is not incompatible with the family's role in habituating virtues. Rather, it works hand in hand, supplementing the family with the objective good needed for good habituation. Such an objective good can provide Confucius with the much needed solution and way out of a corrupt family life. See 1180a29–33 and 1180b4–14 for Aristotle's emphases on the role of the family for one's moral education. For emphases on how habituation is bound up with the political system (in fact, for Aristotle, it is habituation that distinguishes between good and bad political systems), and how the laws continue to play a role in our habituation even after we are grown, see Chapter 6 of this book and Reeve's *Practices of Reason*, 54–55. Also see Sherman's description of the parent's role in habituating the child in Aristotle's ethics in her *The Fabric of Character*, 171–74. The particularity of such a role (which Aristotle stresses) cannot be substituted by the state even though it is the state's role to ensure that such a role is properly fulfilled.

[35] See *Analects* 1.6, 1.9, 2.21, and 12.11.
[36] *Confucius: Confucian Analects, The Great Learning and The Doctrine of the Mean*, trans. James Legge (New York: Dover Publications, Inc., 1893).

any specific universal set of moral virtues, tradition, and exemplary models. One might argue that this rule allows Confucius to reconstruct moral actions without the prerequisite *li* and its corresponding social context as well as without a definite set of moral virtues. Hence the Golden Rule seems to be superior to Aristotle's metaphysical resource for the theoretical reconstruction of the moral virtues. This is because Aristotle's metaphysics only allows him to reconstruct the moral virtues and does not ensure that a person becomes a moral individual or ensure the execution of moral actions because these depend on the dual presence of the social-political situation and exemplary individuals. Confucius' Golden Rule, on the other hand, seems to allow one to perform the moral actions.

That Confucius' Golden Rule, in abstraction from *li* and its prerequisite context, will not provide one with a universal moral rule for action is clear when one attempts to apply this rule. For example, consider a situation where the agent is deliberating about whether he is to use physical force to get whatever he wants. If this agent is a highly skilled martial artist who always wins in violent encounters, he could arrive at the decision that it is right for him to use physical force to get whatever he wants because he welcomes physical force from others. This is a situation where the Golden Rule does not ensure moral action when used by persons who are not already moral. Hence the rule itself presupposes a standard of morality in order to be effective.

Another problem concerning the Golden Rule is its presupposition of equality between the self and others. This is a problem because one is not always faced with a situation of deliberating among equals in actions. For instance, that I respect my parents' admonitions, harsh and strict though they may be, does not mean that I, too, can admonish my parents with the same tones and attitudes. Heiner Roetz[37] points out that if one takes into consideration *Zy* 13, one can derive "more specific rules for different spheres of action"

---

[37] I am indebted to Roetz's discussion of The Golden Rule in Chapter 10, "Humaneness (*Ren*)," in his *Confucian Ethics of the Axial Age*, and to Wang Qingjie's "The Golden Rule and Interpersonal Care – From a Confucian Perspective," *Philosophy East and West* 49 (1999): 415–38, for my reflections on both these criticisms of the Golden Rule. For extended discussions of this topic, see Roetz, 133–48, and Wang's article.

(Roetz, *Confucian Ethics of the Axial Age*, 140) from the Golden Rule. More specifically, *Zy* 13 states:

Zhong and *Shu* are not far from the *Dao*. (My trans.) In the way of the superior man there are four things, to not one of which have I as yet attained. To serve my father, as I would require my son to serve me: to this I have not attained; to serve my prince, as I would require my minister to serve me: to this I have not attained; to serve my elder brother, as I would require my younger brother to serve me: to this I have not attained; to set the example in behaving to a friend, as I would require him to behave to me: to this I have not attained. (James Legge's trans.)

Even though this formulation seems to solve the problem of how one behaves toward unequals, I also agree with Roetz when he says that this solution makes Confucius' Golden Rule into "a rule in the narrower sense which only determines what should be done within the given framework of unquestioned concrete social conditions" (Roetz, 140). What this does to the Golden Rule is similar to my previous criticism in that the Golden Rule becomes dependent on some external correct standard of behavior between unequals and hence we are back to the same problem of having to reconstruct such a standard for Confucius because we are considering his resources for dealing with the absence of such a proper social context.

In considering the tension between an apparently equity-biased Golden Rule and the hierarchical structure of Chinese society, Roetz observes that such a tension can be dissolved in two directions. He suggests that one could either move "in the direction of a gradual extension of the egalitarian dimension – in the final analysis, of the democratization of the life world – or in the direction of the dismantlement of the idea of equality in the Golden Rule itself and its tailoring to the actual inequalities of society" (Roetz, 139). We have seen one of the problems with trying to accommodate social inequalities earlier. Wang Qingjie in his "The Golden Rule and Interpersonal Care – A Confucian Perspective," attempts a radically different way of tailoring the Golden Rule to the inequalities of society. Instead of relying on *li* to provide the modes of behavior in a hierarchically based society, Wang reinterprets *shu* as "interpersonal care and love" and makes it the basis of *zhong*, *li*, *xin*, and the other Confucian virtues. Wang holds that *li* is not unchangeable for

Confucius, and it is *shu* that determines *li*. *Zhong* also, as Wang interprets it, will become "stupid loyalty," and *xin* will become "blind faith," if each of these does not originate from *shu*. Interpreting *shu* individualistically, Wang claims that it is "to follow (*ru*) each individual's heart/mind," in contrast to *zhong*, which is the "center or togetherness (*zhong*) of the hearts/minds (*xin*)" (Wang, 423). Starting from *shu*, Wang maintains that "Without all the particular hearts, there would be no 'middle,' no 'center,' and no 'togetherness' at all." It is noteworthy that though Wang points out that *xin* refers to both the heart and the mind, he elevates the heart and downplays the mind component in his account. Starting from an individual's love and care for those that are closer to him, Wang follows Michael Walzer in arguing for beginning from a "thick" rather than "thin" morality, and he follows Richard Rorty in deriving morality from "what comes naturally in one's dealing with your parents, children . . . respecting the trust they place in you." Is love, as Wang defines it, especially the love for those that are closest to us, the answer to all moral questions? And is this the foundation of *li* and moral virtues, as Wang claims?

First, there seems to be an inconsistency between Wang's starting with an individual and then having to reconstruct the community and *li* from the individual's heart and Confucius' stress on the *li* and community over the individual.[38] Second, that loving and caring (as defined by Wang, where feelings are stressed over thought) for one's family members does not always produce moral actions is clear in many cases where a family member, say a mother, declares her love for her children to such an extent that she would not allow them to do anything for themselves or for others, nor would she do anything that displeases them. This mother may truly love and treasure her children, but such feelings do not necessarily issue in moral actions. Such love can issue in actions that are immoral as well; in the aforementioned case, the mother's actions would have ruined her children's abilities to learn the virtues of caring for others and to acquire other

---

[38] For the overwhelming significance of *li* and its priority over other factors in the establishment of character, see *Analects* 8.8, 16.13, and 20.3. For how *li* seems to perfect and condition other virtues, see 8.2. For how *ren* consists in curtailing one's inclinations and in curtailing the following of one's heart in order to follow *li* instead (one could argue against Wang), see 12.1.

self-directed virtues. Love alone, or following one's heart alone, as Wang defines it, does not guarantee a moral content. Rather, it is a moral content that will provide a proper goal for the heart to follow and hence allow for love or care that is genuine.[39] As such, in order for it to work, love or interpersonal care presupposes an account of what things are good for human beings. Hence we are back to the same challenge of having to reconstruct a set of virtues for Confucius.

Because of the limited scope of this chapter, I could only gesture toward a couple of recent scholars who also recognized the possibilities of supplementing Confucius' thinking with a metaphysics. I suggest that recent authors such as Tu Weiming and Benjamin Schwartz, who recognize or attempt to supplement Confucius' thinking with a metaphysics, show that Confucianism is not at odds with metaphysics. Some kind of metaphysics, then, might be helpful in the reconstruction of Confucian ethics.

In discussing Confucius' rectification of names, Schwartz points out that he is in agreement with commentators such as Angus C. Graham and Chad Hansen that Confucius does not deal with abstractions such as "eternal forms" or "self-subsistent universals." However, Schwartz also noted that the absence of such ontological speculations does not mean that one should "dogmatically deny" such ideas in the neo-Confucians. Schwartz speculates about the difficulties of the relation between the ideal and the real for Confucius and compares his problem to that of Socrates and Plato. Schwartz claims that Confucius provides neither an "explicit 'metaphysical' explanation for the gap between the ideal reality and

---

[39] Wang's interpretation of *shu* as following the heart/mind harbors a world of possibilities in the reconstruction of how *shu* can relate to morality. However, Wang's stress on the bodily and feeling part of the *xin* component of *shu*, at the expense of the mind part, prevents him from taking advantage of such a reconstruction. As Aristotle had realized, love as a feeling is something that even animals and children share. However, love as friendship (*philia*) is something that requires decision and hence is a virtue. This is a topic that needs more space for development and hence will not be undertaken here.

For how Confucius himself recognizes that untailored love goes after beauty rather than virtue, see *Analects* 1.7; see also 8.9, 8.12, and my earlier discussion of love and knowledge in this chapter. See 5.3 for how virtuous men need exemplars of virtue in order to become virtuous. Therefore, *shu* alone, or love for family members alone, is not going to make one virtuous.

corrupt actuality" nor a method for closing the gap. Nevertheless, Schwartz recognizes that such a metaphysical explanation is consistent with Confucius' thinking.[40]

By the same token, Tu Weiming tackles the Confucian problem of the gap between the ideal and the real, about which Schwartz also speculates, as follows.[41] First, Tu points out that the Confucian self is in a "dynamic process of spiritual development" (Tu, *Confucian Thought*, 125). As to why the self should be developing in this way, he maintains that it is because human nature is intrinsically good. Tu then raises the question, "If goodness is intrinsic to human nature, why is there any need for self-realization?" (Tu, *Confucian Thought*, 126). Tu answers the question concerning the apparent paradox between intrinsic human goodness and the necessity of self-realization by drawing a distinction between "ontological assertion" and "existential realization" and maintaining that there is a dialectical relation between the two. As Tu puts it, "Human nature is good so that there is an authentic possibility for dynamic spiritual development and vice versa" (Tu, *Confucian Thought*, 126). Tu holds that the goodness of our nature is "in a latent state" so that it takes much effort to realize this goodness in reality. I am very sympathetic with Tu's attempt to establish a teleology for Confucius and his attempt to get it started. However, to make the starting point a potency (i.e., for him to assert that our goodness is latent) is to weaken his attempt. To say that the self will develop because it *can* become good is not to say that the self will develop and *this* is its good. Such a development of the self, as presented by Tu, is too contingent upon the social context, which Tu recognizes where he stresses the significance of the father–son relationship as a context for self-cultivation (Tu, *Confucian Thought*, 127). However, such a context cannot be presupposed in our attempt to reconstruct the virtues in the absence of these social-political contexts. Thus, what is required is a more adequate metaphysics that will also better accommodate the kinds of distinctions and solutions that Tu is attempting. But, more importantly, what Tu and Schwartz have shown is that Confucianism is not inconsistent with some kind of metaphysics. Furthermore, the

---

[40] See Schwartz, *The World of Thought in Ancient China*, 93–94.
[41] See Tu, *Confucian Thought*, 126–27.

comparison of Aristotle and Confucius on the advantages of a standard of justification for an account of the moral virtues shows that Confucianism could benefit from a metaphysical account.

In conclusion, unlike Aristotle, who could reconstruct his standards of morality by using his metaphysics, Confucius has no similar foundation for reconstructing his moral virtues. If Confucius could, like Aristotle, provide a metaphysical basis for his view of the family, he might be able to distinguish a corrupt family from a normal one, or a corrupt love from a normal one, and hence guard against dysfunctions that would adversely affect the society. There will still be room for dispute because the Aristotelian form is always known in a *generic* way – we cannot deduce specifics from it. But it can nevertheless provide some important guidance of a sort that is not available to the pure Confucian understanding. In short, Aristotle could theoretically rescue his account of the virtues because of their metaphysical or objective basis. Confucius could also reconstruct and defend his account of the virtues only by appropriating such a basis. That this basis is compatible with Confucius' ethics is clear from my discussions of Schwartz's and Tu's accounts of the place of metaphysics in Confucian thought.

That a metaphysical appeal would aid Confucian ethics is a claim that will be fleshed out in subsequent chapters, where I shall consider how it could be used to justify Confucius' account of the virtuous mean in action and to make explicit a sense of substance that is presupposed in his account of the self, who is to act virtuously. No genuine dialogue is one-way, however; the same discussion will bring out some weaknesses in Aristotle's account of ethics and show how Confucius' account could offer resources for rectifying the Stagirite's position. That a dialogue between Confucius and Aristotle might foster mutual aid makes it well worth pursuing. However, the very possibility of such a dialogue is disputed. Therefore, in the next two chapters, I address some methodological issues surrounding the comparability of Aristotle and Confucius. I consider issues of culture and language as well as a vital question about realism.

In this chapter, I have argued that Confucians could reconstruct their ethics, even though the contexts that support it have long since vanished, with the help of a metaphysical appeal of the sort that enables Aristotelians to reconstruct their account when faced with a similar predicament. This is plausible just in case Aristotelians and Confucians could discuss their similarities and differences, and their strengths and weaknesses, and could come to recognize resources in each other for the rectification of their weaknesses. Can these two traditions, so separate geographically and so disparate culturally, with their radically different standards of explanation, interpretation, and justification, really communicate with each other? I take up this issue in Chapter 2.

2

Categories and Commensurability in Confucius and Aristotle

A Response to MacIntyre

Alasdair MacIntyre argues in "Incommensurability, Truth, and the Conversation between Confucians and Aristotelians about the Virtues" that despite certain agreements about the virtues, Confucian and Aristotelian traditions are ultimately incommensurable.[1] By this, MacIntyre means that each of these systems "has its own standard and measures of interpretation, explanation, and justification internal to itself," so that when dealing with rival claims, there are "no shared standards and measures, external to both systems and neutral between them, to which appeal might be made to adjudicate between" them.[2] For instance, a Confucian may notice that an act of giving fails to conform to *li* (ritual propriety) (e.g., one might have neglected to use both hands and bow in the act), a lack that prevents the act from being truly generous and the agent from being *ren* (the highest Confucian virtue – sometimes translated

---

[1] Alasdair MacIntyre, "Incommensurability, Truth, and the Conversation between Confucians and Aristotelians about the Virtues," in *Culture and Modernity: East–West Philosophic Perspectives*, ed. Eliot Deutsch (Honolulu: University of Hawaii Press, 1991), 104–22. The literature against this particular view of MacIntyre is quite substantial. For instance, see David Hall and Roger Ames, prologue to *Thinking from the Han* (Albany: State University of New York Press, 1998), xiff; James T. Brestzke, S.J., "The Tao of Confucian Virtue Ethics," *International Philosophical Quarterly* 35 (1995): 25–41; and Peter J. Mehl, "In the Twilight of Modernity: MacIntyre and Mitchell on Moral Traditions and Their Assessment," *Journal of Religious Ethics* 19 (1991): 21–54, to cite just a few.

[2] MacIntyre, "Incommensurability," 109; see also 110.

as benevolence, humaneness, or authoritative conduct).[3] Such an omission, according to MacIntyre, is necessarily "invisible to the Aristotelian." The Aristotelian, who lacks even the words to translate *li*, therefore would fail to see the moral shortcoming. By the same token, an Aristotelian may notice that an act fails to conform to the order of the *psychê* (soul) for a citizen of a *polis* (state), where both *psychê* and *polis* are understood in very specific teleological ways. The shortcoming is "invisible" to the Confucian because the standard is lacking – the Confucian even lacks the words for *psychê* and *polis*.

Aristotle's ten categories are of undeniable significance in all of his works. Confucius has no explicit list of categories.[4] But I shall argue that these categories – or ones sufficiently similar – are employed and play significant roles in Confucian thought. To show how these thinkers share a fundamental set of categories is also to show that there are grounds for a kind of commensurability and hence for the possibility of dialogue. Their actual specific standards surely differ in important ways. But if the categories employed in their ethical thought are sufficiently similar (implicitly or explicitly), then it is possible for them to communicate their differences, and perhaps try to persuade each other on the specific points of contention. Lacking these more generic categorial grounds, such dialogue – even about disagreements – would be impossible.

Aristotle's ten categories consist of the following: substance (*ousian*), quantity (*poson*), quality (*poion*), relation (*pros ti*), place (*pou* – literally

---

[3] Aristotle may not understand the necessity of the Confucian standard of *li* (such as using both hands and bowing) in the act of giving. Nevertheless, even Aristotle would recognize that one who throws money at the beneficiary, instead of handing him the money, is not acting generously. Thus, even if *li* is not an explicit element in Aristotle's ethics, it does not follow that he cannot be made to understand that the manner in which an act is carried out has moral significance for Confucius. Nor does it follow that he would necessarily disagree with a lesser degree of such a standard.

[4] Angus C. Graham has examined in great detail how Aristotle's use of his ten categories in his inquiry is similar to what has been done in Classical Chinese. Graham follows Emile Benveniste's lead in focusing on the use of interrogatives in his investigation. Whether this is a productive way of examining Aristotle's categories is neither relevant to nor within the scope of this chapter. See Angus C. Graham, "Relating Categories to Question Forms in Pre-Han Chinese Thought," in *Studies in Chinese Philosophy and Philosophical Literature* (Albany: State University of New York Press, 1990), 360–411.

"the where"), time (*pote* – literally "the when"), position (*keisthai*), state or condition (*echein* – literally "to have"), action (*poien*), and affection (*paschein*).[5] I will take each of these categories in turn and show how they are already employed in Confucius' ethics. Substance (*ousia*) will be discussed last because the greatest discrepancy between Aristotle and Confucius is found in this category. My claim is that Confucius uses these categories even when he does not mention them.[6] I focus in this present chapter on showing how each of these ten categories is used in Confucius' *Analects*; that they are used in Aristotle's thinking is a presupposition few, if any, Aristotelians dispute. A more elaborate comparison between these two philosophers' ethical employment of the categories must also be undertaken elsewhere.

Quantities (*posoi*), for Aristotle, are discrete or continuous. Numbers such as three and five are examples of discrete quantities, while lines, solids, places and times, are examples of continuous quantities.[7] The former are discrete because they do not have any common boundary (e.g., three is not joined to five), whereas the latter do share common boundaries (e.g., the past is joined to the present, etc.). Aristotle also maintains that the most unique feature of quantity is that equality (*ison*) and inequality (*anison*) are predicated of it.[8] In its ethical contexts, quantity is a critical category – critical both because without it moral reason is too fluid and also because an overreliance on quantities leads to theoretical and practical troubles. Confucius invokes the category. He says that what worries the ruler of a state or the head of a household is not the people's poverty absolutely considered but "that wealth is inequitably distributed."[9] He goes on to recommend equitable distribution. Confucius speaks

---

[5] Aristotle, *Categories* 1b25–26, *Cat.* hereafter.

[6] One may object to my claim by saying that I am just imposing Aristotle's categories on Confucius. Such a criticism is especially likely from commentators such as Chad Hansen, David Hall, and Roger Ames, who maintain that Confucius is not concerned with objectivity or truth in his use of language but rather with the conventional political or aesthetic phenomena. I argue against these commentators by showing that Confucius' use of language is intertwined with an objective nature and with heaven's mandate about the right *dao* of living in the chapter that follows, "Ritual and Realism in Early Chinese Science."

[7] *Cat.* 4b20–5a13.   [8] *Cat.* 6a26.   [9] *Analects* 16.1.

of quantity (i.e., amount) of wealth, which can either be equitably or inequitably distributed. Depending on its distribution, one either creates poverty or eliminates it and thus is either acting correctly or not. Equity in the distribution of wealth is not merely arithmetic equality. It is a matter that calls for what Aristotle calls particular justice. Likewise, Confucius' view of the appropriate quantity is bound up with the circumstances and parties involved. For example, Ranyou supplies Zihua's mother with ten measures of grain; Confucius suggests two measures instead because he could tell from Zihua's horses and fine furs that he was a rich man. Confucius says, "Exemplary persons help out the needy; they do not make the rich richer" (6.4). Hence equity in distributing wealth for Confucius is not simply a matter of giving everyone equal amounts of wealth. Rather, quantitative consideration is bound up with the relative wealth or poverty of the people and other situational factors. Nevertheless, Confucius uses the category of quantity – and necessarily so – even if he does not dislodge it and hold it up for theoretical examination.

Relative things are for Aristotle explained by reference to something else (*pros heteron*).[10] For example, both habit (*hexis*) and knowledge (*epistêmê*) are of something and hence are explained by reference to something else. Some relatives can have contraries. As Aristotle puts it, "For example, virtue (*aretê*) is the contrary to vice (*kakia*) and knowledge (*epistêmê*) is the contrary to ignorance (*agnoia*)."[11] Some relatives can also vary in degree. For example, things can be more or less relative to each other. Finally, if properly defined, all relatives have correlatives (e.g., master and slave or greater and less are correlatives). Confucius employs the category of relatives extensively. It is also important to note that the features of relatives described by Aristotle are also present in Confucius. For instance, Confucius talks about various virtues such as *ren* (17.6), courage (2.24, 9.92), acting appropriately (*yi*, 4.16, 17.23), living up to one's words (*xin*, 1.6, 2.22) and acting with loyalty and in accordance with the Golden Rule or reciprocity (*shu*, 4.15), just to name a few. So when one is said to have a virtue, he is said, for example, to have the virtue of courage or *ren* and thus his virtue

---

[10] *Cat.* 6a36–37.   [11] *Cat.* 6b15–17. My translation.

is defined with reference to the specific virtue he has. Such relatives as virtue and goodness vary in degree. For instance, Confucius speaks of not befriending one who is not as good as oneself (1.8). His constant contrasts between the *junzi* (exemplary individual) and *xiaoren* (petty or small person) (4.11, 15.21, 6.13, 4.25) also show that virtues and vices are contraries. Such relatives play a significant role in Confucius' ethics because they allow him to identify the virtues and vices and note the variation of degrees in each virtue so that one could get clear about what to pursue and what to avoid and get clear about the degree of one's progress. Another highly significant Confucian use of this category lies in human relationships such as father and son, minister and sovereign, or husband and wife. These are co-defining and correlative so that each has a well-defined role to play (1.4–1.7, 1.9, 2.5, 2.20–2.21, 3.19). Playing one's roles well, especially those beginning in the home, such as fulfilling one's filial and fraternal responsibilities, is the root of *ren* (1.2, 2.2). The category of relation cuts all the way down in Confucius. Aristotle makes quite a lot of human relations[12] and the relativities of virtue,[13] but these are terminated in substances. Substance, the primary category for Aristotle, is not relative and hence is not defined by reference to something outside itself.[14] I shall say more about substance and relation with Aristotle and Confucius later.

Aristotle defines quality (*poion*) as that "in virtue of which men are said to be such and such."[15] Habits (*hexeis*) such as knowledge and virtue are examples of qualities (*poiôn*), for it is in virtue of these that people are said to be knowledgeable and virtuous, respectively. Quality is also the category employed whenever Confucius marks out the abiding habits that qualify one as a person with a certain virtue. A condition for filial piety is: "A person who for three years refrains from reforming the ways of his late father can be called a filial son (*xiao*)" (1.11). Similarly, Confucius distinguishes bravery from *ren* by saying, "The one with *ren* is bound to have courage, but the courageous is not bound to have *ren*" (14.4, my trans.). He also distinguishes loyal actions (*zhong*) from *ren* actions (5.19). Qualities such as relations have contraries. For example knowledge has as its contrary

---

[12] See *NE* VIII–IX.   [13] *NE* III, IV, and VII.   [14] *Cat.* 8a15ff.
[15] *Cat.* 8b25. My translation.

ignorance. Qualities also vary in degree; for example, some people
are more or less virtuous than others. But most importantly for
Aristotle, quality is the only category of which "like" (*homoia*) and
"unlike" (*anomoia*) can be predicated.[16] Confucius observes this
characteristic in his use of quality. For example, he teaches that one
should want to be like someone who is of "exceptional character" and
not want to be like one who is the opposite when he says, "When you
meet persons of exceptional character think to stand shoulder to
shoulder with them; meeting persons of little character, look inward
and examine yourself" (4.17, see also 1.8). Quality then is a category
that is significant to Confucius' ethical thinking because implicitly, he
is constantly delineating the qualities of a certain virtue from those of
another, as well as urging people to become like the exemplary
character rather than the petty person. Quality, plainly, is important
to Confucius both in reference to the variable qualities of habits and
acts and the excellence of one's character. But, more than this,
Confucian thinking observes just those features of qualities Aristotle
highlights – their similarities and dissimilarities, variability, and
contrariety.

Both categories of action (*poein*) and affection (*paschein*) also play
prominent roles in Confucius' thinking. Consider his five attitudes
needed to become *ren*: deference, tolerance, making good on one's
word, diligence, and generosity (17.6). His insistence on *yi* (appropriate) acts (2.24, 7.16, 17.23), as well as *shu* (reciprocated/Golden
Rule) acts (12.2, 15.24), also supports the prominence of action in
his ethics. In conformity with Aristotle's discussion, we find that
actions for Confucius admit contraries (e.g., inappropriate acts, *buyi*)
and variation of degree (4.7). Again, that action is susceptible to
both contraries and variation of degree allows Confucius to encourage the virtuous act instead of its contrary and the act with the
greater degree of virtue instead of the less, hence the usefulness and
significance of this category in his ethics. Confucius believes that an
exemplary person should have certain affections and not others –
should be vexed or glad in the *yi* situations. Affection therefore is
also a commonly employed category in Confucius' work. He says,
"The *ren* are not anxious; the wise are not in a quandary; the

---

[16] *Cat.* 11a16–17.

courageous are not timid" (14.28). Also: "Do not worry over not having an official position; worry about what it takes to have one. Do not worry that no one acknowledges you; seek to do what will earn you acknowledgment" (4.14). Affections and actions, then, are central to Confucius' ethics because there are certain affections that are to be cultivated, which accompany certain virtues, and others that are to be avoided because they accompany vices. If this point of comparison seems too obvious, remember that there are modes of ethical thought that do not make action and affection morally central. Think of Stoicism or (on at least one interpretation) Kantianism. To the extent that they use the category and use it similarly, Confucius' and Aristotle's ethics are to just that extent commensurable.[17]

That place (*pou* – literally "the where") and time (*pote* – literally "the when") are ethically relevant categories in Confucius' thinking is evident in that he distinguishes between places such as the home, the village, the court, the temple, and funeral sites, and discourses about the proper rituals at each of these places (1.6, 1.9, 3.6, 3.15, 9.16, 10.1). Likewise, time is essential to his ethics; Confucius insists a three-year mourning period is necessary for one to be considered filial because that somehow reciprocates the number of years that parents care for children (1.11, 17.21). Both place and time are emphasized when he insists on kowtowing immediately upon entering the hall (9.3). So place and time are relevant categories in Confucius' ethics.

That position (*keisthai*) and state or condition (*echein* – literally "to have") are also very visible in Confucius' highly ritualized system of ethics is exemplified when he talks about wearing a silk cap instead of a hemp cap in observance of *li*. Similarly, both position and state are discussed in a report of how Confucius would stand up and walk quickly when he encountered those wearing mourning clothes (9.10). Such concerns might seem superficial to most twentieth-century observers, but for Aristotle, and even more for Confucius, they show

---

[17] It is not necessary for me to take sides on the issue of whether commensurability is necessarily determinate or indeterminate. Rather, whether two modes of thought are commensurable or not, and to what degree they are commensurable, is to be determined on a case by case basis.

two things. First, they show that character is so pervasive that it is visible even in attire and position (which at least potentially exert an influence on others even prior to actions). Second, they show that matters of manners are ethical issues for both Aristotle[18] and Confucius. Manners and ceremony are on a continuum with other matters of ethical concern. Moral systems that recognize this, by according categories of *situs* (position) and *habitus* (attire) moral pertinence, are again to that extent comparable.

Finally, substance (*ousia*) is the most important of all the ten categories to Aristotle,[19] whereas Confucius gives priority to relations. But if we could identify something in Confucius that satisfies the criteria of substance, then dialogue between the two regarding their strongest difference will be all the more feasible. Aristotle defines primary substances as those that "underlie (*hupokeisthai*) all other things and all other things will be either predicated of (*katêgoreisthai*) or present in (*en*) them."[20] The individual man and individual horse are examples (*Categories* (hereafter *Cat.*) 2a13). But the most distinctive mark (*idion*) of substance is that it can change (*metabolên*) to admit contrary qualities (e.g., virtue or vice) "while remaining one in number (*hen arithmô*) and the same (*tauton*)."[21]

Confucian commentators have often denied that there is any sense of a substantial self in Confucius.[22] Instead of focusing on the self that

---

[18] *NE* 1125a13–15.

[19] In holding substance to be the most important of all the ten categories, I agree with the traditional commentary on Aristotle's *Categories* and differ from Michael Frede's view that substance is not Aristotle's focus in his *Categories*. While Frede relies on the *Topics* to make his case, I also disagree with his reading of the *Topics* on this issue. Please see "Dialectical Communities: From the One to the Many and Back," in *From Puzzles to Principles? Essays on Aristotle's Dialectic*, ed. May Sim (Lanham, MD: Lexington Books, 1999), 183–214, for my position on the centrality of definition and hence the talk of substance in the *Topics*, and subsequently for the centrality of substance in Aristotle's *Categories*. See Michael Frede, "Categories in Aristotle," in *Essays in Ancient Philosophy* (Minneapolis: University of Minnesota Press, 1987), ch. 3.

[20] *Cat.* 2b15–18. My translation.   [21] *Cat.* 4b16–18. My translation.

[22] Fingarette, in "The Problem of Self in the *Analects*," asserts that "Confucius teaches, as central to his way, that we must have no self and not impose our personal will." See Herbert Fingarette, "The Problem of Self in the *Analects*," *Philosophy East and West* 29 (1979): 129–40. Xinzhong Yao is another who denies a metaphysical self in Confucius. His reason is that a metaphysical self necessitates a substance that is fixed and unchangeable. See Yao's "Self Construction and Identity," 179–95.

issues forth appropriate actions (e.g., acting with *shu* or *zhong* in various circumstances), these Confucian commentators focus on the roles that dictate the *li* that is appropriate. These are really distinct issues. Even if one's roles do dictate how to act (with *shu*, *zhong*, or *yi*) in various situations, an account of that which is capable of issuing forth such actions is still needed. Confucius, without theorizing about it, does in discussion invoke a stronger sense of a self than commentators allow. Thus the Confucian self is minimally "substantial"; it persists through various changes, is the source of agency, and can adopt various roles and perform them more or less well.[23]

Confucius' focus is sometimes the individual agent's personal commitment to an action. This requires an even stronger sense of self because it involves an agent's care for her agency and a character's concern for her character. Confucius stresses this personal investment in the performance of actions and quality of character – and puts down the blind following of *li* when he says:

In referring time and again to observing ritual propriety (*li*), how could I just be talking about gifts of jade and silk? And in referring time and again to making music (*yue*), how could I just be talking about bells and drums? (17.11)

Confucius means by this that ritual ceremonies do not merely refer to the motions and materials. On the contrary, appropriateness means that one must tune one's attitude to fit the situation (17.6). This means that one should participate in these rituals with one's entire being. As Confucius puts it, "The expression 'sacrifice as though present' is taken to mean 'sacrifice to the spirits as though the spirits are present' but 'If *I* myself do not participate in the sacrifice, it is as though *I* have not sacrificed at all'" (3.12, my italics). This "I" signifies the source of agency that persists through changes (and so is responsible) and is capable of filling roles. Similarly, Confucius condemns the "village worthy" as the thief of virtue because even though he abides by the conventional standard of morality, his acts are motions that accord with his role without personal commitment

Finally, Roger Ames rejects Aristotle's view because of its teleology. See Ames, TFFS. I discuss these commentators' positions in detail in Chapter 5.

[23] For a detailed discussion of such a minimal substantial self in Confucius, see Chapter 5, "The Moral Self in Confucius and Aristotle."

(17.13). Mere role playing then is not sufficient for Confucius. The distinction between one who fills her roles well and one who does not rests in an investment of the person. A substantial enough self must be presupposed for such an investment. Without such a minimal self, we can have neither personal investment nor ownership of the action, let alone a creative addition to the tradition.[24]

A role tells one what a father does, but a role cannot act. A role needs a bearer who can take responsibility for his acts. Commentators who propose a selfless view or a self-as-social-roles view frequently deny the notion of personal responsibility.[25] To support the stronger sense of a self in Confucius, a self that is an agent or a source of choice and responsibility is required.[26] Similarly, while he focuses on relations, Confucius does not at all deny that relations need something to relate – such as particular mothers and children. The same is true for the other nonsubstance categories. My argument is that texts of Confucius point to a minimally substantial self – that which persists through change, terminates relations, bears roles, initiates acts, suffers, and owns qualities – a "minimal" sense of substance. A substance in the minimal sense is an

---

[24] This emphasis on a self that is sincere and true to oneself is the ultimate virtue in *The Doctrine of the Mean*. See *Confucian Analects, the Great Learning and the Doctrine of the Mean*, trans. James Legge. As Confucius puts it: "It is only he who is possessed of the most complete sincerity that can exist under heaven, who can give its full development in his nature. Able to give its full development to his own nature, he can do the same for the nature of other men. Able to give its full development to the nature of other men, he can give their full development to the nature of animals and things" (22; see also 25.2). For a detailed comparison between Confucius and Aristotle on the mean, see Chapter 4, of this volume "Harmony and the Mean in the *Nicomachean Ethics* and the *Zhongyong*."

[25] This is clear when Fingarette points out the incompatibility of such views and personal responsibility. He says, "The Confucian viewpoint, seeing 'person' as a complex abstraction from the concrete social nexus, does not require or even permit use of our concept of personal responsibility for an act or consequence thereof." See Herbert Fingarette, "Comment and Response," in *Rules, Rituals and Responsibility: Essays Dedicated to H. Fingarette*, ed. Mary I. Bockover (La Salle, Il: Open Court, 1991), 200 (hereafter *RR&R*).

[26] That a more substantial self is already there in Confucian literature is visible when Confucius mentions that filial piety consists in refraining from reforming a father's way for three years after a father's death (1.11). Such talk of refrain or restraint presupposes that there is some figment of a self that is to be restrained beyond that of a son whose role is to adhere to the father's wishes – for what of the years following the mourning?

article that terminates recognized accidents – for instance, it is, whatever else it is, that which bears qualities; acts and receives action; stands in relations; occupies positions; fills roles, spaces, and times; and so on. A more maximal sense of substance is a further theory of what this is: for instance, a hylomorphic theory, an account of teleology, and so forth. The texts of Confucius provide ample evidence for not only the nine accidental categories but also the substance category – but only in a minimal sense (because of his heavy emphasis on the categories of relation and quality). Aristotle not only proffers a maximal sense of substance; he leans on features of this theory of substance in his ethics. That is a prime source of the differences between Aristotle and Confucius.

I began this chapter with MacIntyre's view that Aristotle lacks the words to translate *li* and hence would fail to see any shortcoming from violating the *li* in action. Similarly, MacIntyre holds that Confucius lacks the words for *psychê* and *polis* so that he would fail to see the moral shortcoming of actions that violate the order of the *psychê* and *polis*. Having shown that Confucius has an implicit understanding of Aristotle's ten categories, which also means that they can communicate with each other, let me illustrate how Aristotle would be able to explain the concepts of *psychê* and *polis* to Confucius and how Confucius, in turn, would be able to explain the concept of *li* to Aristotle.

Even though no single term in Confucius' vocabulary translates *polis*, he could understand Aristotle's concept of *polis* because he could grasp that human beings come together to form associations to secure their survival and pursue other goods. That such human associations necessarily occupy certain places, last for a certain period of time, and vary in character and style depending on how people are related are facts that Confucius could grasp.[27] Hence, even if they were to disagree about which kind of human association is best, Confucius and Aristotle could understand each other in the main.

Beginning with his own discourses about rulers relating effectively to the ruled, we can explain to Confucius that the *polis* consists of

---

[27] For an elaborate account of Confucius' understanding of the state and how it compares with Aristotle's understanding, see Chapter 6, "Virtue-Oriented Politics: Confucius and Aristotle."

relations between rulers and ruled. Confucius could understand Aristotle's further claim that good rulers need certain qualities because of his own claims about how rulers and ministers should conduct themselves toward the ruled. More specifically, Confucius' claims such as "Rulers should employ their ministers by observing ritual propriety, and ministers should serve their lord by doing their utmost (*zhong*) (3.19)" and "The ruler must rule, the minister minister" (12.11; see also 12.14) can be used to show that the citizens of the *polis* are the ones who undertake the ruling for Aristotle.[28] Furthermore, given that Confucius also prescribes a hierarchy between the rulers and the ministers, where the ministers are the same in rank, one could also explain to him how Aristotle's ideal *polis* is made up of many rulers who are the same in rank. He need not agree that it is good that the rulers should be the same in rank to be able to understand that it is a possible mode of government. On the other hand, that the ruled are to be governed[29] can be communicated to Confucius by pointing to his own claims that "common people do not debate affairs of the state" (16.2) and how they are to be ordered (2.3, 2.19).

More importantly, the *polis* is to satisfy the needs of the ruler and ruled so that all citizens can pursue the good life (i.e., the life of virtue).[30] This may be explained to Confucius by showing that he, too, believes that the ruler's job is to be concerned with having enough food for the people: one of Confucius' advices about effective government is to "[m]ake sure there is sufficient food to eat" (12.7; see also 12.9). Aristotle's claim, obscure or scandalous to the modern West, that beyond necessity the point of the *polis* – its final cause – is moral education would be perfectly intelligible to Confucius because he maintains that once the necessities are met, the next order of business is to "teach them" (13.9). The ultimate goal of ruling is to make the people virtuous – this is evident in Confucius' constant interest in the effects that exemplary rulers have on the people:

The excellence (*de*) of the exemplary person (*junzi*) is the wind, while that of the petty person is the grass. As the wind blows, the grass is sure to bend. (12.19)

---

[28] Aristotle, *Politics* 1275a22–23, *Pol.* hereafter.   [29] *Pol.* VII, 8–9.
[30] *Pol.* I, 1–2.

Lead them with excellence (*de*) and keep them orderly through observing ritual propriety (*li*) and they will develop a sense of shame, and moreover, will order themselves. (2.3; see also 2.1)

In light of his interest in developing the virtues of the people, Confucius would also be able to understand how there should be a certain quantity of people in the *polis* – not so few that it cannot be self-sufficient, and not so many that it cannot be governed properly.[31] The size of the territory[32] is also a quantitative consideration relevant to the well-being of the *polis*. Confucius asks, "How can one speak of a territory of sixty or seventy – or even fifty or sixty – *li* square, and not be referring to a state?" (11.26). Aristotle and Confucius would be mutually intelligible on such quantitative considerations of place. Finally, Confucius could also understand why Aristotle would also make recommendations for the best kind of place for his ideal *polis*[33] if he considers his own view that states are related to each other, the relations of which are affected by one's location (13.3, 9.14, 3.5, 1.10).

MacIntyre would assert[34] that this does not yet show that Confucius would understand Aristotle's concept of the *polis*. The reason is that MacIntyre has a very different conception of the preconditions for understanding and explaining a concept. He believes that his strict contextualist conception of concept is "stronger" than my more Aristotelian category- (and topic-) based conception.[35] Because Confucius lacks experience with the precise forms of social life that are the matrix for the concept of "*polis*," MacIntyre maintains that Confucius will altogether lack the ability to grasp the concept.

I do not deny that one's understanding and use of concepts are bound up with the context within which they have application and are understood. But I want to argue that it is sometimes possible to communicate enough about a context to make an alien term intelligible. The precondition is that there be enough affinity between the two traditions. Confucius' narrower understanding of political

---

[31] *Pol.* VII, 4; see also *Analects* 13.9.   [32] *Pol.* VII, 4–5.   [33] *Pol.* VII, 11.
[34] And did assert, in a letter dated February 4, 2002.
[35] For details of my Aristotelian topic-based conception of concepts, see my "Dialectical Communities: From the One to the Many and Back," in *From Puzzles to Principles? Essays on Aristotle's Dialectic*, 183–214.

government can be expanded to accommodate Aristotle's concept of *polis* because of the proximity of their views about the good of practical life and how political and social institutions are to serve this good. Moreover, Confucius' implicit use of categories sufficiently similar to Aristotle's categories also paves the way for an explanation of Aristotle's concepts. I do not believe all thinkers or all traditions share categories, but when they do – even when the categories are used but not mentioned – it is an important bridge to mutual understanding.

Plainly, Confucius cannot understand an alien political system by simply being given its name. For instance, to say that a particular society has an "aristocratic," or "timocratic," or "oligarchic" form of government would make no sense to Confucius. MacIntyre rightly points out that Confucius was not exposed to the practices and contexts within which these concepts developed and therefore they could not mean to him what they do to others who have had such exposure – if they mean anything to him at all. MacIntyre believes that concepts develop in a history to which they remain internal; if people do not share a history, they cannot share concepts. I believe that concepts develop in contexts but (once developed) need not remain internal. Some concepts are more strongly "contextual" or "internal" than others. Concepts with objective content are not so internal. My argument is that Confucius and Aristotle happen to share some concepts with objective content. Because these are not strongly internal to a history, shared understanding does not require shared history. In these cases, because the pertinent categories are already implied by Confucius' own discourse, explanations that are couched in them may also make sense to him. So while I agree with MacIntyre that a term like *polis* cannot be understood without a sense of its context and associated practices, I disagree with him that this must be inaccessible to Confucius. Confucius already possesses an understanding of a form of political government such as monarchy. Such a context, though seemingly narrow when compared with Aristotle's grasp of a variety of constitutions, can, *by using the relevant categories*, be expanded to enable him to grasp Aristotle's concept of *polis*. Such an expansion of Confucius' context is even more likely in light of how both share so many views regarding the family and the significance of the state for the well-being of the people. In fact,

I think that a Confucian could more readily obtain an understanding of Aristotle's concept – and may be better equipped to evaluate it – than a modern Western contractarian individualist. That is true despite the lack of a shared history in the Confucian case.

To say that Confucius can understand Aristotle's *polis* is not to say that he needs to agree with Aristotle's specific recommendations about it or with Aristotle's analyses of what features might affect it. My thesis is that the basic dimensions of intelligibility are just the pertinent categories: place and time, quantity and quality, and so on. Once mutual understanding is achieved on the basis of such categories, disagreements will be rife. For instance, for Confucius, neither the size of the territory, nor the number of people, nor its location could affect the well-being of the inhabitants of the state. This is clear when one looks at his repeated assertions stressing the significance of the rulers' virtues in affecting the people (13.4, 13.11, 13.13, 12.17), so that it is ultimately not factors such as wealth, number of people, and place per se that affect their well-being but rather, the quality of the rulers and how they handle these factors. For example, Confucius cites with approval the assertion that the ruler "does not worry that his people are poor, but that wealth is inequitably distributed; [d]oes not worry that his people are too few in number, but that they are disharmonious" (16.1). Consequently, one could imagine Confucius deemphasizing these same factors Aristotle recommends for his ideal *polis* and replacing these considerations with the import of having exemplary rulers. Again, the fact that Confucius could disagree with Aristotle about whether, and to what extent, features such as number of people, place, and prosperity are relevant to the people's well-being is a sign that he could understand Aristotle's position on these features (explicable through the categories of quantity, place, and quality, etc.). It is because Confucius also employs these same categories – even if he neither mentions nor reflects philosophically upon them – that he could understand Aristotle's claims about the *polis*.

The substance category is supposed to be the greatest stumbling block to mutual understanding between these two traditions. But what does substantiality amount to in Aristotle's discussion of the *polis*? The substantiality of the *polis* is nothing Confucius must fail to comprehend: it is the independence and self-sufficiency, the wholeness and unity, the enduringness and stability of the organized political body. Using the minimal sense of substance tacit to his thinking, Confucius could see that Aristotle's ideal *polis* has a high degree of self-sufficiency, independence, and wholeness, and that it remains one and the same *polis* through various changes. It consists of parts (people) who cannot satisfy their needs nor reach their virtues without belonging to this whole. These parts/people are related to each other, act and are acted upon, make up a certain number (quantity), are located in a certain place of a certain size, and pursue certain actions to reach their goals. Consequently, even though Confucius lacks the words to translate Aristotle's *polis*, he could still understand what it is by using the relevant categories, most of which are already employed in his own claims about the state and government, even if they are not explicit in his thinking.

Aristotle's concept of *psychê* could be explained to Confucius in much the same way. Confucius has experience of individual persons, how they live, die, eat, grow, think, act, are virtuous or vicious, become better or worse, possess knowledge or not, and are identifiable as the same persons over time. Aristotle could explain that the *psychê* is the single source of the several functions and the cause of the several capacities. Confucius recognizes the difference between a living body and a dead body. Aristotle would say that the difference between the living and the dead body is the presence of a *psychê* in the former. The *psychê* is an internal source of life and motion, without which a body cannot carry out its functions, such as eating, perceiving, thinking, and acting. I not only want to maintain that Confucius could make sense of this claim but will wager that he would find Aristotle's claim of a single internal source of life and thought *more* intelligible than do post-Cartesian dualists in the West. Aristotle's soul is closer to Confucius' heart-and-mind (*xin*) than it is to modern ideas of consciousness or cognitive mind. Apart from being one, the *psychê* also remains one through various changes. That Confucius could see how a person could change and remain essentially the same is clear when he says:

From fifteen, my heart-and-mind was set upon learning; from thirty I took my stance; from forty I was no longer doubtful; from fifty I realized the propensities of *tian* (*tianming*); from sixty my ear was attuned; from seventy I could give my heart-and-mind free rein without overstepping the boundaries. (2.4; see also 1.11, 19.5)

And again, were Confucius to take up an interest in metaphysical speculation, he might argue with Aristotle about whether the form that accounts for the individual's unity is identical with the species form. My claim is that such disagreements presume sufficient common ground, and "categories" can provide this ground.

Confucius could understand Aristotle's *polis* and *psychê* because of his implicit use of the categories through which these concepts may be explained. Let me show next how Aristotle can understand Confucius' *li* even though he, too, lacks the words to translate this term.

Confucian *li* prescribes the appropriate actions and manners for one in various roles. One could explain *li* to Aristotle by invoking the categories of relation, action, quantity, quality, place, time, position, suffering, *habitus*, and substance. One could say that in relation to his father, a son's obedience is necessary to his moral training. Because Aristotle already believes that the moral virtues are attained by repeating the same appropriate actions in the situations that call for them, he would be able to understand why a prescribed set of actions between, say, father and son will help in cultivating the son and in letting the father exercise his role of nurturing, educating, and ruling over his son.[36] Apart from obedience, deference and respect are also appropriate ways of comporting oneself toward one's parents for Confucius. So acts that show honor toward their parents, such as "contributing their energies when there is work to be done, and deferring to their elders when there is wine and food to be had" (2.8), can again be explained to Aristotle as the appropriate acts children should accord their parents and hence are acts that are to be repeatedly performed in such relations to cultivate the proper way of honoring parents. One could explain, using Aristotelian categories, that *li* is a set of normative action – patterns, habits of social history – something like ethics writ large. Aristotle could understand Confucius' *li* because he already shares with Confucius the understanding that the quality of honor is to be accorded one's superior and already agrees that habituation is key. All Aristotle lacks is a concept for the large-scale cultural pattern. This concept, though lacking, can be encroached upon along the lines laid down by the pertinent categories. Aristotle would have no trouble understanding the

---

[36] *NE* 1161a16–18.

intertwining in *li* of the deepest moral matters with details of manners, dress, posture, and so on – far less trouble, it seems to me, than
most ethicians in the modern West. For instance, he describes the
parent–child relation as a friendship of superiority and says, "that is
why parents are also honored."[37] But it is also crucial that this honor
is manifested by "standing up, [and] giving up seats and so on."[38]
Aristotle would then understand Confucius' *li* as the social pattern of
habits and acts that exemplify the universal virtue of honor.

Li, for Confucius, is not just a set of motions one undergoes in
various situations. He says:

> Those today who are filial are considered so because they are able to provide
> for their parents. But even dogs and horses are given that much care. If you
> do not respect your parents, what is the difference? (2.7)

Again, he says:

> It all lies in showing the proper countenance. As for the young contributing
> their energies when there is work to be done, and deferring to their elders
> when there is wine and food to be had, how can merely doing this be con-
> sidered being filial? (2.8)

Confucius could explain to Aristotle that the *li* is not simply a set of
behaviors to be mindlessly imitated; he, like Aristotle, maintains that
there are internal conditions that make one truly virtuous. These
conditions include knowing that it is a virtuous act that one is carrying
out, deciding on the act for its own sake rather than for the sake of
some gain to oneself, not regretting one's action, and taking pleasure
in the act.[39] Because of these qualities of mind (decisions and states)
that must accompany an act in order for the actor to be considered
virtuous, Aristotle could understand why Confucius would put down
one who adheres to all the moral acts required of him and yet is totally
devoid of any personal investment in carrying out those acts. Such a
person is exemplified in Confucius' discussion of the "village worthy."
He says, "The 'village worthy' is excellence (*de*) under false pretense"
(17.13). The "village worthy" for Confucius is one who appears to be
outwardly excellent in that he abides by all the laws or moral acts
expected of him, but is inwardly bankrupt in that he lacks the
appropriate attitudes and motives that should accompany those acts.

---

[37] *NE* 1161a20–21.   [38] *NE* 1165a28.   [39] *NE* 1105a30–35, 1104b3–9.

Li dictates that one is to act in such and such a manner (exhibiting the qualities of the right attitude and virtue, and attributing the right quantity of honor or respect, or giving the right quantity of gifts), in relation to so and so (one's relatives, sovereign, or subordinates, where each of these persons is understood through a minimal sense of substance that makes them remain who they are), at such and such a place (in the court, home, or at the graveyard), and at such and such a time (of ritual sacrifice, wedding, or funeral). Again, Aristotle could understand Confucius' *li* because (1) Aristotle and Confucius share the categories of quality, relation, place, time, quantity, and even action and passion; and (2) Confucius' concept of *li* can be explained in terms of those categories. Once again, I urge that explainability, not translatability, is the pivotal issue for mutual understanding.

A last sticking point that might seem to block mutual understanding is the Confucian idea that *li* is the final appeal for matters of proper behavior and attitude. But Confucius would want to explain that *li* is not a set of arbitrary prescriptions of ritual propriety but rather is rooted in a *dao* (way) that has been transmitted through tradition. That the *li* exemplifying the proper *dao* (way) will always be captured by people's way of life is evident when we see one of Confucius' students, Zigong, responding to the question "With whom did Confucius study?" as follows:

The way (*dao*) of Kings Wen and Wu has not collapsed utterly – it lives in the people. Those of superior character (*xian*) have grasped the greater part, while those of lesser quality have grasped a bit of it. Everyone has something of Wen and Wu's way in them. Who then does the Master not learn from? Again, how could there be a single constant teacher for him? (19.22)

Even though it may have been modified over time, *li* is preserved not only in the people's way of life but also through written works. For instance, in response to a question about what the *li* in ten generations would be, Confucius says:

The Yin dynasty adapted the observances of ritual propriety (*li*) of the Xia dynasty, and how they altered them can be known. The Zhou adapted the observances of ritual propriety of the Yin, and how they altered them can be known. If there is a dynasty that succeeds the Zhou, even if it happens a hundred generations from now, the continuities and changes can be known. (2.23)

That we rely on written works to know the *li* of a particular dynasty is clear when Confucius says:

> I am able to speak on ritual propriety (*li*) during the Xia dynasty, but its descendent state, Qi, does not provide adequate evidence. I am able to speak on ritual propriety during the Yin dynasty, but its descendent state, Song, does not provide adequate evidence. It is because these states have inadequate documentation and few men of letters. (3.9; see also 17.9 on how the *Songs* can transmit the proper *li*)

Aristotle could understand the variation of *li* in various dynasties because he was attuned to how variations in the types of people who make up the ruling and the ruled, and their characteristics (e.g., their wealth, virtue, and occupations), all contribute to making their constitutions quite different from others. There are even variations within the same type of constitution, and these differences typically reflect variations in the customs and manners of the respective groups. For instance, Aristotle discusses five types of democracies and four types of oligarchies.[40] Democracies can exist where the poor are as qualified to rule as the rich, or where property determines who can rule but because the required property is so minimal, the many qualify, or where one's qualification for office is determined by birth. Apart from these considerations, the occupation of the ruler and ruled will also contribute to the democracy by making it a democracy that is primarily agricultural or trade oriented, hence determining if the law or active political legislation by the rulers is sovereign. Because Aristotle understood the variety of constitutions and how each may require a different kind of rule or way to govern and habituate the people, he could also understand how a different set of *li* may better suit a different set of people for Confucius precisely for the purpose of moral training toward a set of virtues.

Aristotle says, "For law (*nomos*) has no power to persuade (*peithesthai*) besides custom (*ethos*), but this will not come to be (*ou gignetai*) if not through (*dia*) a great length of time (*chronou*)."[41] To the extent that the laws for Aristotle constitute the content of cultivation, he could understand that Confucius' *li* serves a similar function. However, Confucius' understanding of law is different from

---

[40] *Pol.* IV, 4–5, 1291b14–1293b22.   [41] *Pol.* 1269a20–23. My translation.

Aristotle's because he does not conceive of laws as forming the content of cultivation but rather as external and without the kind of impact that *li* has on character formation. As Confucius puts it:

Lead the people with administrative injunctions (*zheng*) and keep them orderly with penal law (*xing*), and they will avoid punishments but will be without a sense of shame. Lead them with excellence (*de*) and keep them orderly through observing ritual propriety (*li*) and they will develop a sense of shame, and moreover, will order themselves. (2.3)

Even better than written law for understanding Confucius' *li* is Aristotle's view of unwritten law or "custom."[42] This is more sovereign in Aristotle's view because it not only encompasses more, and more significant, issues than written law but is also safer than written law because it is immune from the tendency toward tyranny from the rule of a man. As Aristotle puts it:

But laws resting on unwritten custom are even more sovereign, and concerned with issues of still more sovereign importance, than written laws; and this suggests that, even if the rule of a man be safer than the rule of written law, it need not therefore be safer than the rule of unwritten law.[43]

We see again that even without the words to translate Confucius' *li*, Aristotle could understand the concept because it is explicable by the qualities to be cultivated, the significance of differences in place and time, the focal importance of relations (especially relations between the rulers and ruled), the shaping of actions and passions by ongoing customs, and so on. Again I claim that the pivotal issue for mutual understanding is not the translation of terms but the explanation of concepts. Explanation is made possible, in this case at least, because of an underlying similarity in the structure of their categories.

MacIntyre has argued that in spite of their agreements about the virtues, the Confucian and Aristotelian traditions are ultimately incommensurable because they have no shared standard and measures of interpretation, explanation, and justification to adjudicate their differences. These differences, MacIntyre maintains, are radical enough that each lacks the words for the other's key concepts.

---

[42] See Chapter 6 for an elaborate comparison of Aristotle's and Confucius' views on law and habituation.
[43] *Pol.* 1287b5–8. My translation.

He maintains that they necessarily fail even to recognize the other's problems and moral shortcomings. I have shown how Confucius' text provides ample evidence for the nine Aristotelian accidental categories, and even the substance category in a minimal sense. Even supposing these two ethical systems do not share all standards and measures, it does not follow that they are so radically disparate that they employ no kindred concepts or must necessarily find utterly unintelligible what the other advocates or repudiates. My point is that given the significant role of these categories in both views, MacIntyre exaggerates the distance between them. Those ten little concepts Aristotle presents as our basic modes of predication are used by both thinkers and so can help us to investigate their similarities and differences. Thanks to the ten categories, dialogue between these two great and culturally diverse traditions of thought is possible. Thanks to their different perspectives on kindred topics, it can be fruitful.

The minimal basis for shared speech is the use of common categories. I have shown in this chapter that Aristotelians and Confucians can, at least in principle, have a dialogue about their similarities and differences because Confucius uses Aristotle's ten categories even though he never holds them up for reflection or even mentions them. The availability of categorial commensurability is but a minimal condition of dialogue, and we must compare the two in greater detail with respect to topics such as the mean or harmony, which characterizes virtuous acts, and the moral individual, who is the agent of the virtuous actions. Much of the book is dedicated to these more detailed explorations. There is, however, one nagging preliminary issue.

I have claimed in the present chapter that Confucius makes use of categories that an Aristotelian could recognize and have argued, moreover, that a Confucian could recognize these same categories as somehow her own. It is this second claim that needs further underwriting, not least because I have based my argument on the objectivity of these categories – or rather, at this point, on the idea that members of both traditions could be brought to see this objectivity. The nagging difficulty in this is that many contemporary Confucian commentators deny outright that the Confucian tradition is in any way concerned with objectivity in this sense.

For example, recent commentators maintain that when Confucius speaks about the rectification of names (*zhengming*), he is engaged in a social act of adjusting rituals – something that should not be understood in any epistemic or metaphysical way at all. They wish to claim that instead of capturing some truth or objective condition in the world, Confucius' interest in naming is directed toward the practical outcome of increasing social harmony. In the next chapter, I will argue that Confucius' use of language – and his rectification of names in particular – is oriented not only toward practical social tuning but also toward an objective nature. Settling this point will help to clinch my argument about comparability. After that, I shall proceed to the more detailed comparisons of the moral self, the mean, and so on.

3

Ritual and Realism in Early Chinese Science

Is it a prejudice merely of Western thinking to suppose that learning and knowledge want definition and a due measure of objectivity? Given that learning is such an important element in Confucian thought, it might seem strange that commentators such as Hall and Ames and Chad Hansen deny that Confucius is interested in the pursuit of definitions. They contrast Confucius with ancient Greek thinkers such as Aristotle, for whom definitions are key. I want to show that definition and what we call "objectivity" are among the goals of name rectification for Confucius and for practices of study in classical China. Name rectification, in turn, is best understood to be a matter of adjusting language with its objectives so that a harmony of the human and the nonhuman orders, as well as human social harmony, is the outcome. Naming is not merely a political or aesthetic phenomenon. I begin this chapter with Aristotle. It is well known that concern with definition permeates his entire corpus, but it is not so well known why definition is crucial. I say why and then contrast this with Confucius and his tradition. Although the rectification of names always serves practice, I disagree with commentators such as Ames and Hansen, who insist that Confucius is never interested in getting the "right" name that would, like a definition, align language with nonhuman nature. I argue that Confucius is concerned with this alignment, which is served by rectification. To make my case, I offer the negative point that clear definitions need not hinder practice: on the contrary, sharp definitions help pinpoint states of character, features of situations, and kinds of actions that ought to be taken. I then offer the more positive point that rectification of names is essential to the pursuit of knowledge of nature. My examples here are traditional Chinese astronomy and herbal medicine.

Consider the following comparison, which I offer as an analogy.[1] In 1790, still gripped by revolutionary fervor and full of universalistic Enlightenment notions, the National Assembly of France commissioned its academy of science to recommend a system of measures intended for use by all nations. This was the metric system (essentially that of Gabriel Mouton devised a century earlier). France officially adopted the system in 1795, and by 1875, fifteen countries had followed suit. Few nations today use a different system. (The United States has yet to adopt the system, even though it should be familiar with the advantages of a decimal system because its currency was the first decimal currency.) Not only does a decimal system have internal advantages in terms of simplicity of reckoning, but there are large advantages in terms of coordination and efficiency of transaction. Nations that have not adopted the system continually need to adjust and recalibrate in order to interface with nations that have.[2] The declaration by a political authority that a particular system of measures is to be adopted is not a declaration that bears on or reflects a natural and objective order. Some systems may be more useful or efficient for some purposes rather than others, but this is a practical point, not a claim that a given system is more "natural" or more "objective" than any other.[3] Systems of measure can be used in reference to objective nature, but none is in itself more objective than any other, even though some will be *authoritative* by virtue of being adopted as normative by some cultural group.

Compare this with a second case. In 1582, Pope Gregory XIII issued the bull *Inter Gravissimas*, which resulted in calendar reform.

---

[1] I owe this comparison to Wes DeMarco, whom I also thank for urging the point about the harmony between human and natural orders.

[2] In 1959, for instance, the definition of "inch" was altered slightly so that one inch would equal exactly 2.54 centimeters. That is an obvious attempt to harmonize two sets of conventions.

[3] It may *seem* miraculous that the speed of light in a vacuum is exactly 299,792,458 meters per second, with no remainder. But that is merely because the "meter" has recently been redefined to be the distance light travels in a vacuum in 1/299,792,458 seconds. Here again is a paradigmatic entwining of fact and convention.

The need for reform flowed from the fact that the Julian calendar (adopted in 46 B.C.E. to replace the more ancient *ab urbe condita* calendar) had been slipping. The calendar year was increasingly out of synchrony with the equinoxes and solstices, and the Roman Church especially was concerned that the date for Easter was nudging toward summer by the sixteenth century. The central innovation of the Gregorian calendar was to have a leap year not every four years (as in the Julian calendar, based on the system of Aristarchus) but every year divisible by four and not by one hundred, or every year divisible by one hundred but not by four hundred. This reform had a large impact on the whole series of holy days and public festivals. Moreover, Easter came to be normalized, and the first day of the new year came to be January 1, instead of March 25 as was the case with the Julian calendar. Italy, Spain, Portugal, and Poland adopted the system immediately; other countries followed suit little by little, though it was not until 1752 that Britain and its colonies adopted the Gregorian system. In every case, official adoption or nonadoption had religious, social, political, and economic consequences.

Notice that there is a difference between the case of the authorization of the metric system and the authorization of the Gregorian calendar. In the calendar example, the Julian system was drifting out of sync with an objective condition – the solstices and equinoxes – and the new system was as a matter of fact better able to track this natural condition than was the previous system. Any calendar reform surely involves a large dose of pragmatics: political issues and even intrigues are part of the story, and certainly a calendar is a social construction. But reform also involves reference to a natural condition to which our practices of timing must adjust, and some systems adjust better than others. Now here is the point of my analogy. Prominent contemporary Confucian commentators claim that the "rectification of names" is ultimately to be understood on something like the model of the conversion of measurement systems. I want to argue that in some cases – in fact in many and the most important sorts of case – name rectification is instead to be understood on the model of calendar reform. The rectification of names is on the whole more like the case of calendar reform than it is like the case of measurement conversion because it has political causes and consequences, but also makes reference to objective conditions that it must track and to which it must adjust.[4]

I shall show that traditional Chinese astronomical study involves ritual social authorization and a healthy dose of convention, but it also aspires to a correct depiction of the movements of heavenly bodies, even as it is at the same time closely bound up with a declaration of standards and measures by the incoming ruler and with ritual or even magical purposes. Both the purpose of "objectivity" and the practical point of the study are, I shall maintain, crucial to the classical Chinese way of examining the heavens. I shall discuss more briefly the traditional pharmacopoeia of herbal medicine, which similarly betrays both a concern with getting the right correlations between names and things – frequently a matter of life and death in this case – and with ritual or even magical practices. In all such cases, the "rightness" toward which we rectify is an alignment both with authoritative practice and with the facts of the matter.

It is crucial to see that there is no tension between these concerns in the Confucian mind, not least because of the conviction that when something is "right" relative to ritual it is right relative to nature, just as the way of the Zhou *li* is the way of heaven. It is the modern commentator who feels it necessary to champion one side or the other and to argue practice at the expense of truth or science at the expense of ritual. But such selective reading winds up turning the rectification of names into either a protoscience divorced from ritual concern or performative pragmatics servicing ritual divorced from objective knowledge of nature and the right way of life mandated by heaven. The Confucian, on the other hand, would simply find that names rectified with respect to harmonious social practice are ipso facto rectified with respect to the order of nature or the way of heaven. These must be understood to be two sides of the same coin. The Confucian way of naming stands in the

---

[4] No rule-based calendar system is entirely adequate. Moreover, there is a further and inescapable element of convention or choice in the decision to adjust a calendar to the mean tropical year or the vernal equinox year. These are different, and we simply must choose. The modern Eastern Orthodox calendar is more accurate than the Gregorian with reference to the first; the Gregorian is more accurate than the Orthodox with respect to the latter.

middle. Names stand between definition and description. The rectification of names involves theory-like and practice-like aspects. Ignorance of either aspect will distort our understanding of the Confucian way. The rectification of names serves authoritative practice but it also serves truth. Its goal is a *rightness* that is at one and the same time harmony with other people in an order of social relations and a harmony with nonhuman nature under the order of heaven.

I turn now to the role of definition in all this, and, since Aristotle is so often a favorite foil for East/West contrasts, to Aristotle. In *Posterior Analytics* I,2, we read that scientific knowledge consists in knowing the cause (*aitian*) from which a thing (*to pragma*) is, which in the focal case cannot be other than it is (*Posterior Analytics*, hereafter *APo* 71b9–13). Knowing causes as causes is scientific knowledge. Science proceeds from definitions and advances through causal demonstration. Causal demonstration is rather more than deduction; it proceeds through establishing the middle term of a syllogism as the proper cause of the phenomenon under study. As Aristotle puts it, "By demonstration (*apodeixin*) I mean a syllogism (*sullogismon*) productive of scientific knowledge (*epistêmonikon*)" (*APo* 71b17).[5] He argues that the primary premises of such a syllogism must be true, primary, immediate, and in a sense better known than the conclusion (*APo* 71b20–21). The primary premises of a demonstrative syllogism must themselves be indemonstrable to avoid, in Geoffrey E. R. Lloyd's words, "the twin problems of circularity and infinite regress."[6] Inference from necessary premises results in scientific knowledge that is also necessary. What then constitutes these necessary first premises of scientific demonstration? Aristotle tells us that these must be the

---

[5] *Aristotle: Posterior Analytics, Topica*, The Loeb Classical Library from Aristotle, trans. Hugh Tredennick and E. S. Foster (Cambridge, MA: Harvard University Press, 1960).

[6] As G. E. R. Lloyd puts it: "It was Aristotle, as is well known, who first clearly defined and classified the various types of indemonstrables, that is, in his view, definitions, axioms and hypotheses. That demonstration must ultimately be based on primary propositions that are themselves indemonstrable is clinched, in the *Posterior Analytics* I 2, 71b9ff, I 3, 72b5ff, with arguments that show that this must be so, to avoid the twin problems of circularity and infinite regress." See G. E. R. Lloyd, *Adversaries and Authorities: Investigations into Ancient Greek and Chinese Science* (Cambridge: Cambridge University Press, 1996), 55.

essential attributes of the kind of thing under consideration by that science, causes that make a thing to be what it is. As he puts it:

> Since in each genus it is the attributes that belong essentially (*kat' auta*) to that particular genus that belong to it of necessity (*ex anankês*), it is evident that scientific demonstrations (*apodeixeis*) are concerned with essential attributes and proceed from them. For accidental attributes (*sumbebêkota*) are not necessary (*ouk anankaia*), and therefore we do not necessarily know why the conclusion is true. (*APo* 75a28–34; see also 74b5–12)

Definitions capture these essential attributes. Aristotle says that definition [*horismos*] is "of the essence [*ti esti*]" or "of being [*ousias*]" (*APo* 90b30). The being or essence is expressed in an attribute that is definable (*APo* 75b30–31, 82b36–37). In sum, causal demonstration is the vehicle of Aristotelian science, and definition is crucial to demonstration as its starting point. As Aristotle puts it, "the starting points [*archai*] of demonstrations are definitions [*horismoi*]" (*APo* 90b24).

Definitions are intended to capture essences, and essences are not demonstrated but rationally intuited. A statement of essence is never the conclusion of a syllogism, though it may enter into its premises and figure in the conclusion. Nevertheless, a demonstration may be invoked to show that an essence is in fact functioning as a cause and in that way may enter into the demonstrative content of a syllogism. In this sense, Aristotle speaks of proving that essential attributes (*kat' auta*) belong (*huparchei*) to things (*tois pragmasin*) (*APo* 84a12). For example, the following demonstration relies on the definition of man, which forms the middle term of the syllogism:

> Premise 1: All Greeks are men.
> Premise 2: All men are rational animals.
> Conclusion: All Greeks are rational animals.

Such a demonstration exhibits the nature of the Greeks, their rational animality, by inferring it *as a cause* from the basic premises that Greeks are men and all men are rational animals. The demonstration does not show what Greeks are as Greeks but what they are in their essence as human beings. Moreover, the demonstration leans on a previous recognition of the human essence captured in the definition. (Even here, this definition formulates the species being and not yet the specific difference focal for human being, which is rationality per se.) We can proceed further with the following syllogism:

> Premise 1': All Greeks are rational animals.
> Premise 2': All rational animals are animals.
> Conclusion': All Greeks are animals.

And from that we can advance to a third syllogism:

> Premise 1'': All Greeks are animals.
> Premise 2'': All animals are mortal.
> Conclusion'': All Greeks are mortal.

This last demonstration leans on advance knowledge about the mortality of animals, which itself turns upon both inductive inferences from observation (see *APo* II,19) and insights into the necessity of change and destruction in all material beings. Here is another example of Aristotelian demonstration:

> Premise 1: The moon is not casting shadows on a clear night.
> Premise 2: It cannot cast shadows when the earth is acting as a screen.
> Conclusion: The moon is not casting shadows because the earth is acting as a screen.

This syllogism, like the others, relies both on definitions (what an eclipse is, for instance) and on some insight into the phenomenon. The point of the syllogism is to demonstrate that the earth's acting as a screen – the "middle term" in the syllogism – is functioning as the *cause* of the phenomenon, here the eclipse. This syllogism can lead to a second:

> Premise 1': An object that casts a circular shadow in all orientations is spherical.
> Premise 2': The earth casts a circular shadow in all orientations.
> Conclusion': The earth is spherical.

Aristotle argues that a successful causal demonstration, leaning on real definitions, exhibits something that holds *of necessity*. It is necessarily the case that if the earth screens the moon, the moon can cast no light of its own. It is necessarily the case that if the earth casts a circular (at least roughly) shadow in all orientations, it is (at least roughly) spherical. It is necessary that Greeks – whatever their sometime pretensions to the contrary – are mortal animals. Causal demonstration affords insight into the phenomenon in such a way as to answer the essential "why" question (*di-'oti*): why Greeks are mortal, or why the moon is eclipsed. In each case, the demonstration hinges on one or more definitions. Consequently, definition is the sine qua non of scientific knowledge for Aristotle.

For traditional Western thought, these are paradigm cases of knowledge, and it should come as no surprise that in this line of thought there would be no knowledge without definition. Now commentators have urged that Confucius is not concerned with definitions. This would imply either that Confucius has some route to knowledge that does not involve definition or that he is not concerned with knowledge, at least not in any sense that implies an interest in what we would call truth or objectivity. This last opinion is the more common among contemporary commentators. Even when Confucius is talking about the rectification of names (*zhengming*), living up to one's words (*xin*), or language (*yan*), commentators such as Hall and Ames and Hansen claim that Confucius' concern is practice and *not* truth or objectivity. Hall and Ames characterize *zhengming* for Confucius as follows: "The name/thing correlation does not seem to concern Confucius. The act of ordering is not one of achieving appropriate reference to things in the world, but is an act of tuning the language, the practical consequence of which is to increase harmonious activity."[7] Similarly, Hansen writes: "Ancient Chinese philosophy contrasts with ancient Greek philosophy in lacking a preoccupation with meanings as expressed in definitions. Socrates and Plato regarded their attempts at definition as the crucial method of gaining real knowledge. Neither Confucius, Lao-tzu, nor Mencius ever viewed the philosophical task in that way or used definition as a discovery of a deeper truth." Hansen declares, "We might best understand the thrust of Chinese thought in this period by thinking of the philosophical schools as being interested in the use of language; they would be interested *only* in accounts of the way words functioned in,

---

[7] Hall and Ames, *TTC*, 264.

say, socialization, problem solving or behavior modification" (my emphasis).[8]

I agree with these commentators that Confucius has a practical orientation in this matter as in everything else but disagree that this implies Confucius has no interest in getting the "right" reference or definition or in aligning language with nature. Far from being antithetical to the practical uses of language, definition is indispensable to them. Good definitions further practical uses of language by helping one pinpoint where one stands and see clearly what one must do. To show that definition is important to Confucius, I examine the *Analects*. Confucius' discussions of *zhengming*, *xin*, and *yan* are not groundless individual adaptations of cultural patterns. His injunctions for one to become *ren* (an authoritative person) and act with *yi* (appropriateness) do not consist entirely of pragmatic advice addressed rhetorically to particular individuals. Rather, his intended meaning is often general enough that he is striving to capture broad characterizations of *ren*, *yi*, *de* (excellence, virtue), and so on – characterizations that are comparable to the quest for definitions in ancient Greek thought, if by no means identical in all respects.

To provide some context for these claims about Confucius, I discuss examples from early Chinese science to show that an interest in realism and truth is not foreign to these practices. By "realism" here I mean a commonsense attitude that implies, for instance, only that knowledge of the course of some planet is knowledge about how that planet moves as a matter of fact. This minimal sense of realism is neutral on the issue of whether human practices might alter the facts. It is also neutral on the question of whether the object of knowledge must be unchanging and necessary – a key supposition of Platonic and Aristotelian science. Finally, it is neutral on the question of the ultimate purpose to which "objective" or realistic knowledge is to be

---

[8] Chad Hansen, *Language and Logic in Ancient China* (Ann Arbor: The University of Michigan Press, 1983), 58. See also Hansen's *A Daoist Theory of Chinese Thought: A Philosophical Interpretation* (New York: Oxford University Press, 1992), where he says: "When Chinese philosophers worry about change, they do not worry about what object or individual *survives* substantial or property change. They notice how we might change linguistic practices. We might draw the partitioning boundaries in the world in different ways. Constancy is an issue of linguistic pragmatism, not metaphysics."

put: practical, technological, scientific, contemplative, or something else. Similarly, my interest in definitions is an interest in uses of language that express real characteristics of things. And again, this sort of definition is part and parcel of a commonsense realism and not confined to the formulation of essences. Nor is it my contention that definitions must formulate a set of necessary and sufficient conditions – that is, a highly specialized and technical understanding of "definition." I want only to show that if Confucius and some of his contemporaries are concerned with definitions and objectivity in commonsense ways, then commentators such as Hall and Ames and Hansen are mistaken in asserting that the Chinese in general and Confucius in particular are unconcerned with definitions, truth, or correctness of references to things in the world when they name things or rectify their names.

Most comparisons between Greek science and Chinese science stress the absence in Chinese thought of rigorous demonstration of the sort I discussed earlier in reference to Aristotle. While admitting that definitions are not quite so sharp and rigorous, and acknowledging that they are not pressed into logical service, I wish nevertheless to stress the significance of definition for the Chinese and, in particular, for Confucius.[9] Even though I maintain that Confucius and some Ancient Chinese are concerned with a sort of realism, I do not at all want to deny that they are concerned with the practical use of language.[10] Confucius is concerned with how particular names and language are used and misused and how they can help harmonize

---

[9] Commentators who point out the lack of demonstrative proof on the part of the Chinese include Nathan Sivin, as quoted by Angus C. Graham in "China, Europe, and the Origins of Modern Science: Needham's The Grand Titration," in *Chinese Science: Explorations of an Ancient Tradition*, ed. Shigeru Nakayama and Nathan Sivin (Cambridge, MA: MIT Press, 1973), 62. See also Lloyd, *Adversaries and Authorities*, 75 and 207.

[10] After quoting Donald Munro's claim about how truth or falsity in the Greek sense has not been important to the acceptance of any "belief" or "proposition" by the Chinese but rather it is the behavioral implications of the belief or proposition for social action that count, Hansen follows by saying, "The stress on behavioral implications of doctrines can be seen as a natural consequence of the underlying view that the function of words is to engender and express attitudes with implications for action rather than to express some 'content' such as the speaker's thoughts which either reflect or fail to reflect reality." See Hansen, *Language and Logic in Ancient China*, 60.

one with other people and with the nonhuman world. When asked what he would do if the Lord of Wey asked him to administer his state, Confucius replied, "It would be to insure that names are used properly (*zhengming*)" (13.3).[11] Improper use of language will adversely affect matters, the observance of *li* (ritual propriety) and playing music (*yue*), laws and punishments, and the ability of people to act properly. So whether names and language are used properly severely affects the functioning of both the individual and the community. But what counts as the proper use of names and language? According to the commentators who stress that Confucius is not interested in correlating names and things, correctness in naming consists *only* in the way words function in speech acts to harmonize behavior. It is like promulgating a system of measurement in the name of social coordination. It is the ruler's job, these commentators would say, to use words performatively to bring about certain actions and modify behavior. On their account, the ruler has no concern whatsoever with whether words have references to specific things in the world or whether assertions have meanings that might be true or false. The ruler is the standard of what words mean; words do not have meanings independent of the ruler's use. This is like saying the ruler's foot is the standard of "the foot," and while the measure can of course be used to measure *things*, the unit itself is a matter of convention, stipulated by the customary authority. These commentators are right to say that *zhengming*, or the rectification of names, is primarily the ruler's job and that this job is primarily practical and social. They are wrong, however, to suppose that this practical concern implies an indifference to things in the world to which words are properly correlated. Against interpreters who downplay the role of definition and truth for Confucius, I offer two points.

First, Confucius encourages his students to study the *Songs* because they allow them to know the names of birds, beasts, and plants; that is the "distinctions in the world around" (17.9). As I shall show later in my discussion of horticultural nomenclature, there is nothing sloppy about such knowledge, even if it lacks what *we* might consider scientific precision. One either knows or does not know that an osprey is an osprey. The most persuasive speaker is wrong to call

---

[11] *Analects*.

an ostrich an osprey even if he could convince everyone that it is and they could eat it because it is tasty. This is why a stress on the performative role of language, independently of an *equal* stress on the truth of an assertion, blurs the distinction between glib talkers and authoritative speakers, a distinction Confucius would be loath to relinquish (see 5.25). Names do not institute such distinctions but ought to track them.

Second, action and thought about action (such as one finds in the *Analects*) require correct names that amount to adequate definitions of states of character, social roles, and so on. One must know what a glib talker is and what an authoritative speaker is (even if one does not try to formulate a set of necessary and sufficient conditions for them) and must refer the proper meaning, to the proper person – otherwise, practice will misfire. The importance of knowledge for action is evident when Confucius discusses the six flaws that shadow the six desirable qualities of character. (And note that this concern with definition and enumeration is a typical gesture.) These are the six flaws that haunt the six virtues of acting authoritatively, with knowledge, truth, boldness, firmness, and living up to one's words. The flaws arise when one does not have a due regard for learning (17.8). And learning here involves being informed about what each one of these six virtues is. When we know "what" each virtue is, we know – in the sense of "know" pertinent to the most commonsensical sort of realism – its real definition.

Definitions in this sense are pertinent not only to the virtues but also to social roles. Confucius says, "A person who does not understand words (*yan*) has no way of knowing (*zhi*) others (*ren*)" (20.3). Even though this passage talks about *yan* (words/language) instead of names, passages where Confucius talks about *yan* are often interchangeable with those that talk about *ming* because, as Hansen puts it: "In Chinese semantic theory, *ming* 'name' is rather like English 'word.' It encompasses not only proper names but all nouns and adjectives."[12] I take this Confucian passage to mean that names and words are connected to the world and the types of characters there actually are so that knowing the former will bring knowledge of the latter. Such knowledge guides one's actions. Confucius says,

[12] Hansen, *Language and Logic in Ancient China*, 35.

"The ruler must rule, the minister minister, the father father, and the son be a son" for there to be social harmony and effective government (12.11). Implied here is that there are appropriate actions that come with each of these personal roles. It is crucial to this Confucian conception that each role has a distinctive character and limits of its own: a father is not a son; a son is not a daughter. And obviously enough, which roles one adopts is not entirely arbitrary. A son cannot simply assume the name of "father" toward his own father and take on the father's role toward him. Names such as "father," "mother," "son," "brother," "ruler," "minister," "elder," "younger," and so on already have relatively determinate content and are to be correlated with definite persons in the world. Confucian teaching presumes both a realism of meaning and a realism of reference, in the minimal sense I have recommended, in regard to these roles.

If language use for Confucius were entirely pragmatic and performative, then any definition of roles should serve as long as it is adopted by others and useful for social coordination. This is not Confucius' view. If it were, he would have no grounds to reject certain positions put forth by some of his interlocutors in the *Analects*. For instance, consider Confucius' disagreement with the governor of She's claim that the true person in his village reported his father's theft of sheep. The claim is that, by stealing, the father has become a thief instead of a father deserving of respect; moreover, by acknowledging the father's theft and reporting him, the "true" person would bring about more harmony for his village. This pragmatic renaming of the father as "thief" and the rather utilitarian reasoning that ensues are rejected by Confucius. Instead, he said: "A father covers for his son and a son covers for his father. And being true lies in this" (13.18).[13] At this point, an Aristotelian might observe that Confucius seems to manifest an interest in the *being* of the father (what a father is "as" a father), which is as it is regardless of

---

[13] Confucius does preface his alternative by saying that "Those who are true in my village conduct themselves differently." However, I do not believe that Confucius' intent is merely to contrast one set of customs with another set of customs, neither of which is morally better or intrinsically more "right" than the other. Rather, Confucius adduces considerations throughout to show that the Zhou *li* is the way of heaven and hence intrinsically preferable. Confucius does not advance under the banner, "My village right or wrong!"

his behavior. Let us say more neutrally that Confucius exhibits an interest in delimiting the roles and defining the names that correspond to those roles. He infers from the nature of being a son that a son is to "cover" for his father. This man is a son; therefore, he is to cover for his father. Such reasoning is the functional correlate, in Confucius, of the practical syllogism in Aristotle.

The harmony between knowing words and knowing things is again shown in Confucius' response to the question of what knowledge (*zhi*) is: it is to *zhi ren* (i.e., to know others) (12.22). Here, he says that promoting the true above the crooked will make the crooked true. This expresses the practical *point* of knowledge in Confucius. The point is to bring about a harmonious situation where the crooked is made straight. But the straight is also the "true" and the crooked is what distorts the true; knowledge here is best understood in the minimally and commonsensically realistic sense noted earlier. Confucius is saying that knowing the various types of people, and knowing which person is which type in fact – knowing the meanings and the references – are crucial for action.

An emphasis on relations between words and the world is evident in Confucius' assertions about truth and correctness (as in his injunction to study the *Songs*) and discernment (as in his discussions about the true person and the opposition between the true and the crooked). It is all the more manifest in his accounts of virtues such as *de*, *ren*, and *yi*. These accounts display Confucius' own *zhengming* that rectify names of virtues used by others. For instance, Confucius distinguishes the actions of one with *ren* from others who might perform some of the same actions but who are not *ren*. He says, "The authoritative person (*ren*) is certain to be bold, but someone who is bold is not necessarily authoritative" (14.4). I take this to be a general point, not limited to members of his village. Similarly, when Confucius says, "The 'village worthy' is excellence (*de*) under false pretenses" (17.13), he is criticizing the way *de* is understood and used. *De* here refers to one's obedience to the rules or laws in society. But adherence to the laws does not imply that one is acting properly for the right reasons. Thus "*de*" is not correctly applied to such cases. Another example is Confucius' discussion of *yi* (appropriateness). *Yi* is opposed to *li* (gain) so that in situations where personal profit can be gleaned, the one with *yi* thinks about acting with appropriateness, whereas the small man thinks about gain (4.16, 14.12; see also 15.21). Confucius' repeated emphases on the opposition between acting with *yi* and *li* (gain) are also attempts to delimit the conditions for the proper use of the name *yi*. These attempts at definition are not directed toward formulation of a set of necessary and sufficient conditions (neither are Aristotle's attempts at definition in his *Ethics*). Nor, on the other hand, are they examples of performative declarations that bring the phenomena into existence along with the stipulation of the name. In fact, sometimes Confucius admits to unclarity about the name or its application. For instance, Yuansi asked, "If in one's conduct one refrains from intimidation, from self-importance, from ill-will, and from greed, can one be considered authoritative *(ren)*?" (14.1). Confucius replied that these actions are difficult, but he does not know if these are adequate to make one authoritative. This confession of uncertainty abandons neither the quest for definition nor objectivity. Quite the contrary, by confessing to uncertainty, Confucius shows that extant practices may *not* suffice to define a virtue. Therefore, the definitions of virtues – like the definitions of roles – cannot be referred solely to extant practices. Nor is Confucius' admission of doubt a confession of indecision, as if once he decides his very performance will make it the case that *ren* consists in whatever he announces it to consist in.

To the extent that Confucius aims to delimit and specify the characteristics of specific virtues and roles, and to the extent that reference to extant practices fails to suffice for this aim, he is seeking definitions – if definitions of an informal sort. To the extent that Confucius neither stipulates nor merely codifies extant practice, his informal definitions are intended to be real definitions that express a content that is independent of the linguistic act that expresses it. Again I must emphasize that the search for definitions is not synonymous with the attempt to formulate necessary and sufficient conditions of a sort that might satisfy a mathematical logician. (And again I note that Aristotle's definitions of virtues do not meet – and according to his own doctrine could never meet – that standard of exactitude.) Confucius disagrees with the way others have come to use names such as *ren*, *yi*, and *de*. He also disputes the application of these names: the reference of the meanings to particular people.

Contrary to the suggestions of commentators such as Hall and Ames and Hansen, Confucius does seem to be concerned with rightness because he knows that the right definition helps one to effect the right action. To think that *de* is achieved by simply adhering to the rules or laws in a society, or that *ren* is simply self-restraint, is to misunderstand the definitions of these names and the real character of the virtue. The real character of the virtue is what is to be expressed by the rectified name. Hansen is entirely correct that language can "engender and express attitudes with implications for action" (Hansen, *Language and Logic in Ancient China*, 60), but he seems to miss the point that Confucius' championing of certain virtues *generally* (and not just for his village) implies a correspondingly general understanding of those virtues and roles.

I have opposed commonsense realism to a performative pragmatism that implies a kind of conventionalism about language and a sort of social harmony utilitarianism in ethics. The quest for definition and a sort of objectivity need not imply mathematical exactitude or claims to certainty, and the alternatives are not so dichotomous that a rejection of this exactitude and certainty must leave one with social conventionalism. I want next to provide a bit of background for my claim by showing that some early Chinese investigations into nature support the view that names are bound up with things even as they are bound up with custom and ritual.

Human life stands in the middle – and mediates between – heaven and earth. In ancient times, heaven was personified in the sense that it was regarded as having a sort of will that may be angered or appeased. Oracle bone documents of Chinese astronomical records that date back to the Shang dynasty (ca.1520–1027 B.C.E.) have shown that heaven's will is intimately bound up with the human world. Heaven is responsible for both the regular and irregular celestial phenomena. Mitukumi Yosida writes: "As is well known, this oracle-bone writing was the script used in divinations addressed to the celestial Lord and spirits. This Lord held the power to make the rain fall, bring drought, and control the abundance of the year's harvest. He was the powerful spirit who controls nature."[14] Not only

---

[14] Mitukumi Yosida, "The Chinese Concept of Nature," in Nakayama and Sivin, *Chinese Science*, 72.

does the Lord control nature, but he also controls human conduct. Again Yosida quotes the oracle bone documents, where the diviner makes the following inquiries of heaven:

> This spring when the King makes a tour of his lands, will the Lord give us his protection? Will the Lord sanction the King's establishment of a city? . . . Will the Lord send down misfortune? (Yosida, "The Chinese Concept of Nature," 72)

While the regular orderly movements of the sun and stars, and the moon and planets, along with the cyclical seasonal changes, are easily observed, other movements are more complex and difficult to predict. Other events such as the appearances of comets are so irregular they could not be predicted at all but could be observed and interpreted. The more regular phenomena are documented in the calendar studies (*li fa*), while the less regular phenomena are documented in the astrological studies (*tian wen*). Both sets of astronomical phenomena are tied up with human life, though in different ways: the more regular provide a relatively constant background of influences, while the more irregular provide omens and portents. As Kiyosi Yabuuti puts it, "The object study of *li-fa*, calendrical science, was not only the composition of calendars for daily use, but also the calculation of all other known celestial regularities, for instance eclipse prediction and computation of planetary positions." On the other hand, astrological study, in Yabuuti's words, was "judicial in character. . . . Its main function was to prognosticate the fates of rulers and states . . . not to foretell the fortunes of individuals."[15] Because in both sorts of cases the human order is bound up with the heavenly order, Chinese rulers were responsible for maintaining the harmonious relation between heaven and earth. Regulation of the calendar affects the way that agriculture is conducted, and that conduct may be more or less harmonious with respect to the seasonal changes dictated by heaven. Astrological studies inform the rulers about the ominous and irregular. Those occasional phenomena show whether their acts are being sanctioned by heaven. This in turn

---

[15] Kiyosi Yabuuti, "Chinese Astronomy: Development and Limiting Factors," in Nakayama and Sivin, *Chinese Science*, 94. See also Lloyd, *Adversaries and Authorities*, 166.

affects subsequent actions and decisions of the rulers. Astronomy is extremely important to the rulers because it both provides information about the natural condition with which their decisions must try to harmonize and information about the signs that indicate whether the attempted harmonization was successful. As Yosida puts it:

Thus the ruler must depend upon observing the signs in the sky in order to infer the will of Heaven with respect to the world which he rules. And insofar as mundane human conduct was controlled by Heaven, necessarily through human conduct as well the will of Heaven is known. Thus nature and human society, inseparably, coexist in accord with the laws by which Heaven exerts its control. (Yosida, "The Chinese Concept of Nature," 73)

Similarly, G. E. R. Lloyd says:

In China, the whole study of the heavens, both *li fa* and *tian wen*, was of intense importance to rulers.... This is because rulers were personally responsible for keeping the order of the heavens and order on earth in harmony with one another.... The regulation of the calendar was not just a matter of practical concern, for instance for agriculture, but one of far-ranging implications for the order of the state. (Lloyd, *Adversaries and Authorities*, 167)

Because of the significance of astronomy for rulers, it is not surprising that one of the most common practices for a new ruler is to rectify the calendar to legitimize his rule. As Yabuuti puts it:

The founder of a new Chinese dynasty had to demonstrate the transition of legitimacy, after his victory, partly by his performance of certain imperial rituals and partly by reforming certain institutions which were closely related to the imperial charisma. One such practice was "correcting the beginnings of years and months" – that is, calendar reform. (Yabuuti, "Chinese Astronomy: Development and Limiting Factors," 95)

G. E. R. Lloyd also makes this observation when he says:

Thus it was often represented as common practice for a new ruler, or a new dynasty, to assert their authority by the introduction of a new calendar taking a new month as its starting-point. (Lloyd, *Adversaries and Authorities*, 167)

Such a practice is not an arbitrary act but rather is bound up with the observations and interpretations of astronomers. As Ho Peng-Yoke explains:

Because of the close connection between the calendar and state power, the emperor would view with alertness the activities of independent astronomers, fearing that they might be engaged secretly in calendar-making, which could be of use to rebels interested in setting up a new regime. Furthermore these rebels could have employed astronomers to interpret celestial events contrary to the interest of the existing dynasty.[16]

That our science has no place for astrological divination, much less the magical influence of the emperor upon the heavens, should not obscure the fact that men of this age aimed to know the heavens as objectively as they could and to adjust their actions and plans to it. This is not the image of an authority's fiat decrees of names that are to be judged solely with reference to their consequences for social harmony. That view – shall I call it Copernican? – ascribes too large a role for human decision and will. It is instead the Chinese view that humans are in the middle. Men, and the emperor above all, mediate between heaven and earth – and while human action can affect the order of heaven and earth, this order is something to be known as objectively as one can. Chinese astronomy had always strived for accuracy in observation. Chinese theory, as Nathan Sivin says, "imposed on the history of astronomy an insatiable demand for increased precision – far exceeding, in the area of the calendar, any conceivable agricultural, bureaucratic, or economic necessity."[17] Similarly, Yabuuti claims that the "breadth of the Chinese ephemerides reflected the grave concern of Chinese rulers constantly to expand the demonstrable order of the sky, while reducing the irregular and ominous" (Yabuuti, 94).[18]

[16] Ho Peng-Yoke, *Li, Qi and Shu: An Introduction to Science and Civilization in China* (Hong Kong: Hong Kong University Press, 1985), 120.

[17] Quoted in Lloyd, *Adversaries and Authorities*, 167.

[18] Further evidence of the sophistication of Chinese astronomy can be gleaned by looking at the breadth and keenness of their observations in the early astronomical records. For instance, Ho and Lisowski tell us that the earliest oracle bones astronomical records (ca. 1339–ca. 1281 B.C.E.) included the names of stars such as the "Bird Star," the "Fire Star," and the "Great Star." These oracle bones also contained the most ancient record of a nova, while another oracle bone recorded the identification of a solar eclipse in 1217 B. C. E. See Ho Peng-Yoke and F. Peter Lisowski, *A Brief History of Chinese Medicine*, 2nd edition (Singapore: World Scientific, 1998), 120. Another earliest record pertained to the sighting of Halley's comet in 611 B.C.E. (Ho and Lisowski, *A Brief History of Chinese Medicine*, 121).

This discussion of ancient Chinese astronomical practice suggests two things. First, in astronomy, names are to be correlated with heavenly bodies and celestial occurrences, and name rectification is to improve that correlation (though it has other functions as well). Second, the ruler's practice of authorizing names makes explicit reference to real events in the celestial realm. His rectification of the calendar – a paradigmatic case of name rectification – needs to be sanctioned by astronomical observations and interpretations. It is not a matter of stipulation or fiat, as if he were instituting or reforming a system of measures. This point extends to the ruler's ordering of agriculture. It even pertains, if in more subtle ways, to his ordering of sacrifices and ritual ceremonies, morality, and music. It is the modern commentator, not the ancient practitioner, who believes that one must make a choice between objectivity and social practice, between ritual and realism. The practitioner's belief is that harmonious practice is at one and the same time productive of social harmony and harmony with the real order of heaven. Given that such practices remained the norm during Confucius' time, it is highly unlikely that his talk of *zhengming* as the ruler's primary task understood that task to be divorced from reference to the nonhuman order. It is far more likely that we should understand Confucius' ethical rectifications in the light of the actual practices of *zhengming* such as we find it in calendar reform. Both sets of practices bind a practical ritual concern with concern for what we must call truth and objectivity.

Confucius' focus upon harmony between heaven and earth, and human activity – including name rectification – should be understood in this context. His hierarchical, kin-centric vision of social order finds that this harmony flows downward. For that reason, heaven's order is the ruler's model for action. This is evident in passages as follows:

The Master said: "Governing with excellence (*de*) can be compared to being the North Star: the North Star dwells in its place, and the multitude of stars pay it tribute." (2.1)

The fixity and constancy of the North Star in the celestial realm become the fixity and constancy of the ruler's *de* in governing. Such an order in the ruler's own life will affect how the people are ordered toward him. Confucius goes on to say:

Lead them with excellence (*de*) and keep them orderly through observing ritual propriety (*li*) and they will develop a sense of shame, and moreover, will order themselves. (2.3)

That heaven is Confucius' model for what is great and expansive, as well as being the source of human culture, is evident in this passage:

The Master said, "How great indeed was Yao as ruler! How majestic! Only *tian* is truly great, and only Yao took it as his model. How expansive was he – the people could not find the words adequate to praise him. How majestic was he in his accomplishments, and how brilliant was he in his cultural achievements." (8.19)

If *tian* is the cause of everything and hence the reason for our ceremonies and sacrifices and everyday ritual propriety, it is no wonder that Confucius would compare Yao's cultural achievements to *tian*. Finally, Confucius also appreciates the way in which heaven accomplishes all that it does effortlessly. For instance, when asked by Zigong how his followers will find the proper way if Confucius stops speaking, he responded by saying:

Does *tian* speak? And yet the four seasons turn and the myriad things are born and grow within. Does *tian* speak? (17.19; see also 15.5)

Respect for the natural order of the celestial world is extended to respect for the natural order in the human world, so the ruler's respect for the heavenly order will result in his people's respect for him. This will affect, in turn, how people in various roles will conduct themselves respectfully toward each other (e.g., the proper accordance of honor, deference, and love between the father and son, husband and wife, younger and older brothers, and friends). Actions in the human realm are appropriate when they harmonize with the heavenly-ordered nature. The four seasons and the natural cycle of birth and death dictate when certain sacrifices and ceremonies are conducted. Ritual propriety and ceremonies are dependent on the orderliness of the celestial and natural worlds. (Some texts suggest the reverse is also true. I say more about this in Chapter 4.)

Chinese herbal medicine is another instance of early investigation into nature that supports the view that names are involved with and referential to a world of real things and processes. This is a tremendously involved topic, and while I can obviously just touch the surface, contact with this topic is useful because it is another area of traditional thought and practice that supports my contention about ritual and realism in names and their rectification.

Just as good rulership consists in maintaining a harmonious relation between heaven and earth, the health of the human body consists in a harmonious relation between the factors and phases that are ingredients to the body. Like everything else in the world, man is composed of nature's five agents (*wuxing*): wood, fire, earth, metal, and water. Wherever they are found, these active factors undergo a continuous cycle of mutual production (*xiangsheng*) and conquest (*xiangke*) that helps to explain the specific kinds of transformation peculiar to the phenomenon under study. For example, on the principle of mutual production, water produces wood (by making trees grow), which in turn produces fire (by fueling it), which in turn produces earth (by leaving ashes), which in turn produces metal (as for instance ores in the earth). On the principle of mutual conquest, water puts out fire, which melts metal, which cuts wood, which breaks up the earth, which soaks up water. The general pattern of change, including its phases or stages, and the kinds of factors that constitute natural phenomena are both typified in the five agents.

The five agents are ingredients of all natural phenomena. Their intertransformations give rise to changes in things. Agricultural processes such as germinating, growing, ripening, harvesting, and storing are conducted in harmony with seasonal cycles understood on the model of the five factors, understood as stages or phases in a single ongoing process. They are also used as basic categories to classify an astounding range of phenomena. On the traditional view, corresponding to the five agents of nature are five seasons, five phases of development (beginning, rising, approaching, cresting, declining), five directions, five colors, and so on. Similarly, man has five sense organs, five tastes, and five *yin* and five *yang* organs with suitable functions. Moreover, in the context of the human organism, the five give rise to five states of energy. These are states of anger, joy, sorrow, puzzlement, and fear – understood as qualitative modifications of basic energy patterns of the organism. The application of the five factors, as categories, to human and nonhuman phenomena gives rise to a series of associations or parallels of the farthest reach. As Dominique Hoizey and Marie-Joseph Hoizey note, "Thus wood corresponds to spring, germination and wind, as well as to the liver, gall-bladder and mouth, and to anger."[19]

Processes of cyclical production and destruction (and reinforcement and hindering) are governed by deeper and more fundamental principles found in all organisms and processes and relationships. These are *yin* and *yang*, the mutually opposing yet mutually dependent cosmological principles of change. As is well known, *yin* is a negative principle that is identified with the earth, the moon, the female, darkness, and passivity; and *yang* is a positive principle identified with heaven, the sun, the masculine, light, and activity. Any of the five agents can play the role of active producer or passive recipient and so can function as "*yin*" or "*yang*." In each case, the active producer (*yang* phase) is subverted (or becomes *yin* and passive) by its product. So, for instance, the wood that fuels fire gets burned up, and the fire will eventually burn out, leaving earth/ashes. In this way, a "*yang*" role gives rise to a "*yin*" and vice versa. All things change and interchange according to such general patterns.

This cycling process, so say the sages, is always seeking its point of greatest harmony and balance. This point in the human organism is what we call "health." Health consists in a harmony and balance of the factors and phases internal to the body but also a harmony of the organism with its environment as a whole. Both sets of relationships are proper objects of Chinese medical study. Changes in the external environment affect human health and well-being. Sickness is often a result of the body's inability to adjust to sudden changes or unwelcome influences. When the weather changes suddenly from hot to cold, health may suffer unless the right "heating" foods are taken or warming exercises performed. And as early as the Shang dynasty, stone probes (*bianshi*) were used to stimulate cavities of the body to relieve pain and stimulate energy circulation. Again, Chinese medicine treats both the body's internal balance and the harmony of the body with the larger body of nature.

Herbal medicine is one of the ways the Chinese physician restores to harmony and balance the factors governing the body. Herbs are useful not only for restoring a patient to health and for counteracting

---

[19] Dominique Hoizey and Marie-Joseph Hoizey, *A History of Chinese Medicine* (Vancouver: Edinburgh University Press, 1993), 25.

diseases but also as nourishment for preserving health and as an elixir for prolonging life. The process of medication is understood largely on the model of the five agents and phases moving according to the *yin-yang* pattern. A particular herb might function as restraining (or under-restraining or over-restraining) or suppressing (or over-suppressing or under-suppressing), for example depending on dosage, preparation (including time of harvest), state of the patient, time of year, and so on. Evident throughout is the idea of illness as an objective condition of imbalance and health as a balance of real factors and agents.

I want to argue that these practices invite and solicit a certain realism about health and illness, about materials and the environment. Names in this connection refer to real objects and processes (if often in ways that reflect a concern with ritual preparation and administration), and rectification of names has among its goals accuracy and veracity. From the earliest times, Chinese were interested in accumulating knowledge of medicinal herbs and their effects. This is evident when we look at the *Shennong bencaojing* (*The Heavenly Husbandman Pharmacopoeia*), attributed to Shennong, a legendary emperor who lived in 2700 B.C.E. Shennong was said to have "personally tasted the hundred types of plants in order to discover their medicinal values."[20] The pharmacopoeia, compiled during the Western Han dynasty, lists 365 medicines derived from plants, minerals, and animals. Ho Peng-Yoke and F. Peter Lisowski say, "This pharmacopoeia explains the *yin* and *yang* and the indications of each medicinal substance and notes that certain combinations of two or more different substances will have a beneficial effect while other combinations will be counterindicative."[21] The 365 medicines are in turn categorized into three classes. The first includes those that nourish and prolong life, the second includes those that restore the patient to health without toxic side effects, and the third includes the toxic substances for fighting diseases. That Chinese interest in accumulating pharmaceutical knowledge arose quite early is further supported by the Mawangdui archaeological findings of the early 1970s. These discoveries – predating the Spring-and-Autumn period (770–476 B.C.E.) – include the *Wushier Bingfang*,

[20] Ho and Lisowski, *A Brief History of Chinese Medicine*, 9.   [21] Ibid., 22.

a document with 52 prescriptions to cure 52 illnesses. This is "one of the earliest Chinese pharmaceutical documents."[22] Not only does it list 242 types of medicines derived from plants, minerals, and animals, but it also "contains a description of a condition that in all likelihood resembles leprosy."[23]

Both the *Wushier Bingfang* and the *Shennong bencaojing* attest to the fact that names of Chinese medicinal materials correspond to things and their parts as well as to their uses and their effects. (The realist would fix on the former, the pragmatist on the latter. I am trying to suggest that the two interpenetrate and harmonize in the classical view.) Moreover, the standard classifications of these materials, which use plant, animal, and mineral categories, are naturalistic and realistic for the most part. Some of these substances produce tonic effects, whereas others are toxic. A good set of medical names will refer both to features of the materials and to features of their human effects.

Naming and classifying well were part and parcel of medical knowledge in ancient China. Medicinal practices prior to the Spring-and-Autumn period were still bound up tightly with magic and were practiced by shamans.[24] But even shamans, however, combined their ritual and symbolic healing with herbal medicine. And they proved quite knowledgeable concerning herbs and their tonic or toxic effects. Perhaps this should not surprise. Our science still has things to learn from pretechnical peoples concerning medicinal properties of plant, animal, and mineral materials.

Traditional Chinese medical knowledge consists in the systematic classification of natural materials according to their sources (animal, vegetable, and mineral) and effects. These medicines were gathered, prepared, and administered according to a scheme of thought (*yin-yang* and the five agents) that applies – according to the intended interpretation – to nonhuman as well as human phenomena. They are named and classified according to procedures that have a sort of check: the health or illness of the patient. (Granted, this is an imperfect "check" because of placebogenesis and the role of

---

[22] Hoizey and Hoizey, *A History of Chinese Medicine*, 20.   [23] Ibid., 21.
[24] Hoizey and Hoizey, *A History of Chinese Medicine*, 16–17, and Ho and Lisowski, *A Brief History of Chinese Medicine*, 11.

symbolic healing in shamanistic practices.) One needs to define terms clearly and describe materials accurately so that they can be identified and reidentified, sought and found. One needs to describe accurately and classify clearly their therapeutic indications and counterindications.

Confucius urges us to study the *Songs* because they allow us to know the names of birds, beasts, plants, and so on. Now is this admonition to be taken as a command to master the ways we customarily use names, purely only for the sake of increased social harmony? Or might it also serve as an injunction to study nature with a more realistic intent? Against the background of existing medical practices, Confucius' talk about the names of things and "distinctions in the world around" (17.9) is best understood to be talk that has a sort of realism as at least a part of its intent. For instance, among the fifty medicinal plants listed in the *Songs*, the kudzu vine is used to treat "influenza, acute gastritis and enteritis, infant diarrhoea and dysentry."[25] Other plants include the "madder-wort, artemesia, and various fruit trees such as those of the jujube, pear, peach and the plum, whose seeds and flesh are used in traditional medicine."[26] Both the peach and Japanese plum seeds are documented in the *Shennong bencaojing* for their therapeutic effects. Over thirty of these seeds were discovered at a Shang site in Taixi in 1973,[27] suggesting that they were likely used in medical practices of the day.

Names are involved with study and with ritual practice; they are meaningful and referential. The Chinese have a long-standing tradition of keen observation of nature. It is not likely that talk about naming and name rectification in Confucian ethical discourse was intended to be divorced from social practices, considered as isolated from the likes of astronomy or medicine. In fact, these provide a traditional focus for what Confucius and his audience would understand by naming and name rectification. The task, then, for an interpretation of Confucian ethics is to come to appreciate how naming (and name rectification) blends and harmonizes ritual and reality. What appear to us in retrospect to be scientific investigations were specializations to be sure, but nevertheless continuous with other areas of study and practice. These investigations not only

[25] Hoizey and Hoizey, *A History of Chinese Medicine*, 21.   [26] Ibid., 21.   [27] Ibid., 15.

comprise an important window into Chinese thought in their own right but form an indispensable background for understanding Chinese ethics and philosophy generally. The point in either case is a harmony of ritual and reality.

I remarked earlier that some well-known Confucian commentators present the rectification of names in a way that suggests the model of the institution and modification of systems of measure. I have argued, to the contrary, that some cases – more cases than these commentators would admit – are instead comparable with the model of calendar reform. That is because when it comes to measures, even though some may be more useful for certain purposes than others, none is intrinsically more objective than any other. All are equally conventional devices that serve social coordination. These commentators believe that all language is like this, all naming, and hence all rectification of names. I have argued for an alternative model of naming and name rectification and have recommended a different model for comparison that involves elements of social practice and objective definition and description. I have urged that in the most central and most important cases (such as ethics and astronomy) there is at the same time a concern for ritual propriety and a concern with definition and objectivity. These concerns not only are not inimical but are deeply entwined in the Chinese mind. When the modern ear hears the claim that the Zhou *li* is the way of heaven, it wants either to make of this an adumbration of a set of universal rules to which the reference to the *li* is inessential (a stopgap that is at best pedagogical) or an endorsement of a particular set of customs in the context of which the reference to "heaven" is but a rhetorical flourish.[28] Either choice distorts and falsifies the sense of the original. Rather, it is the Confucian conviction that a human harmony will reflect and maintain a real harmony of heaven and earth. The idea that the right human order will in the nature of the case reflect and maintain the nonhuman order may seem queer or hopelessly naive in our times, but it is the Confucian conviction. The imperative to rectification is the imperative to adjust our relationships to each other and to the nonhuman environment. These are

[28] This would also be Robert Eno's view. See his *The Confucian Creation of Heaven* (Albany: State University of New York Press, 1990).

two sides of the same harmony. Therefore, the rectification of names is not opposed to the search for definitions or to what we call objectivity: it is in itself a harmony of ritual and reality.

Having shown that Confucius' thinking about language is not antithetical to definition in a rough and ready sense of that term, or to objectivity, it is more likely that Confucian ethics is comparable with Aristotelian ethics because that comparison would falter if Confucius had no interest in objective nature and if name rectification served only a social function. Having addressed, in this chapter and the last, methodological questions about categories and realism, I can now move on in the next couple of chapters to compare the two philosophers' views of virtue, the mean, and the moral self that is to seek such a mean.

4

Harmony and the Mean in
the *Nicomachean Ethics* and the *Zhongyong*

Aristotelians and Confucians stress virtue and the necessity of training to cultivate virtue. Aristotelians describe virtue as a disposition to achieve a mean between extremes, a middle path between an excess and a defect in the possibilities of action and emotion. Something like this idea is evident in Confucian traditions.[1] Confucians, however, emphasize the idea of harmony. Aristotelians have something like the idea of harmony in virtue's effects on one's internal and external relations, but it remains underemphasized. My aim in this chapter is to show that the Aristotelian mean and Confucian harmony (and the principle of that harmony, the *zhong* or crux) are not only comparable but complementary.

What Confucian term – if any – corresponds to Aristotle's "mean" (*meson*)? The most natural correlate might seem to be "*zhong*." Legge's time-honored 1893 translation of the *Zhongyong* renders it

---

[1] The most prominent defender of this view is Richard Bosley. See his "What Is a Mean? – The Question Considered Comparatively and Systematically," *Philosophy East and West* 36 (1986): 3–12, and his *On Virtues and Vices* (New York: Peter Lang, 1991). Kanaya Osamu, in "The Mean in Original Confucianism," in *Chinese Language, Thought, and Culture*, ed. Philip J. Ivanhoe (La Salle, IL: Open Court, 1996) also places the mean between opposite extremes. I agree with Bosley that the Aristotelian mean and the Confucian "mean" are comparable, but I disagree with elements of his treatment of the Confucian tradition and strongly disagree with his treatment of Aristotle. These agreements and disagreements will play out in due course.

The Doctrine of the Mean.[2] And it does seem as if a mean or middle is the target of actions and desires in the *Zhongyong*. Wing-Tsit Chan explains the term "*zhongyong*" by saying that it "literally" means "'centrality and universality', [and] has been translated as moderation, the mean, mean-in-action, normality, universal moral order, etc."[3] Chan continues: "According to Cheng Hsuan (127–200, Confucian Commentator), *yong* means the ordinary and *zhongyong* means using the mean as the ordinary way. According to Zhu Xi (1130–1200, Confucian commentator), it means neither one-sided nor extreme but the ordinary principle of the mean" (Chan Wing-tsit, *A Sourcebook in Chinese Philosophy*, 98–99, my parentheses). Even though the mean is the right way for the most ordinary of actions, most people err by either exceeding (*kuo* – literally "to go beyond") the mean or by falling short of (*bu zhi* – literally "not to come up to") the mean and hence fail to attain the good (*Zy* 4; see also *Zy* 9). Hence it seems, at first blush, that the *zhong* is a kind of mean for the essential feature of a mean is that it is a good triangulated between iniquitous extremes. Confucius attributes this useful middle (*zhongyong*) to the *junzi* (the one with exemplary virtue) and the opposite to the petty person (*xiaoren*). This shows that virtue exemplifies the mean or middle for him. As he puts it, "The *junzi* [acts according to] the mean, *xiaoren* [petty person] the opposite" (*Zy* 2).[4] This mean or middle consists in acts that are neither too much nor too little (i.e., neither excessive nor defective for any situation). The *Zhongyong*

---

[2] The authorship and coherence of the *Zhongyong* have been disputed. More recently, there seems to be some agreement about the coherence of the text. Even though scholars question if and how much of the text is attributable to Confucius' grandson Zisi, they are agreed that this text belongs to the Confucian tradition. Ames and Hall in their recent translation and philosophical interpretation of the text date some of the materials attributed to Zisi to before 300 B.C.E. For my purpose in this chapter, it is sufficient that this text represents the Confucian tradition and that it presents a coherent teaching. For more detailed reflections on the authorship, coherence, and dating of the text, see Tu Weiming, *Centrality and Commonality* (hereafter *CC*) (Albany: State University of New York Press, 1989), 12–17; *Focusing the Familiar*, trans. Roger Ames and David Hall (Honolulu: University of Hawaii Press, 2001), 26–27, 143–46; and *Confucian Analects, the Great Learning and the Doctrine of the Mean*, trans. James Legge, 35–55.

[3] Chan, *A Sourcebook in Chinese Philosophy*.

[4] All translations of the *Zhongyong* (Zy hereafter) are mine unless otherwise indicated, and I follow Legge's chapter and section numbers. I will use *FF* to refer to Ames and Hall's 2001 translation of the *Zhongyong*, *Focusing the Familiar*.

asserts, "The *junzi* acts according to his present station, he does not desire to exceed [*wai*, literally "outside"] his station" (*Zy* 14). This passage continues to describe how the *junzi* always does what is proper regardless of whether he is in a position of wealth or poverty, superiority or subordination. The *junzi* avoids the trappings that are common to certain positions such as treating one's subordinates with contempt when one's station is superior or courting the favor of one's superior when one's station is subordinate. Again the *zhong* marks that middle which is either exceeded (*kuo*) or not attained (*bu zhi*).

The situation, however, is more complex and more interesting. For the Confucian, *zhong* is not directly and unproblematically an Aristotelian mean. I want to argue that *zhong* (the crux, the "mean" for Legge, "centrality" for Tu) and *he* (harmony, concord, attunement) must be taken together both in reference to the teaching of *Zhongyong* and in relation to Aristotle's mean. I shall try to explain how *zhong* and *he* are to be taken together in the *Zhongyong* and, once taken together, how this can clarify the ways in which Aristotelian and Confucian teaching are comparable and complementary.

I begin by noting some of the most obvious differences between the Confucian *zhong* and the Aristotelian mean. The *Zhongyong* portrays the mean as the beginning as well as the norm guiding both human action and all things under heaven. It states:

Prior [*wei*] to the happening [*fa*] of joy, anger, sorrow and pleasure is called *zhong* [equilibrium/mean]. When these feelings have happened and they are regulated according to *zhong* is called *he* [harmony]. *Zhong* is the basis of all under heaven [*tian*] and *he* is the way [*dao*] of all under heaven. (*Zy* 1.4)

The *Zhongyong* asserts that *zhong* is prior to feelings and actions and that *zhong* is the "basis" of all. In its prior state, it is an "equilibrium" or central tendency; in its role as basis, it is the ground of harmony. *Zhong* dictates the way of human beings and all things in this world, and *he* is that way. When things, actions, or relations accord with *zhong*, harmony (*he*) is achieved. Notice that *zhong*'s significance is not restricted to human beings, or even limited to nonhuman nature, but also extends to heaven itself. As the *Zhongyong* puts it, "When there is *zhong* and *he*, heaven (*tian*) and earth are in place and all things (*wanwu*) are nourished" (*Zy* 1.5). Hence, *zhong* (equilibrium) is both the beginning and the norm of harmony (*he*) of the whole cosmos.

Actions and passions regulated by *zhong* are in harmony (*he*) with themselves and with others. For this reason, the individual who pursues the way (*dao*) based on *zhong* is not only seeking a state of *he* (harmony) for himself but is also contributing to the harmony of all things – animals, the earth, and heaven (*Zy* 22, 25.3). That *zhong* should have an effect on heaven by keeping heaven in its place is not surprising because *Zhongyong* tells us that the command of heaven (*tian*) is called *xing* (nature) and to accord with *xing* is called *dao* (way) (*Zy* 1.1). Because the genuine *dao* is the way that is based on *zhong* (*Zy* 1.4), any *xing* that is commanded by heaven is also to be regulated by *zhong* (*Zy* 1.1, 1.4). When such a regulation takes place, then the place of heaven as the commander of nature (*xing*) is maintained (*Zy* 1.5).

Unlike Aristotle's mean, the Confucian *zhong* precedes everything in this world and is an almost metaphysical principle with cosmic significance. The mean in action for Aristotle is not something that precedes human actions and feelings. Aristotle explains that virtues of character such as courage, temperance, and mildness are concerned with feelings and actions that admit of excess, deficiency, and a mean or intermediate state (*NE* 1106b16–18). He claims that the best way to have these appetites or feelings is the mean, and the habit of choosing the intermediate state is virtue (*NE* 1106b28). In contrast to the Confucian *zhong*, which denotes a state or principle that is prior to all things, Aristotle's mean is limited to the sphere of human action; while the *zhong* is prior to and devoid of all feelings, the Aristotelian mean is a state of *having* feelings and appetites appropriately (i.e., having them neither too much nor too little, toward the right people, in the right way, in the right circumstances, and for the right end).

The *Zhongyong*'s *zhong* is the norm of all things; it is the basis for regulating not only human feelings but all under heaven. As the ground that regulates all things, including actions and feelings, *zhong* is not a human goal to be attained. Aristotle does not portray the mean as having cosmic significance. In contrast to *Zhongyong*'s cosmic view of the mean, Aristotle's view seems very limited in that it is only applied to the ten virtues to delimit the mean between two extremes in each case. For instance, the virtue of courage is a mean state between the excess of rashness and the defect of cowardice in a situation where one could react either with fear or confidence. Similarly, the virtue of temperance is a mean state between the excess of intemperance and the defect of insensibility in a situation where one's bodily desires with respect to touch and taste are at stake. At best, Aristotle's virtuous person, or one who acts according to the mean at all times, is able to attain an essential good of his own soul, and achieve happiness, if additional external conditions are met. His virtuous acts also extend to those around him and perhaps to the whole *polis* (if he has the relevant power). But Aristotle neither claims the virtuous person affects heaven and earth nor posits equilibrium as a first principle. Hence Aristotle's view of attaining the mean is narrower in scope than the *Zhongyong*'s view.

According to the Confucian, it is rather a state of *he* (harmony) that marks the specifically human good. But *he* is, if distinct, not separable from *zhong*. Most precisely, in *he*, feelings and things are regulated according to *zhong*. *Zhong* is prior to all things and is the basis for *he*, which is in important respects more like the Aristotelian mean. This is because *he* is accomplished when the human feelings are regulated according to the *zhong*.[5] In the case of *he*, human feelings are present

---

[5] This distinction between *zhong* as a "given reality" and *he* as a human achievement is recognized by Tu. As Tu puts it, "And it is only to that inner self, 'before the feelings of pleasure, anger, sorrow, and joy are aroused,' that the term centrality can be adequately applied. Harmony, on the other hand, symbolizes an actual human achievement when the aroused feelings 'each and all attain due measure and degree'" (Tu, *CC*, 20).

Even though I agree with Tu's distinction between *zhong* as a given reality and *he* as an achievement, I disagree with him that such a state exists as an inner self or as a "state of mind wherein one is absolutely unperturbed by outside forces" (Tu, *CC*, 20). This is because nowhere does the *Zhongyong* mention human beings in a state without feelings (i.e., man's being in a state of *zhong*). On the contrary, the *Zhongyong*'s claims that *zhong* is the basis of all under heaven and its being that according to which feelings are to be regulated attest to its being a "given reality" having priority over humans and all things under heaven. The many claims about *xing* (nature) and *dao* taken with *he* (harmony) also support Tu's and my claim that *zhong* is given reality. However, there is no textual evidence for Tu's claim that *zhong* exists in an inner self. Such an interpretation would also lessen the coherence of claims about *he*, *dao*, and *xing* in this same text.

Another reason why Tu cannot plausibly claim that *zhong* exists as a state of mind where one is totally unperturbed by outside forces is because such an ideal is unreachable for the Confucians and is contrary to their constant attempts to act appropriately in various situations. To try to attune one's acts to one's situations is to be affected by various feelings, and to order them well is the human achievement of *he* rather than the total absence or negation of all feelings. (See *Zy* 27.6 for the

and ordered according to the norm (*zhong*). In sum, to the extent that the Aristotelian mean also involves feelings and their proper ordering, Aristotle's mean is more like the *Zhongyong*'s *he* than its *zhong*.

Associated with the *Zhongyong*'s cosmic view of the *zhong* is its universal applicability to everything under heaven (human beings, things, and animals; see *Zy* 1.4, 1.5, 22). Aristotle, on the other hand, quite sharply distinguishes the mean for inert objects, a sort of tendency toward equilibrium found in physical nature, from the mean for human beings. Even beasts are excluded from the mean in the proper sense (*NE* 1099b33). Nonhuman nature exhibits among its tendencies a proclivity toward an equilibrium state, but according to Aristotle this is a quantitative or numerical mean, not the qualitative mean that is proper to human feeling and action. A numerical mean in an object or process is an arithmetic middle that is "equidistant from each extremity; ... (and) is one and the same for everyone" (*NE* 1106a30–31). However, the mean proper to human action and emotion is an intermediate state that is (a) qualitative, (b) something like an extreme in itself, and (c) multiply relative. It is qualitative because no mathematical formula determines it: the mean of action is neither arithmetic nor geometric. The mean of action is something like an extreme (*NE* 1107a6–8); that is, it does not lie on the same line.[6] Most important of all, the mean is, as Aristotle says, "relative to

junzi's constant striving for self-improvement and 27.7 for his appropriate actions in various situations.) Also see 25.3, where the one with sincerity (*cheng*, meaning integrity or sincerity – as a way to self-cultivation) seeks to unite what is within himself and what is outside. To the extent that what is outside oneself can never be completely devoid of feelings and so on (think about animals), *zhong* as absence of feelings is not a realistic goal for human beings. Rather, it is better understood as a norm that regulates our feelings and all under heaven so that they become a harmony that is a full, relational likeness of the original empty equilibrium.

[6] This simple point seems to be a stumbling block not only for beginning readers of Aristotle but for certain scholars as well. Saying that the mean does not lie on the same line as the extremes means that, even though the mean, the excess, and the defect are all possibilities for the same dimension of feeling or action, the mean does not amount merely to less of the excess or more of the defect. The mean that is "courage" is not merely a lesser amount of rashness, nor is it a larger amount of cowardice or a middling amount of fear (much less a mediocre amount of confidence). The definition of the mean requires a specification according to Aristotelian categories: courage amounts to being confident about the right things regarding the right persons in the right ways at the right times and places, and so on.

us." That means it is relative to the species form of human beings, to the *phronimos'* actual embodiment of the virtues, and to the individual agent with his peculiar abilities and circumstances.

Expounding Aristotle's assertion that the mean is "relative to us," commentators too often restrict their explanations to one or two of these three factors rather than seeing that all three are essential to Aristotle's own account. These commentators can of course find texts for their favored factor because Aristotle invokes all three. What is needed is not a defense of one factor over against the other but an interpretation that shows why we need all three and how each factor makes an essential contribution. That the peculiarities of the individual and his circumstances are relevant to Aristotle is clear when he compares the different amounts of food needed by Milo the athlete and the beginner in gymnastics. Whereas six pounds of food may be too little for Milo, this same amount may be too much for the beginner. So the mean amount of food to take is relative to the individual's ability (training level), size, and activities (*NE* 1106b2–5). This is for Aristotle a direct analogue of virtue. A dramatic rescue that is courageous for one man may be rash for an old, frail man to attempt. Similarly, Aristotle's discussion of generosity and magnificence also shows that these virtues are relative to individuals' resources as well as their circumstances. With respect to magnificence, he says:

Magnificence is expenditure that is fitting in its large scale. But large scale is large relative to something; for the expense of a warship captain and of a leader of a delegation are not the same. Hence what is fitting is also relative to oneself, the circumstances and the purpose. (*NE* 1122a22–26)

In general, Aristotle says, "We fix the right amount by reference to the agent [as well as the task] – by who he is and what resources he

---

When drawing the mean for students, it is not good – though it is customary – to draw a single straight line and then mark off its ends (the vices) and its middle (the virtue); it is better to mark three vertices of a triangle with the two vices at the base and then make the line connecting the vices slope up asymptotically to the top vertex. This is a graphic representation of Aristotle's assertion that the mean is a sort of extreme in respect to goodness. Once one allows the top vertex degrees of freedom of location relative to the base, one has a diagram of Aristotle's assertion that the mean admits some variation and is "relative to us."

has; for the amounts must be worthy of these, fitting the producer as well as the product" (*NE* 1122b24–26).[7]

And yet, it is plain that the mean in Aristotle's account is not solely determined by individual abilities and circumstances. The "us" to which the mean is relative is not simply distributed across individuals. Aristotle also uses "us" to refer to us collectively as a single species. That the "us" in the relative to us has reference to the species form is clear when Aristotle defines virtue as the mean state that is defined by reason.[8] We know that the rational soul is the form of the

---

[7] Commentators who recognize that the relativity of Aristotle's mean includes the peculiarities of the individual and his circumstances include Stephen Leighton, "Relativizing Moral Excellence in Aristotle," *Apeiron* 25 (1992): 49–66; Peter Losin, "Aristotle's Doctrine of the Mean," *History of Philosophy Quarterly* 4(3) (1987): 329–41; and William A. Welton and Ronald Polansky, "The Viability of Virtue in the Mean," in *Aristotle, Virtue and the Mean*, ed. Richard Bosley, Roger A. Shiner, and Janet D. Sisson (Edmonton: Academic Printing & Publishing, 1995), 79–102, see especially 91–92. Stephen Leighton, in "The Mean Relative to Us," in Bosley et al., *Aristotle, Virtue and the Mean*, 67–78, further distinguishes between "circumstance relativity" and "character relativity" and maintains that the latter is superior because it does not deny the former but goes beyond the former in accounting for the relativity of Aristotle's mean. Lesley Brown, in her "What Is 'the Mean Relative to Us' in Aristotle's Ethics?" *Phronesis* 42(1) (1997): 77–93, denies that Aristotle's mean is to be understood as relative to individuals. Rather, she defends the position that relativity for Aristotle means "relative to us as human beings" (Brown, 78); that is, what I call the "species form" factor.

[8] That the *logos*, or reason, is not an invariable general principle or rule is clear in that Aristotle further refers to the *phronimos* as the standard for this *logos*. Because the *phronimos* is known for his ability to deliberate well about changeable objects (as opposed to eternal objects), it would not make sense to talk about deliberation at all if the *logos* or reason were an invariable rule or general principle. It is the insight that the *logos* or reason needs to deal with particulars that led an interpreter such as Alfonso Gomez-Lobo to maintain that it is "a particular proposition" that is true and deny that it is either a rational capacity, a rule, or a norm. See Alfonso Gomez-Lobo, "Aristotle's Right Reason," in Bosley et al., *Aristotle, Virtue and the Mean*, 15–34, especially 16–17. I think that Gomez-Lobo strays too far in denying anything general in interpreting Aristotle's *logos*. After all, Aristotle himself defines the *phronimos* as one who is able to deliberate about "what promotes living well in general" and not simply about what is good for himself or about some specialized area (*NE* 1140a26–28). Furthermore, Aristotle claims that *phronêsis* is a virtue of one of the rational parts of the soul. Thus, in defining virtue as the mean that is relative to us, relativity that is defined by reason/*logos*, it is quite reasonable to understand *logos* as the deliberative part of the rational soul – not just the deliberative part of any rational soul but that of the *phronimos*, for his is the perfected rational part. For this reason, even though I am sympathetic with the attempt by Thomas Tuozzo, in his "Contemplation, the Noble, and the Mean: The Standard of Moral Virtue in Aristotle's Ethics," in Bosley et al., *Aristotle, Virtue and the Mean*, 129–54, to

human being and that its excellent functioning is the human good
(*NE* 1098a6–17, 1106a21–24).⁹ It is important for Aristotle to
include the species form in his definition of the mean because this
prevents the relativity – which for Aristotle amounts to the dependence of our good on a series of human conditions – from slipping
into individual relativism. By having reference to a species form that
is the same for all human beings, Aristotle is able to make assertions
about what is good for us in general and moreover is able to defend a
set of virtues such as courage, generosity, truthfulness, and mildness,

introduce the general into the *logos* by seeing it as "a principle expressing the end
specific to each particular virtue: namely, the noble in the relevant sphere of human
life" (Tuozzo, 136), I disagree with his claim that "Aristotle cannot intend *logos* to
refer to reasoning as to how to act in a particular situation" (Tuozzo, 135). What
Tuozzo attributes to *logos* here as the principle expressing the end is more rightly
attributed to the moral virtues (which the *phronimos* undoubtedly possesses), while
the *logos* is more appropriately attributed to the deliberation about the proper
action while aiming at these principles. This is clear from Aristotle's assertion that,
"Further, we fulfill our function insofar as we have intelligence and virtue of
character, for virtue makes the goal correct, and intelligence makes what promotes
the goal [correct]" (*NE* 1144a7–10). Because "intelligence," or *phronêsis*, is what
deliberates about the changeable things and hence action, Aristotle's reference to
the *phronimos' logos* at 1107a2 must be a *logos* that deliberates about particular
situations and actions. But because *phronêsis* is a virtue of one of the rational parts of
our soul, our good is not arbitrary but prescribed by our species form.

⁹ The thesis that the form of the human soul determines its goodness or virtue has
been defended by commentators who insist that Aristotle's *Ethics* has a metaphysical
basis. For instance, Terence Irwin says that Aristotle's "argument begins with his
assumptions about happiness; and ... these are not arbitrary assumptions, and not
merely common beliefs, but consequences of his general theory of the soul, form,
and essence.... The argument of the *Ethics* depends on more than common sense.
It depends on the whole view of natural substances outlined in Aristotle's
metaphysics and psychology" (Irwin, "The Metaphysical and Psychological Basis
of Aristotle's Ethics," 51).
  For more essays defending metaphysical readings of Aristotle's ethics/politics,
see my "Senses of Being in Aristotle's *Nicomachean Ethics*," in *The Crossroads of Norm
and Nature*, and chs. 1, 2. Also see Tuozzo, "Contemplation, the Noble, and the
Mean: The Standard of Moral Virtue in Aristotle's Ethics," where he subordinates
all human activities, especially the moral virtues, to contemplation, the highest
human activity. He says, "One of the advantages of this interpretation is that it
brings Aristotle's theory of human activity into line with his metaphysics, according
to which there should be some single, unitary activity, the active potentiality for
which is the essence of a natural substance, and from which all other activities
characteristic of that substance are in some way derived" (Tuozzo, 131). With
respect to Tuozzo's interpretation, I want to say that it is right in what it affirms (a
species-universal content) and wrong in what it denies (determination of the mean
by social and individual factors).

for example, that correspond to the universal premises in our deliberations about right actions or feelings.[10] Premises such as "truthfulness is to be pursued" and "courage is to be pursued" are the ends toward which all human beings ought to aim because these are what allow us to function well and live well. And yet, while courage is to be pursued, it would be rash for a firefighter with a broken back to attempt a rescue even though it would have been cowardly for the same man (prior to the injury) to forego it. The species form tells us what is good in general; this needs specification and sometimes modification by reference to individual abilities and circumstances.

Finally, the *phronimos'* actual embodiment of the virtues is also a necessary factor in understanding Aristotle's mean. This is clear from his reference to the *phronimos* in his definition of virtue as a mean that is relative to us, defined by reason (*NE* 1106b36–1107a3),[11] where

[10] Lesley Brown in, "What Is 'the Mean Relative to Us' in Aristotle's Ethics?" agrees with the normativity of the mean when she claims that we should understand Aristotle's mean that is relative to us "not as 'relative to individuals' ... but as 'relative to us as human beings,' and that Aristotle uses the phrase to convey a normative notion, the notion of something related to human nature, needs or purposes, and which is the object of a certain kind of expertise and judgement" (Brown, 78). Again, she claims that she finds "no suggestion in the ethical works that each excellence itself is multiple, being different for different types of person" (Brown, 81). While I agree with Brown that each moral virtue (*êthikê aretê*) is fixed for Aristotle, I disagree with her objection to relativizing the mean to individuals, for I have shown how Aristotle does allow for different ways of arriving at the mean depending on the differing resources, situations, and abilities of individuals.

[11] In spite of Aristotle's explicit reference to the *phronimos* in his definition of virtue as a mean, there are commentators who deny the significance of the *phronimos* in *determining* the mean or virtuous state. Gomez-Lobo, in "Aristotle's Right Reason," attempts to disabuse readers of the following "misunderstanding": "It is tempting to infer from this that Aristotle has in mind some privileged individual who would actively determine the intermediate and thus the noble thing to choose. He would be the person we should look to and imitate because, in so far as he is the preeminently prudent person, whatever he does would be the prudent thing to do. That we would have to rely on the evidence of prudent choices to identify the prudent man generates, of course, a well-known circularity problem" (Gomez-Lobo, 32–33). I argue that the circularity is Aristotle's, and it is not vicious. Leighton, in "Relativizing Moral Excellence in Aristotle," ascribes to Aristotle an "attribute relativism" that "makes no supposition of an ideal standard or paradigm of excellence equally applicable to all of excellence. Rather a concatenation of relevant subgroups set in terms of species boundaries determines the mean, the mean that is relative to us" (Leighton, "Relativizing Moral Excellence in Aristotle," 55). See note 14, this chapter, for some of my disagreements with Gomez-Lobo's view of the *phronimos*. Though Leighton, in "Relativizing Moral Excellence in

reason is understood in the way that the *phronimos* has it. This triple
formulation of Aristotle is not redundant. The reason why the *phronimos* is needed is because virtuous actions are not just the following
of universal rules.[12] Rather, as I pointed out earlier, the specific
mean of a particular action is also contingent on one's abilities,
activities, and circumstances. Familiarity with such particulars is
gained through an experience (*NE* 1141b15) that is not fully teachable. Furthermore, the ability to *nous* what is required in particular
situations (a kind of natural intuition or immediate cognitive grasp)
is another requirement that escapes formulation in rules.[13] The
phronimos acts as a kind of concrete universal, exemplifying how the
right ends are pursued in particular instances by using the right
means. By seeing concretized right actions, at the right times, in the
right situations, toward the right persons, and so on, one could
model how the *phronimos* acts in particular situations and thus be
guided in subsequent deliberations about the mean. This is the way
we learn to be moral, according to Aristotle. One might not be a
phronimos; nonetheless, by reminding oneself that a *phronimos* aims at
the good life and attains such a goal through particular noble acts,
one could decide against a particular act because such an act is not
one that a *phronimos* would do. Thus, despite the fact that the *phronimos* can never decide our actions for us, nor can we just do what he
does (because our abilities, circumstances, and activities are always

Aristotle," is right to find a tacit appeal to "subgroups" in Aristotle's analysis, he is
wrong to think that this reduces the need for appeal to the *phronimos* because it is
precisely the *phronimos* who shows a "subgroup" how the common principles can
be particularly embodied in ways that are particularly relevant to them.

[12] That the virtues are not just a set of universal rules to be adhered to in actions is a
point many interpreters have recognized. As James E. Tiles, in "The Practical
Import of Aristotle's Doctrine of the Mean," in Bosley et al., *Aristotle, Virtue and the
Mean*, 1–14, puts it: "One cannot specify a set of rules conformity to which
constitutes virtuous character. Virtuous character is what is needed to interpret
rules, fashion rules for those who need them as well as deal with difficult cases. The
standard is not a rule but the person with a crucial intellectual virtue" (Tiles, 13).
Also see Losin's "Aristotle's Doctrine of the Mean," where he claims that Aristotle's
mean "cannot fairly be regarded as a rule or set of rules designed to tell us what, in
particular cases, to do" (Losin, 340).

[13] Aristotle stresses the salience of the ability to *nous* particulars in the following
passages in the *NE*: 1142a26–28, 1143a25–28, and 1143a36–1143b5. See Losin,
"Aristotle's Doctrine of the Mean," 339–40, for more discussions regarding the
significance of the particulars to the *phronimos*' deliberations.

different from his), he could nonetheless affect our deliberations by acting as a concrete standard or reference for correct deliberations and actions.[14] We do not learn what the "mean" is merely by considering our individual situations; nor does a set of universal rules suffice. We learn by modeling the ways in which exemplary persons embody the general truths in particular ways in situations relevantly like our own. Again, all three factors are needed to make sense of Aristotle's view of the mean: the species form supplies the general content, the *phronimos* shows us how to embody this content in pertinent ways that are paradigmatic for a culture, and the individual with her abilities and circumstances limits and modifies the meaning of the "mean" in this circumstance here and now.

There are counterparts to all three factors in Confucian thought about virtue and the mean, though Confucians seem to leave a bit less room than Aristotle for individual agency and individual differences. (Scholars, inevitably, dispute this. I shall return to the issue at the end of this chapter.) A heaven-endowed nature (*Zy* 1) corresponds to Aristotle's species form, the *junzi* or moral exemplar corresponds to Aristotle's *phronimos*, and finally, Confucius' focus on appropriate conduct (*yi*), which hangs on doing what befits one's station and abilities, corresponds to Aristotle's individual abilities and circumstances.[15] Nevertheless, the *Zhongyong*'s cosmic view of the mean and its universal applicability to everything under heaven (human beings,

---

[14] Because the *phronimos* can remind us about our general goal of the good life as well as exemplify to us concretely the carrying out of right acts by the right means, I disagree with Gomez-Lobo's skepticism about the *phronimos'* role in attuning us to the remote end of the good life. As he puts it: "If the good life consists in contemplation, then the prudent man would be expected to determine the intermediate by deliberating about what is conducive to this privileged activity. As I have already suggested, this is highly implausible because in many instances the action according to a vice, e.g., cowardice or illiberality, may be the most conducive to future contemplation" (Gomez-Lobo, 27; see also 28–29). Contrary to Gomez-Lobo's claim, cowardice or illiberality will never be exhibited by the *phronimos* because he is concerned not merely with the right end of life in general but also with the right means to attain this end. In other words, Gomez-Lobo is quite right to call into question that "a picture of happiness is *the* major contribution prudence makes to the determination" of right action (Gomez-Lobo, 28, my italics). However, he is mistaken to reject that this picture of happiness is *a* major contribution of the *phronimos* in determining right action.

[15] I discuss Confucius' exemplary individual, or *junzi*, and appropriate conduct (*yi*) in Chapter 1.

things, and animals) renders it different from Aristotle's mean for human beings.

Even though the *Zhongyong* does not discuss the *he* (harmony) in as particularistic a way as Aristotle, it derives three universally binding virtues and five universal obligations from a knowledge of heaven and the heaven-bestowed human nature (*Zy* 1 and 20.7–8). These three virtues are knowledge (*zhi*), humaneness as authoritative conduct (*ren*, the highest virtue), and courage (*yong*). The five universal obligations are duties between rulers and ministers, fathers and sons, husbands and wives, older and younger brothers, and friends. Although the *Zhongyong* admits that knowledge of these obligations and virtues may be inborn or simply acquired through experience (*Zy* 20.9), its primary and most important source is ritual propriety (*li*) (*Zy* 20.5). *Li* in the *Zhongyong*, as in Confucius' *Analects*, is derived from past traditions.[16] *Li* tells the individual how to behave toward his superiors, elders, peers, and subordinates. Depending on the individual's role, *li* will dictate how he behaves in various situations. Again I want to say that this is a matter of emphasis: all three factors – individual, social, and natural – can be found in the classical Confucian texts, but there is a heavy emphasis on the social (ritual or ceremonial) factor. In contrast to a traditional *li* that dictates almost entirely the ways to act relative to an individual's role, Aristotle's mean (as I have argued) is a vector determined by three factors, each of which makes a generous contribution. Whereas the Confucians rely more heavily on a ritualized tradition,[17] Aristotle, while making appeal to social *ethos* and social roles, tries to be explicit about the ways in which these might specify a generic, species-wide

[16] See Chapter 1, note 9, about Fingarette's interpretation of Confucius' *li*.

[17] See Chan Wing-tsit, in his "The Evolution of the Confucian Concept *Jên*," *Philosophy East and West* 4 (1955): 295–320, where he says, "*ren* becomes meaningless unless it is involved in actual human relationships" (ibid., 311) and *ren* "is essentially social, active, and dynamic" (ibid., 319). See also Hall and Ames, in their *The Democracy of the Dead* (Chicago and La Salle, IL: Open Court, 1999), 42, where they say, "The dominant models of Western individualism are resourced in transcendent principles that do not directly depend upon any social or cultural institutions for their development. In China, individual as well as national identity is realized through shared language, customs, and rituals." In my view, Hall and Ames' claim about the Chinese is correct. Their claim that Western models of the individual do not acknowledge a dependence upon any social or cultural institutions, however, is simply not true of Aristotle.

moral content. For this common content, Aristotle turns to his soul doctrine and ultimately to his metaphysics of teleological form.[18] For Aristotle, our form dictates what our virtues are in general and what the shape of human happiness is on the whole. As he puts it, "Both intelligence and wisdom must be choiceworthy in themselves, even if neither produces anything at all; for such is the virtue of one of the two [rational] parts [of the soul]."[19] In spite of the frequent references to knowledge of heaven in order to know *li* and the proper ways of self-cultivation in the *Zhongyong* (*Zy* 20.7–8, 1.1, 1.4), and in spite of the claim that *zhong* is the basis of the proper way (*he*), this tacit metaphysics is not developed in the *Zhongyong*. The *Zhongyong* could elaborate the metaphysical (or at least protometaphysical) notion that *zhong* is the universal basis of every harmony by giving an explicit account of how the *he* that is founded on the *zhong* is best achieved by one particular *li* because its rituals best capture the harmony and balance exemplified by *tian's* (heaven's) way. By uniting the form that is *zhong* with the content that is *li*, the *Zhongyong* could not only espouse the *li* but justify it with a universal norm such as the *zhong*. That move is consistent with, but not explicit in, the *Zhongyong*.[20]

Now we are in a better position to return to the doctrine of the mean. The *junzi*, we are told, takes the middle path (*zhong*) of strength (*qiang*). This middle lies between the defective way of those Southerners who characteristically fail to retaliate when the way does not prevail (*wu dao*, literally "without way") and the excessive way of those Northerners who seem always to rush in to meet death without regret (*Zy* 10). The Confucian view of strength is a middle path that harmonizes (*he*) the two extremes. Getting clear about what precisely

---

[18] See Chapter 1, note 21. [19] *NE* 1144a1–3.

[20] This way of uniting *li* and *tian* could also avoid a charge made by Robert Eno, in *The Confucian Creation of Heaven*, that talk of heaven is simply a rhetorical sanction for the *li* that has been inherited from the Zhou. As Eno puts it in discussing the role that *tian* plays in the early Ruist texts: "Their primary concern is not to fashion a theory of *Tian* that can stand as an intellectual artifact. They borrow or invent in each instance any theory which serves their immediate purposes. . . . What all uses of the word "*tian*" share is the rhetorical force which that word possessed as a primary term of *Zhou* religious and political practice" (Eno, 79). Eno's view is that when the Zhou declined, the Confucians tried to replace the Zhou values of "kingship and hereditary roles" by elaborating on the surviving *li* and tried to sanction it by employing the rhetoric of *tian* (Eno, 28).

is brought into a Confucian harmony and what is excluded as inappropriate to that harmony will help us to be clear both about the *Zhongyong* and about the ways in which the Confucian view is comparable to Aristotle's. We read: "The *junzi* [acts according to] harmony.... He stands in the middle [*zhong*] and does not incline to either side" (*Zy* 10). At first blush, this might seem paradoxical: how can the *junzi* stand in the middle and harmonize the sides at the same time as he avoids them and does not even lean toward or "incline" to them? In the example from *Zy* 10, the middle is neither a position of meekness, exemplified by the Southerners, nor one of rashness, exemplified by the Northerners – and yet it is somehow a harmony. Again, what is being harmonized and what is being excluded? The answer to this question will clarify the relation between the mean and harmony and between Aristotle and Confucius.

Think about harmony and the mean in relation to taste and flavor.[21] The *Zhongyong* compares the way of the mean to knowing the flavor of food and drink, asserting that everyone eats and drinks but only a few really know the flavor of food and drink (*Zy* 4).[22] Notice first that a given dish can be oversalted or undersalted, too sweet or not sweet enough, too sour or lacking in tang, too hot or too bland, and so on.[23] A good dish is a harmony of flavors. It is a concord of just the right amounts of salt and sweet and hot and sour and such – and naturally enough a "hot and sour" dish will *require* pepper and vinegar in amounts that would simply ruin bitter gourd or winter

---

[21] I owe this analogy to the best Chinese cook of Italian extraction known to me personally.

[22] The defect in this gustatory example could refer to those who stuff themselves with food and fill themselves with drink but never stop to appreciate the flavors, while the excess could refer to those who try so hard to analyze the flavors that they, too, miss the real flavors. This is a plausible reading of this assertion because its context is the claim that both the stupid and intelligent (*zhi*) do not act according to the mean; the former fail by falling short, while the latter fail by going beyond. Applying this analogy to actions, Confucius means that everyone acts but only few can act in the moderate way.

[23] The same point can be made with appeal to the more traditional, more medicinal qualities of foods that are "heaty" and "cooling," and so on. This was (and often is) taken very seriously. By the time of the Zhou, imperial families were attended by court dieticians. Tastes were categorized according to the five elements or phases – sweet being associated with earth, with the pancreas and stomach, and with pensive temperament, salty with water and kidneys and bladder and a fearful temperament, and so on. I say a bit about diet and medicine in Chapter 3.

melon soup. While it is the case that flavors are harmonized (according to what is apt for the particular dish), it is nevertheless not at all the case that what is being harmonized is "oversalty" and "undersalty."[24] The right amount of saltiness for this dish will always be a rightness judged in reference to a particular harmony of salt and pepper and the other flavors of the dish; it will never be a "harmony" of oversalty and undersalty. Such extremes are excluded from the harmony, and there can be an appropriate harmony only on the condition that the extremes are eschewed. In relation to this harmony of flavors, there will always and inevitably be such a thing as oversalty and undersalty, and these extremes must in the nature of the case be avoided if a harmony is to follow.

Considering the moral life, Confucians recognize the inevitable penumbra of extremes – as is evident by the "too much/too little" contrasts in the several preceding examples – but they emphasize the focal harmony.[25] Aristotelians, on the other hand, recognize the harmony – as is evident from their explicit recognition that virtue enhances our relationships and builds community – but they emphasize the means/extremes structure in discussions of virtue. Both traditions recognize the mean and harmony, though with different emphases. Confucian harmony and the Aristotelian mean are not only comparable but complementary.

With this clarifying distinction in view, I take up a final point of comparison, the relative ease or difficulty of attaining to virtue. For both the *Zhongyong* and *Nicomachean Ethics*, the way to the mean is a process of self-cultivation or habituation. For both thinkers, this starts from the individual's own family. In his discussion of paternal friendship, Aristotle acknowledges the significant role of the father in causing his children's existence and benefiting them by nurturing and educating them (*NE* 1161a15–18). As a result of these benefits, Aristotle also acknowledges that more benefits are owed to one's father and mother than to one's brothers, fellow citizens, and other companions. As he puts it:

---

[24] This may seem obvious, but failure to appreciate just this distinction seems to mar the bulk of discussions of harmony and the mean.

[25] The focus here, remember, is human actions and relations, where *he* is prominent; in other ways, the *zhong* that is the principle or "basis" of harmony is prominent.

It seems that we must supply means of support to parents more than anyone. For we suppose that we owe them this, and that it is finer to supply those who are the causes of our being than to supply ourselves in this way. And we should accord honor to our parents, just as we should to the gods, but not every sort of honor; for we should not accord the same honor to father and to mother, nor accord them the honor due to a wise person or a general. We should accord a father's honor to a father, and likewise a mother's to a mother. (*NE* 1165a22–28)

Aristotle's talk of familial responsibility sounds very similar to the Confucian filiality (i.e., expression of reverence toward one's parents and forefathers; see *Zy* 19), and his talk of amity (*philia*, standardly translated as "friendship") sounds similar to the Confucian *ren* (authoritative conduct, the highest virtue of humanity, achieved by extending love by degrees from one's family to others; see *Zy* 20.4, 20.5, 20.8).[26] The *Zhongyong* also begins self-cultivation with filial piety toward one's own family. The *Zhongyong* compares the cultivation of the *junzi* to traveling, where, in order to go far, one must first start with the nearer space, and in order to ascend to a height, one must first start from the ground (*Zy* 15.1). In order to cultivate oneself so that one could become a sovereign able to govern a kingdom, one must first cultivate harmonious relations with one's family and relatives. The *Zhongyong* compares such harmonious relations with one's family members to "the music of lutes and harps," which bring one pleasure and delight (*Zy* 15.2; cf. Aristotle's standard analogy between virtue and art). Just as the common and ordinary music of lutes and harps can be harmonized to bring forth enjoyment, so can the common and ordinary relations with one's family and relatives be harmonized to bring forth pleasure and delight. One also learns how to extend one's love from her relatives to others in the society, a love that decreases in proportion to the degree to which the other is less related to one (*Zy* 20.5). Such a virtue culminates in *ren* (the highest Confucian virtue), which allows one to

---

[26] See my discussion of the first of three senses of *ren* in Chapter 1, note 7. See also Chan, in his "The Evolution of the Confucian Concept *Jên*," 319, where he says, "Confucius was the first to regard *ren* as the general virtue and to make it the foundation of ethics" and "This love is universal in nature, but there must be distinctions, that is, an order or gradation in application, beginning with the love of parents."

have a graded love for all human beings (*Zy* 20.5). *Ren* issues from *li* (ritual propriety), which begins with the family, telling us what degree of love is proper to others and the appropriate amount of honor to accord another based on her worth. The recognition of another's worth and the appropriate amount of honor to accord another culminates in the virtue *yi* (appropriateness). These relations between *li* (ritual propriety) and the virtues of *ren* and *yi* are stated in the *Zhongyong* as follows:

> Authoritative conduct (*ren*) means conducting oneself like a human being (*ren*), wherein devotion to one's kin is most important. Appropriateness (*yi*) means doing what is fitting (*yi*), wherein esteeming those of superior character is most important. The degree of devotion due different kin and the degree of esteem accorded those who are different in character is what gives rise to ritual propriety (*li*). (Ames and Hall, *FF*, 20)[27]

In short, the *Zhongyong* claims that in order to cultivate oneself, one must cultivate service toward one's parents.

The *Zhongyong* also connects self-cultivation with knowledge of human beings and heaven. Because all human beings have the same heaven-endowed nature (*xing*) (*Zy* 1.1), knowledge of human nature in turn entails a knowledge of *tian* (heaven) (*Zy* 20.7; cf. *Analects* 14.42). Knowledge of *tian* allows one to know human beings because *tian* has conferred upon human beings their nature (*Zy* 1.1). Moreover, knowledge of *tian* is bound up with the *li* of ceremonies and sacrifices that entail a reverence toward one's ancestors. In short, knowledge of heaven entails the knowledge of *ren* and *yi*, which are accompanied by the reenactment of one's forefathers' ceremonies and music such that they end up showing "respect to those whom they (the forefathers) esteemed, extending their affections to those of

---

[27] For a couple of insightful discussions on the relation between *ren* and *li*, see Shun Kwong-loi, "*Jen* and *Li* in the *Analects*," *Philosophy East and West* 43 (1993): 457–79; and Chong Kim-Chong, "The Practice of *Jen*," *Philosophy East and West* 49 (1999): 298–316. Ultimately, because of the significance that Confucians attribute to *li* for cultivation, coupled with the insufficiency of the *li* by itself to settle all moral problems, I agree with Eno's (Eno, *The Confucian Creation of Heaven*, 69) view that *ren* is "ethically prior to *li*" even though *li* is "sequentially prior" to *ren*. However, to the extent that *ren* stems from *li*, the lack of justification for *li* (see notes 40–42, this chapter) also extends to *ren*.

whom they (the forebears) are fond" (Ames and Hall, *FF*, 19). This reenactment of the sacrifices and ceremonies is so significant to the Confucians because in them one identifies with his forefathers and continues to carry out their wishes (*Zy* 19.2, 19.5). This is filial piety. Because the human ideal has been achieved and embodied in the *li* of past traditions, reenactments of ceremonies and sacrifices handed down by the *li* also reenact the virtues (such as harmony, piety, and actions that accord with the *zhong*). Such reenactments not only have a habituating or socializing effect on the participants who have identified with their forefathers and their virtues but also have an inspirational effect on their onlookers (*Analects* 8.2).

Beginning from the home or one's family is the way to proper self-cultivation for both Confucius and Aristotle. The attainment of harmony (*he*) in the *Zhongyong*, or the mean in the *Nicomachean Ethics*, however, seems to be difficult according to both thinkers. Let me explain why it is so difficult for each.

For Aristotle, once one starts habituating a virtue, there are many ways whereby one can err. It is not simply a matter of avoiding excess and deficiency and finding the intermediate – a task that is difficult enough in itself. Rather, many other conditions must be satisfied in order for one's actions to hit the mean. For instance, Aristotle thinks that just doing the right action in a particular situation is not enough to make one virtuous. Rather, to be virtuous, one must first know that she is doing a virtuous action.[28] So if one accidentally gives money to the needy, one is neither acting generously nor is one in possession of generosity. Second, one must decide or choose to do the virtuous action for itself and not, say, for some utilitarian purpose such as to get money or fame.[29] In order to achieve this second condition, one needs to know the proper ends or goals that constitute the virtues; that is, universal principles such as "courage and temperance are to be pursued." Such decisions are also to be made in accordance with reason – for Aristotle, a human being's function is to use the rational part of his soul to tell the nonrational part what functions are good for it. For example, neither rashness nor cowardice is good for one's feelings of fear and confidence; neither intemperance nor insensitivity is good for one's feelings of pleasure and pain. To become

---

[28] *NE* 1105a31.   [29] *NE* 1105a32.

virtuous, one needs to build constancy: one needs to be firm and without regrets about her action.[30] Finally, Aristotle thinks that one needs to take pleasure in virtuous actions in order to be a virtuous person. If one acts generously but is pained by one's act, then one is not virtuous according to Aristotle but continent or something of that sort.[31]

Given Aristotle's understanding of its prerequisites, virtue is quite rare and the mean quite difficult to attain. It is difficult first because we need to know ourselves and our own tendencies. Self-knowledge is an especially difficult task given the common tendency to think that whatever we are pursuing is good. Furthermore, our perception of what is good has also been largely shaped by our upbringing. People with a bad upbringing tend to have a skewed view of what is good. Second, the mean is difficult to attain because we normally do things because of pleasure.[32] We are, according to Aristotle, already biased toward pleasure and the sources of pleasure that cause us to lean toward intemperance and associated excesses. Controlling ourselves or pulling ourselves back from such common inclinations is another difficult challenge. Finally, the mean is difficult to achieve according to Aristotle because we are concerned with particular cases in every instance. Only universals and unchanging objects are definable for Aristotle because particular cases rely upon perception. The mean may be defined with reference to reason, but Aristotle argues explicitly that it is grasped in the thick of circumstances by perception. We cannot simply follow extant rules or rely on a preexisting account or definition – even Aristotle's definition of the mean makes reference to the concrete action of exemplary individuals. Only our own experience over time can shape a deliberate desire for what is neither too much nor too little – and that presumes we have had the opportunity of being well brought up.

It is hard work to be excellent, since in each case it is hard work ... to find what is intermediate; e.g., not everyone, but only one who knows, finds the midpoint in a circle. So also getting angry or giving and spending money is easy and anyone can do it, but doing it to the right person, in the right amount, at the right time, for the right end, and in the right way is no longer easy, nor can everyone do it. (*NE* 1109a24–29)

---

[30] *NE* 1105a33.   [31] *NE* 1104b3–8.   [32] *NE* 1109b7–9.

At first sight, it seems that the *Zhongyong*'s *he* (harmony) is not as difficult to achieve as Aristotle's mean. One reason for the apparent relative ease of hitting *he* for the Confucians is that people seem to be supplied with directives for how to behave in the form of the *li* (ritual propriety). As we saw earlier, *li* shows us what is *ren* and *yi*; that is, how in particular to express our love for our relatives and extend this love to others not related to oneself, how to honor the worthy, and so on (*Zy* 20.5). Moreover, these actions in turn are classified in various relatively tidy ways. For example, there are said to be five universal obligations: those between rulers and ministers, fathers and sons, husbands and wives, older and younger brothers, and friends. In addition, there are three virtues needed to accomplish these obligations: knowledge (*zhi*), authoritative conduct (*ren*), and courage (*yong*) (*Zy* 20.8). Furthermore, there are nine rules for cultivating one's character – the virtues are said to result from practicing these nine rules. The nine rules range across specific ways of conducting oneself toward the virtuous, one's relatives, various levels of subordinates (ministers and officers), the mass of the people, artisans, distant travelers, and princes of the states. So in contrast to Aristotle, the *Zhongyong* seems to offer no end of rules regarding appropriate behavior and attitude.

Notice, however, that these Confucian rules and universal obligations are not definitions of the mean. The Confucian classifiers are not definitions or a theoretical account; they moreover prescribe appropriate actions without giving an account of how each action is an intermediate between two extremes. Nonetheless, the Confucian leans rather hard on clear-cut roles and sharply delineated relationships. These might suffice so long as one's actions and sense of self are adequately defined by a role and so long as situations are sufficiently unproblematic and straightforward. Assuming a highly ritualistic and relational society, perhaps there is little need to problematize one's roles and situations. Even choice – as we might understand it – may not need to be thematized. The text states:

In all things preparation leads to success, no preparation leads to failure. If speech is fixed beforehand, then there will be no stumbling. If things are fixed beforehand, then there will be no difficulty. If actions are fixed beforehand, then there will be no sorrow. If the way is fixed beforehand, then there will be no exhaustion. (*Zy* 20.16)

There seems to be no need for decision in this *Zhongyong* passage. The *li* fixes conduct beforehand and one is simply to follow the *li*. Aristotle, on the one hand, stresses that one needs to choose or decide on the right action and do so for the sake of the act itself. The right action seems to be clear to the Confucian novice, and instead of choice, it is just practice. One gets a sense that, for Confucians, as long as one knows beforehand how one is to speak and conduct oneself according to one's roles, one will automatically speak and act correctly every time. Talk of choice is absent; discussion of agency and agent knowledge are absent from the *Zhongyong*. Exactly how *li* is to shape action so that choice is not problematized and decision does not become an issue is a difficult matter, much discussed by contemporary Confucian commentators.[33] My point here is that, however it occurs, action without dilemmas and without vexing life alternatives or heavy deliberation would certainly seem to make the mean rather easier to attain.

The *Zhongyong*'s harmony also looks easier to attain than Aristotle's mean because of the proximity of the way to such a harmony. The *Zhongyong* reports Confucius' claim that, "The way is not far from man" (*Zy* 13.1). In fact, he says that what is far from man cannot be the way. Again, he says that even the most ignorant people can know and practice the way (*Zy* 12.2). This makes the *Zhongyong*'s vision of harmony more accessible than Aristotle's mean, at least in the sense that it is available to more people. The *Zhongyong* cites the *Book of Songs*, which says, "In hewing an axe-handle, in hewing an axe-handle – the model is not far away" (Ames and Hall, *FF*, 13). The point is that we need to handle an axe handle in order to make

---

[33] Commentators disagree about whether there is a self in Confucius. Common to many of their views is the recognition that the "self" is intimately bound up with her roles; what is at issue is whether the self is exhausted by her roles. See Chapter 2, note 22, for my discussion of Fingarette's view. Roger Ames holds that the moral self is ultimately unique because it is good at playing roles in a community. His talk of the "focus-field," which determines the self, is not at odds with Fingarette's notion that it is "the social nexus" that determines the self. See Ames, TFFS, and Fingarette, "Comment and Response," in Bockover, *RR&R*. See also Henry Rosemont's "Rights-Bearing Individuals and Role-Bearing Persons," in Bockover, *RR&R*, 90, where he maintains that one is the totality of roles in relation to others and that there is no self independent of these roles. Finally, see Chapter 5, "The Moral Self in Confucius and Aristotle," for a more robust self than that allowed by the aforementioned commentators.

another axe handle. So the pattern of what we are making is right before us. Likewise, in attempting to govern human beings, all the *junzi* needs is to look at human beings, and the pattern of what that should be is quite obvious to perception.[34]

A final issue that suggests that the practice of *he* in the *Zhongyong* is easier than the mean in Aristotle's *Nicomachean Ethics* is that while the former can practice the mean in the most ordinary everyday business, the latter is restricted to the privileged citizen of the *polis*, whose public life is sharply delineated from that of the private household.[35] More elaborately, the focus on *li* in the *Zhongyong* is also a focus on *yong*, which could mean the ordinary or common. According to Tu, *yong* for Zhu Xi means "ordinary" and "common." Tu says, "It should become clear in the course of our discussion that *yong*, which we will translate as "commonality," must be taken to include such connotations as "practicality" and "unchangeability" (Tu, *CC*, 16–17). *Yong* is also the way toward *zhong*. Similarly, Ames and Hall say, "The expression *zhongyong* suggests that the locus for achieving harmony and equilibrium is *yong* – the ordinary business of the day" (Ames and Hall, *FF*, 86–87).

The claim that *he* (harmony) in the *Zhongyong* seems to be more accessible than the mean in Aristotle boils down to the greater range of persons to whom a life of virtue is available in the Confucian way. In a different respect, however, there is also evidence that the *he* (harmony) in the *Zhongyong* is either as elusive or even more so than the mean in Aristotle. The elusiveness of *he* (harmony) in the *Zhongyong* is evident in passages such as:

The Master said, "I know why the way is not traveled. Those who know go beyond it and those who don't know don't reach it. I know why the way is

---

[34] Of course, the axe-handle analogy might also be taken in another way, from the standpoint of the ordinary agent who is not a sage. Here the model would be the *junzi* himself, shining as an exemplar for others. This way of taking the analogy is entirely compatible with Aristotle, for whom the *phronimos* functions as the exemplary individual. Aristotle says that ordinary human action is not sufficiently guided by abstract rules but by the *phronimos* or *spoudaios* (the sincere man, the man with *cheng* who is the living rule and measure).

[35] See Anthony Kenny, *Aristotle on the Perfect Life*, 43, for the necessity of a *polis* for habituation. For Aristotle's emphasis on how habituation is bound up with the political system and how the laws continue to play a role in our habituation even in adulthood, see Reeve, *Practices of Reason*, 54–55. See Chapter 6 of this volume for my analysis of both issues.

not clear. Those of superior character go beyond it and the unworthy don't reach it. Man eats and drinks, but few can know flavors." (*Zy* 4; see also *Zy* 5)

The way to *he* seems to be near and available – as near and available as the taste of food – yet few get it. Common men and women know something about the way and can act according to some of the way (*Zy* 12.2); however, the depths of the way are commonly missed, and sometimes the way is missed altogether. The *Zhongyong* seems to hold that few take the way and no one ever reaches a state of perfected virtue. Aristotle holds that some few do reach the goal.

Confucius holds that the virtues (*de*) come from one's adherence to the *zhongyong* in his actions (*Analects* 6.29). Given that one rarely has such virtues, one finds it difficult to hit the *zhong*. Even if one pursues the equilibrium, the *Zhongyong* maintains that she would find it difficult to adhere to it even for a month (*Zy* 7). The reason it is difficult is because it takes fortitude to stick to the middle without relaxing when the way prevails and when the way does not prevail (*Zy* 10.5; see also 11.3). What is easier for human beings in general is to relax their efforts when they are successful and to give up their efforts when they are not being honored appropriately, when they are under some kind of duress, or when their lives are at stake. Only the most disciplined *junzi* with *ren* can stick so closely to the *li* that he neither looks, nor listens, nor speaks, nor does anything that violates it (*Analects* 12.1). The *Zhongyong*'s *junzi* seems to be caught up in a life of ceaseless working with, and for heaven and earth to nourish, not only himself but others and all things between them (*Zy* 26.1–5). Even though the sage seems to accomplish his tasks with ease (*Zy* 26.6, 27.1), the constant extension of one's actions to others and the constant inquiry and learning (*Zy* 27.6, *Analects* 17.8) seem to make his life a constant challenge. There is no completion of the moral task for the Confucian because he is suspended between heaven and earth in the eventful world of change and action.

The tasks that are demanded of exemplary persons in the *Zhongyong* and *Nicomachean Ethics* vary greatly. In spite of the fact that the *Zhongyong*'s view of *he* seems easier to attain because the resources required for self-cultivation are available to everybody, the breadth of the *junzi*'s actions makes his task more daunting than that of Aristotle's *phronimos*. Notice that Aristotle's individual needs to undertake virtuous actions in order to cultivate his virtues. But apart from developing himself and other human beings, nowhere is he required to develop the natures of animals and things. In contrast, the *Zhongyong* states:

It is only he who is possessed of the most complete sincerity that can exist under heaven, who can give its full development in his nature. Able to give its full development to his own nature, he can do the same to the nature of other men. Able to give its full development to the nature of other men, he can give their full development to the natures of animals and things. Able to give their full development to the natures of creatures and things, he can assist the transforming and nourishing powers of Heaven and Earth. Able to assist the transforming and nourishing powers of Heaven and Earth, he may with Heaven and Earth form a ternion. (*Zy* 22, Legge's trans.)

Cheng (sincerity or integrity) becomes the ultimate virtue in the *Zhongyong* (*Zy* 25.2). This virtue not only allows one to complete himself but also allows him to complete others and all things. His self-completion is manifested in his possession of *ren*, and his completion of all things is manifested in his possession of knowledge (*zhi*). The *Zhongyong* asserts that *cheng* is a virtue that belongs to human nature and also is the way that enables the one with this virtue to unite the outer and inner (*he wai nei*) (*Zy* 25.3). *Cheng*, then, is "the end and beginning of things; without *cheng* there would be nothing" (*Zy* 25.2). Moreover, *cheng* makes one the coequal of earth and heaven, like a spirit (*Zy* 24), and gives one the infinity (*wu qiang* – literally "without boundary") to assist in the transforming and nourishing powers of heaven and earth (*Zy* 22, 26.5, 31.3–4, 32.2). Even though Aristotle compares the life of contemplation to the life of the god (*NE* 1177b27–35), neither the man of action nor the contemplative one in his self-sufficiency is as broadly effective in the universe at large as the Confucian sage.

Having examined the mean in Aristotle and how it compares with the *Zhongyong*'s harmony (*he*), how one starts cultivating each, and the relative ease and difficulty of achieving each, let us examine the rationale of each view in a bit more depth.

When Aristotle says the mean is "relative to us," he refers to three irreducible determining factors that shape it. Aristotle's mean is a vector determined by a common human nature, living paradigms who exhibit concretely the moral meaning of that nature, and individuals with peculiar abilities and circumstances.[36] The *phronimos* or *spoudaios* (the sincere person) is Aristotle's exemplary individual, the living paradigm who behaves well for the right reason (*orthos logos*) and displays it for others in his own person. We know about human nature in its morally relevant aspects thanks to Aristotle's metaphysics of the soul (*psychê*). There are, according to the Stagirite, discernible functions of the *psychê*, each of which may function well or ill; human well-being consists in the excellent functioning of these "parts of the soul," with the fullest functioning of the best and most distinctively human parts defining the human purpose. Hence we are above all to pursue the perfections of the two rational parts of the soul, namely the speculative part and the deliberative part. These parts are to train or persuade the nonrational parts of the *psychê*, which consist of the appetites, emotions, and desires. These points of Aristotelian doctrine have three important consequences for his view of the mean. First, when thinking about the mean, we need to acknowledge all three determinants: individual agents, social paradigms, and common human nature. Second, there is some "give" or slack, some play between these, so that there are several more or less legitimate ways that social paradigms can specify the common nature and different ways that individual agents can specify a single social paradigm (within the limits set by the two other factors). Third, there is a metaphysical grounding for the whole thing in Aristotle's soul doctrine and teleological metaphysics that argues that there is a specifically human function and why it is that the excellent functioning of the human being in political life with others is that in which the moral life consists.

---

[36] There are moral wrongs that do not have the character of extremes at all, according to Aristotle. There is no mean of theft, murder, or adultery. There is no right way, right time, and right person in regard to theft, murder, or adultery. And even in reference to qualities that are either excess or defect, Aristotle argues that there is no *further* mean for them. One cannot claim to be a coward in just the right way and in the right circumstance, for instance. Nor ought one to use the latitude required to take moral stock of abilities and circumstances as a slacker's excuse: one ought not to say that one is by nature a timid person so that one's mean should be to refrain from any courageous acts whatsoever. Such would be an act of cowardice.

The *Zhongyong*, too, has a metaphysics; *Zy* 1 starts out with the claim that nature (*xing*) is conferred by heaven (*tian*). The middle path (*zhong*) is the proper way for the most ordinary (*yong*) of actions. This injunction seems to have its sanction and justification from *tian*. Everything holds the middle way (*zhong*) in common (*yong*). Heaven in the *Zhongyong* is all-encompassing, extending from the sun to the moon, stars, and everything else under it (*Zy* 26.9). Heaven, together with earth, nourishes everything in such a way that everything is harmonized. In the human order, a harmonization of our appetites and desires (internally) and our actions and relations results from our pursuing actions (externally) according to the *zhong* (*Zy* 30.3). The way of heaven is *cheng*; likewise, this is the ultimate virtue in man. By acting according to *cheng*, a human individual becomes the coequal of heaven and earth and assists them in nourishing other human beings, animals, and all things under heaven (*Zy* 20.18, 22). The sage not only wins the favors of heaven (*Zy* 17.4–5) but is also the proper one to "order ceremonies, to fix the measures, and to determine the written characters (*wen*)"[37] (*Zy* 28).

Although both appeal to the divine, the *Zhongyong* and Aristotle part company in their conception of it. Aristotle has an account of God as an unmoved mover who moves all things as if their seeking their own forms of good were at the same time a love of divine perfection. Aristotle's God is the primary *ousia* (being, standardly translated as "substance") and *energeia* (enactment, standardly translated as "actuality"), to which everything else that has form and activity is focally related.[38] The *Zhongyong* does talk about heaven (*tian*) and about a human nature that is conferred by heaven. Moreover, its declaration that a knowledge of heaven allows one to know human nature suggests a most intimate intertwining of divine nature and human nature.[39] However, apart from telling us that heaven is all-encompassing and that it nourishes everything, that its way is *cheng*, not much else is said about what it is or how we know it. Nor is there any suggestion about how we are to bring this way of

---

[37] *Wen* can mean both written Chinese characters and Chinese culture.
[38] See Halper, *One and Many in Aristotle's Metaphysics*, quoted in Chapter 1, note 22, of this book.
[39] *Zy* 1.1, 20.7. See also *Analects* 14.42.

heaven to human practice except by practicing the *li* of authoritative tradition in an earnest manner. One can see how serious practice of the *li* in ceremonies and sacrifices may lead to the cultivation of general moral sincerity (*cheng*); one can see how reverence and love toward one's ancestors can be extended to others (*ren*). However, we are never provided with a rationale for why the Zhou *li* is over all others the *li* to be practiced, other than the assertion that it does in fact embody heaven's way.[40] Of course, blind adherence to the *li* does not always lead one to act correctly. I argued earlier that the Confucian way, like the Aristotelian way to virtue, makes room for individual differences in abilities and circumstances, as well as for social paradigms and a common human nature that somehow connects us to a suprahuman divine. Appeal to elements other than the *li* occurs when we find Confucius amending the *li* (*Analects* 9.3) and commentators calling for supplements to the *li* by appealing to other Confucian virtues such as *shu* (reciprocity)[41] and *yi* (appropriateness).[42] Cases where an individual's roles conflict such that he needs to choose between two roles or prioritize one over the other also show that *li*'s revelation of heaven and human nature is limited.[43] But, on the whole, the Confucian way leans mainly and focally on authoritative tradition far more than it leans upon individual agency and choice or metaphysical verities.

To the extent that the Confucian appeals to *li* and *tian* are more like appeals to authority than justified and justifying reasons, hard moral cases such as conflicts in an individual's roles cannot be resolved by those appeals. In recognition of this point, commentators have invoked "creativity," for it takes creativity to deal with

---

[40] Confucian commentators discuss the lack of justification in following the Zhou *li*. See Chapter 1, note 28.

[41] Philip Ivanhoe claims that *shu* is needed to make the right judgment, and one needs enough experience before one can appropriately amend the *li* (Ivanhoe, "Reweaving the 'One Thread' of the *Analects*," 28).

[42] Schwartz, in *The World of Thought in Ancient China*, claims that "The prescriptions of *li* do not always clarify what is right (*yi*) in the infinite variety of life situations, and 'righteousness' is just as essential an attribute of *ren* as is a submissiveness to *li*" (Schwartz, 80). See also Hall and Ames (*TTC*, 107–9) for their discussion of the necessity of *yi* for supplementing *li* in particular actions.

[43] See Heiner Roetz's *Confucian Ethics of the Axial Age*, ch. 8, 99, for his examples from the fifth and sixth centuries B.C.E. I discuss these examples in Chapter 5.

unanticipated contingencies. Creativity seems to allow one to trans-
cend the conflicting roles and to assume some other standpoint that
might resolve them. Tony Cua invokes moral "creativity" in this sort
of way. For Ames and Hall, the *Zhongyong*'s concept of sincerity is all
about creativity. However, because they understand creativity to be
opposed to rational choice rather than supplementary to it,[44] the
ability of their model to resolve real-life dilemmas and conflicting
roles is questionable. Despite their appeal to the language of creativity, it seems to me that the way of life Ames and Hall describe is
designed to function when roles are not conflicting and affairs of the
day are familiar. Such a model reaches its limit, therefore, with
situations where there are no moral dilemmas but only noncon-
flicting roles and appeals that neither solicit nor require rational
justification. I hasten to add that this is, quite likely, not so much a
defect in Ames and Hall's interpretation of Confucian tradition as a
shortcoming in that tradition. The Confucian way is simply not
designed to handle human action outside of clearly defined roles, or
situations that are rife with alternatives, or affairs that are not terribly
"familiar." It is difficult enough for the Confucian way to handle a
situation where a son's filiality toward his father is at odds with his
official loyalty toward the emperor, much less all the many crossroads individuals face in the tangle of modern affairs. There are
situations that cannot be handled by focusing on the familiar or by
adjusting one's *li*-informed dispositions precisely because one is
dealing with the unfamiliar, or with conflicting dispositions that call
for deliberation and choice rather than "unstinting attention to
proper roles" (Ames and Hall, *FF*, 151), for reason rather than "*li*-
informed affect" (ibid.), or for individual initiative rather than
"dispositional adjustments in communal *li*-living" (ibid.).

Tu Weiming attempts to put his finger on the common root of the
Zhongyong's ethics and metaphysics by looking to the concept of
sincerity (*cheng*). Tu points out that sincerity is what human beings
share with heaven (Tu, *CC*, 72, 82). As he puts it:

Cheng definitely points to a human reality which is not only the basis of self-
knowledge but also the ground of man's identification with heaven. This

---

[44] "It is not reason, but *li*-informed affect, that directs experience" (Ames and Hall,
    FF, 151).

seems to imply that that which enables a person to fully realize himself and to understand heaven is inherent in his own nature. (Tu, *CC*, 72)

In spite of the identification of human nature with heaven's nature, Tu claims that there is no guarantee that human beings will unite with heaven. Rather, this is an ideal to be actualized by moral self-cultivation. According to Tu, heaven is the "transcendent anchorage" of morality in the *Zhongyong*. But this does not make it inaccessible. Rather, Tu says that the *Zhongyong* "maintains that common human experience itself embodies the ultimate ground of morality, thus providing the theoretical basis for actualizing the unity of heaven and man in the lives of ordinary people" (Tu, *CC*, 69). Furthermore, Tu explains that *Zhongyong*'s metaphysics advocates that the ultimate reality is transparent and attainable by everyone because human nature shares in the reality of heaven and thus can manifest this reality (Tu, *CC*, 70). What Tu is saying is that human beings share the same inherent nature that is established or realized in the same common or ordinary way. As he puts it: "The Way of the sage therefore is centered on the commonality of human nature. And it is this sameness inherent in each human being that enables the sage to establish others and to enlarge others as a way of establishing and enlarging himself" (Tu, *CC*, 83). Because this commonality of human nature shares in heaven's reality, Tu claims that heaven is the "transcendent anchorage" of morality. This subtle claim is not to be confused with the claim that there is a "transcendent reference" of morality. Tu denies that there is a transcendent reference for morality. He says:

Having no transcendent reference to rely upon, the profound person cannot be absolutely sure whether that which is best for him is necessarily of equal value to others. Although he envisages his own quest for his inner self as a universal path, he does not presume to have a privileged access to esoteric truths.... He reflects on things at hand with the intention of establishing himself so that others can also be established. He hopes that his fellow human beings will appreciate what he believes to be true and valuable, but he has no compulsion to see to it that his "world view" is universally accepted. (*CC* 36)

Having already clearly asserted that heaven (*tian*) is the transcendent anchor, Tu's denial that there is a "transcendent reference" amounts to a denial that there is any moral content to the notion and hence no way to appeal to this metaphysical principle for action guidance. Therefore, "heaven" plays no justificatory role, offers no specific guidance for action, and is devoid of moral content. Without a way to determine what is best for the human being, how is the profound person to assess if others are being established, too, and by what means he is to establish them? Tu speaks of a "higher morality," "the morality of the sage-king," (Tu, *CC*, 44) while justifying King Wu's neglect of the proper mourning ritual for his father while campaigning against the tyrant and the Duke of Zhou's campaigns against his own brothers while trying to unify the dynasty. Tu's claim to a "higher morality" seems to conflict with his claim that because there is no way to use the "transcendent anchor" (heaven, *tian*) as a "transcendent reference" for moral guidance and justification, the profound person will have to respect all *li* (Tu, *CC*, 84). Tu, however, goes on to claim that what he calls the "higher morality" actually prevents the sages from fulfilling the *li* associated with their family relations when the two conflict. It is not at all clear how heaven (or sincerity, its inward counterpart) allows us to resolve such conflicts in the way that Tu has them resolved, by prioritizing one's roles in the state over one's familial roles. Tu's claims about the lack of a transcendent reference for morals leave one with nothing more than groundless intuition.

Perhaps the Confucian concepts of heaven and sincerity need some sort of supplement in order to develop the metaphysics they tacitly imply.[45] The *Zhongyong*'s views of heaven and human nature that ultimately sanction the *zhong* could be strengthened by a more elaborate account of heaven as a source of more determinate moral norms. Just as Aristotle's account of God as the primary substance or form allows him both to make sense of his teleological ethic and to justify the rational soul as the highest part of man and hence to sanction its judgment of the mean, a similarly definite account of heaven and how it is related to human nature could help the *Zhongyong* to sanction the *zhong* and justify a more definite range of *li* practices as the proper way. Such a development could also more clearly delimit the human good and so rescue the Confucian ideal from vagueness and baselessness.

---

[45] This is, arguably, a key part of the project of Song neo-Confucianism.

A Confucian could profit from Aristotle's example of a more explicit metaphysics and elaborate on the *Zhongyong*'s metaphysics of heaven. Similarly, Aristotle could benefit from the Confucian example in at least two ways. First, Aristotle could learn from the *Zhongyong* that the exercise of human virtue can take place in a full-fledged way in the most ordinary everyday business within the family. One need not rely on the aristocratic life of the citizen in the *polis* to exercise the virtues. Aristotle already knows that doing good for others begins in the home; he seems to need reminding that it can also be fulfilled there. Second, Aristotle could learn from the Confucians how development of the mean accords with harmonizing one's relations not merely with other human beings but also with nonhuman animals and with the natural world at large.[46] Such an approach will rescue his view from an exclusive emphasis upon human being. This is desirable. We are increasingly becoming aware that our well-being is affected not only by the social and political world but also by our natural environment.[47] The challenge for an ethic of virtue is to develop an understanding of the mean relevant to this larger picture. Aristotelian and Confucian traditions both have much to contribute to this project.

I have considered central concerns of Aristotelian and Confucian ethics to argue their comparability and complementarity. That is not at all to say the two traditions will agree or even that they will share central concepts. Concepts of the "mean" provide a striking example of this point. It is not the case that the Aristotelian mean maps neatly onto either *zhong* or *he*. Certain aspects of the mean are more pertinent to *zhong* and others more pertinent to *he*. None of these terms

---

[46] See Tu's discussion of Confucian filiality and reverence as principles in the "Confucian anthropocosmic worldview" that function as "ecological principles" today. As he puts it, "Filial piety and reverence are not conservative but conservationist ideas; they attempt to establish a pattern of mutual dependence and organismic unity between Heaven and humankind" (Tu, *CC*, 107). Also see Tu's "Beyond the Enlightenment Mentality," in *Confucianism and Ecology*, ed. Mary Tucker and John Berthrong (Cambridge, MA: Harvard University Press, 1998), 18–19, for more on his view of the Confucian anthropocosmic vision.

[47] Such a point might also be teased out of the Stoic appropriation of Aristotle. An alternative argument for the ecological pertinence of Aristotelian tradition can be found in C. W. DeMarco, in *The Greeks and the Environment*, ed. Laura Westra and Tim Robinson (Lanham, MD: Rowman and Littlefield, 1997).

translates the others. What we find instead is a web of similarities and differences. The Confucian *zhong* is the principle or "basis" of *he*, and it is *he* – a harmony of the person with herself, with other persons, and with nature at large – upon which we are to focus in human moral life. In practice, ideas of equilibrium and balance remain in the background. Nevertheless, it is Confucius and not Aristotle who points to a cosmological or metaphysical principle that grounds this practice: *zhong* as a principle of nature in which we might participate through moral practice and the ritual observances that focus and intensify moral practice. An encounter with Confucian tradition can and should invite Aristotelians to notice that they need a metaphysical basis for their doctrine of the mean.

In the *Zhongyong*, we read: "The *junzi* [acts according to] harmony.... He stands in the middle [*zhong*] and does not incline to either side" (*Zy* 10). Confucians recognize what I called the inevitable penumbra of extremes and recognize that extremes are to be avoided, but they emphasize the focal harmony. Aristotelians, on the other hand, recognize the harmony – as is evident from their explicit recognition that virtue enhances our relationships and builds community – but they emphasize the means/extremes structure. In fact, the mean and harmony go together hand in glove. Both traditions recognize the mean and harmony, but with different emphases; each tradition can benefit from the extra attention the other has accorded to an essential element of virtue.

Just as a harmony of flavors in an appetizing dish is a suitable blend of ingredients that avoids extremes (so that it is neither too salty nor not salty enough, and similarly for the other ingredients), a harmony of action and feeling is a concord of human relationships that avoids the extremes of vice. This is comparable to an Aristotelian mean: the mean that is courage is not a smaller amount of rashness or a larger amount of cowardice; nor is it a mediocre amount of confidence or a middling amount of fear. Every mean is in itself an extreme in respect to goodness that is defined in reference to appropriate actions performed in appropriate ways in relation to appropriate persons in the appropriate places with the appropriate timing (and so on for the other categories). Every Aristotelian mean is triangulated between an excess and a defect by appeal to a common human nature, social paradigms, and individual differences in abilities and circumstances. The mean that is "relative to us" is shaped by all three factors and profiled against extremes to be eschewed. Such extremes are excluded from the elements that are to be harmonized, and there can be an appropriate harmony only on the condition that the extremes are eschewed and the ingredients find their proper proportions. Every harmony is a harmony of differences, but no Confucian harmony is a harmony of extremes.

While the *Zhongyong* is not a "doctrine of the mean" in Aristotle's sense, it could use one. Aristotelian claims about the mean resonate with Confucian claims about harmony, but Aristotle's observations about the structure of the mean are more explicit and more numerous. A Confucian should recognize the value of these observations for her own practice within her own tradition. This is an excellent example, I believe, of the way in which – with a little groundwork – one philosophical tradition can find useful resources in a quite alien philosophical tradition, even though term–term translations are wanting. In this chapter, I have shown that though Aristotle's mean (*meson*) does not translate either Confucius' "mean" (*zhong*) or harmony (*he*), Aristotle's account of the mean can provide a needed supplement for the Confucian account. Furthermore, a Confucian can and should be brought to appreciate this fact. An Aristotelian can and should be brought to appreciate that the *Nicomachean Ethics* needs a metaphysics of the mean. Only a genuine and genuinely mutual dialogue can make such appreciations possible. It is the aim of this book to contribute to this dialogue.

5

The Moral Self in Confucius and Aristotle

Both Aristotle and Confucius stress that paradigmatic persons exhibit the nature and content of ethical standards. For that reason, their views of what it is to be a paradigmatic person – and what it is to be a person at all – take on a decisive importance. Conversely, because ethics for both authors centers upon character, getting clear about the self that is formed in character will help clarify the nature of ethics in each case.

One of the starkest differences between Aristotle's and Confucius' views of the self or person is the presence of a soul doctrine in Aristotle and the absence of such a doctrine in Confucius. The soul is the primary substance or form that causes an individual to be the kind of being he or she is.[1] Confucius does not have a soul doctrine; he never speaks of a principle of self that is distinct from, and understood by abstracting from, the body and is the cause of the individual's existence. My purpose is to make three arguments. First,

---

[1] Aristotle holds that the substance or form, or essence of something, is its nature (see *Metaphysics* 1015a6, 1014b36, 1022a24–28 and also 1031b19–23, 1041b29–32, hereafter *Met.*) and its cause (see *Met.* 1041a27–30, 1041b7–9 and 25–28). Because he holds that the soul is the form of the human body (*De Anima* 412a22) and that the function that is uniquely human is the activity of the rational part of the soul rather than the nutritive or perceptive parts (*Nicomachean Ethics* I, chs. 7 and 13), it follows that human nature, or the cause of the "what it is" of a human being, is the activity of the rational part of the soul. See Chapter 1, note 21, for commentators who argue that the primary substance or formal cause (e.g., the human soul) is the form or essence for Aristotle.

habituation into virtue, social relations, and paradigmatic persons are central for both Aristotle and Confucius. Both therefore need a notion of self supportive of them. Second, Aristotle's individualistic metaphysics cannot account for the thick relations this requires. Third, the Confucian self, if entirely relationistic, cannot function as a locus of choice and agency; if fully ritualistic, cannot function as a source of moral norms that might help assess existing social proprieties. I shall suggest that each offers some corrective for the others and so urge further dialogue between the friends of Confucius and Aristotle. In order to appreciate fully the difference between Confucius and Aristotle on this issue, let me elaborate on Aristotle's soul doctrine.

Aristotle, like Plato before him, is concerned with being and intelligibility. Because things that change are not amenable to knowledge, the task is to find an essence or substance that is unchangeable.[2] Plato found his answer in the forms that are exempted from change and play the role of principles of being and intelligibility. Aristotle also found his unchanging primary substance in a separate unmoved mover who thinks his own thoughts (i.e., God). God is primary substance because as an eternal unmoved mover of other substances, He satisfies the criteria of completeness and self-sufficiency that in turn make Him definable, knowable, and prior in time to anything else (*Met.* 1028a30–1028b1). Unlike Plato, who was content to relegate the rest of this world to the realm of appearances or imitations that participate in the forms, Aristotle sought to give a more prominent place to the concrete beings in this world by speaking about various senses of being that are focally related to primary substance or form. He then demonstrated that God is the ultimate cause and principle of primary substance.[3] Because God's activity is to think His own thoughts (for only in this way could He be immaterial, complete, and self-sufficient as opposed to being dependent on something else about which he is thinking), human beings are most like God when we contemplate things

---

[2] For a good exposition of how Aristotle's notion of "actuality" (*energeiai*) satisfies the conditions of completeness and hence knowability, see Halper, *Form and Reason*.

[3] See Chapter 1, note 22, for Halper's account on the relation between primary substance and God as the principle and cause of primary substance.

eternal. For Aristotle, then, the substance of a human being lies in his rational part of the soul, for this is the part that can become most like God in contemplation. Aristotle dismisses the nutritive and perceptive parts of the soul as uniquely human because they are shared with plants and animals, respectively (*NE* 1098a3–5). This does not mean that human beings do not partake of nutrition and perception, for it is obvious that they do. What Aristotle means is that the rational soul unites and organizes all that human beings do, including their nutrition and perception. Just think about how we eat and perceive differently from plants and animals because these activities are controlled by our reason.[4] Despite Aristotle's position that the ultimate human function is to perform that most Godlike function of contemplation, one need not be actively contemplating God to be human. Otherwise, one would not be human when one is asleep, or is a child, or is a slave. Rather, what suffices for being human for Aristotle is simply the possession of the rational soul, which makes possible its exercise when needed.[5] This is clear from Aristotle's *De Anima*, from which we know that the soul is the actuality or form of the body (412a22). Here, Aristotle goes on to distinguish two senses of actuality and to claim that the soul's actuality corresponds to one of these senses. The two senses of actuality correspond respectively to the difference between the possession of knowledge (i.e., the first

---

[4] Terence Irwin and Ed Halper make this point. See Chapter 1, note 13, for their assertions.

[5] That it is the presence of the rational soul that is sufficient to make us human is also supported by Halper when he says: "The form of human being is an actuality; and, since it is complete, the end of a human being is just to be a human being. There is no need to look for an end of human life beyond the fulfilling of those human functions that constitute our nature. If thinking or the *capacity* for thinking is the function which is our essence, then the *end* of human life for each of us is just to exercise this capacity for thought." (Halper, *Form and Reason*, 102, my italics.) Irwin, too, recognizes that it is the first actuality or the mere presence of the rational soul that makes someone the human he is rather than the way in which he has actualized his rationality (i.e., his character or virtue). As Irwin puts it: "The particular form of a rational agent is the first actuality that is his soul. If it is like other particular forms, it does not require the persistence of a coherently changing system of desires and aims. A particular person's persistence does not consist in the persistence of any particular first order desires or aims, but in the persistence of the same particular soul that organizes them. The organizing desires are the agent's conception of his good; but this may change without his ceasing to exist.... The persisting self, therefore, cannot be identical to the character" (Irwin, *Aristotle's First Principles*, 377–78).

actuality) and the actual exercise of knowledge (i.e., the second actuality). Aristotle likens the soul's actuality to that of the possession of knowledge; that is, the soul is the first actuality of the body because its presence in the body is what makes the body a human body. Just as one who possesses knowledge need not be using it actively (e.g., when one is asleep), one who possesses the rational part of the soul need not be using it at any moment. Thus, it is the soul as the first actuality, rather than its exercise or the second actuality, that makes one a human being (*DA* 412a23–26). This is also consistent with Aristotle's claim in the *Categories* that substance does not "admit of variation of degree" (*Cat.* 3b32). As Aristotle puts it, "One man cannot be more man than another" (*Cat.* 3b38). Because Aristotle also holds that the substance, form, or essence of something is its nature (*Met.* 1015a6, 1014b36, 1022a24–28; see also 1031b19–23, 1041b29–32) and its cause (*Met.* 1041a27–30, 1041b7–9, 25–28), it also follows that human nature, or the cause of "what it is" of a human being, is the rational soul, where one man's rational soul cannot be greater or more than another man's (see *Met.* 1044a11, 1037a7–9, 1029b14–16).[6]

---

[6] Stephen R. L. Clark, in his *Aristotle's Man* (Oxford: Clarendon Press, 1983), points out that even though in the *Categories* 3b33ff Aristotle "denies that substance can admit of degrees," he is prepared to admit that the composite individual does admit of degrees at *Met.* 1044a11(Clark, *Aristotle's Man* 27). Clark uses the latter point to support his claim that the *ergon* (function) and *eidos* (form) are identical so that one may be more or less human. Hence, as Clark puts it, "It is the Aristotelian saint who is *most* especially *human*" and "best shows the nature of man" (Clark, *Aristotle's Man*, 26–27).

While I agree with Clark that the nature of man is best exhibited by the *phronimos*, I do not agree that 1044a11 supports the claim that human beings, as possessing the first actuality, could vary in their degree of humanity. By identifying *ergon* and *eidos*, Clark is collapsing Aristotle's distinction between soul as the first actuality and second actuality. Such a move results in the variation in degrees of being human. Clark adheres to this variation in his discussion of the differences between the master and the slave, but he will have to adhere to it as well in his discussion of children, despite his recognition of children as human beings. Aristotle's definition of a human being as possessing a first actuality that does not differ in degree is supported by 1044a10–11, where Aristotle says that "substance in the sense of form (*eidos*)" does not admit of degree. That composite substances admit variation simply means that the matters of different composite substances differ in degree. This makes sense because matter is what is variable (*Met.* 1027a14–15, 1032a20–23), whereas form qua first actuality or substance that makes something the thing it is is not variable for Aristotle, as we have seen. That the matters of composite substances differ in degree simply means that there is more

In contrast to Aristotle's elaborate remarks on the soul's making one a human being, there is only a single claim regarding human nature in Confucius. He says, "Human beings are similar [*jìn*, literally "near"] in their natural tendencies [*xing*], but vary greatly by virtue of their habits" (17.2).[7] Even though he does not tell us what these natural tendencies are or whether absolutely all human beings have them, we are told that there is a human nature that is developed differently depending on one's habits. Confucius does not elaborate a view of human nature; perhaps he downplays its import. Nonetheless, he does mention it, and I shall argue that it has some pivotal roles to play. We can infer features of a Confucian human nature by reasoning to the traits necessary for ethical qualities – even when Confucius does not frame these in terms of a common human nature. For instance, all people have a capacity for virtue. Therefore, we may fairly infer that human nature for Confucius consists of a potentiality to develop just these virtues of which he speaks, such as acting with authoritative conduct or humanity (*ren*), being appropriate in one's actions (*yi*), living up to one's words (*xin*), or acting with deference, tolerance, diligence, and generosity, just to name several. In short, what it is to be a human being is to be equipped with certain faculties or capacities that can be developed into such virtues. Whether these capacities are innate moral tendencies with a natural inclination to the good or morally indifferent tendencies that need to be mastered and crafted before one could acquire morality is a debate for later Confucians such as Mencius and Xunzi.[8]

But we can say that for Confucius there are natural tendencies and basic capacities for virtue that we have simply because we are human.

matter in some individuals than in others, such as between a man and a child and between a large man and a small man.

[7] *Analects*.

[8] For an account of how the goodness or badness of human nature became an issue for Mencius because of the universalistic tendencies of the Mohists and the individualistic tendencies of Yang Chu and the Nurture of Life School, see Angus C. Graham's *Studies in Chinese Philosophy and Philosophical Literature* (Albany: State University of New York Press, 1990), 18–22. See also Bryan W. Van Norden's "Mengzi and Xunzi: Two Views of Human Agency," *International Philosophical Quarterly* 32 (1992): 161–84, for a good discussion of the goodness or badness of human nature in Mencius and Xunzi.

Mencius is an advocate of the first view, which Ivanhoe calls the "development model of self-cultivation," whereas Xunzi is an advocate of the second view, which Ivanhoe calls the "reformation model."[9]

Mencius held that man has four innate moral tendencies that incline him toward the four virtues of humaneness or authoritative conduct (*ren*), appropriateness (*yi*), propriety (*li*), and wisdom (*zhi*) (*The Works of Mencius*, 2A6).[10] He maintains that all men will feel alarm and distress when they see a child suddenly fall into a well. This feeling is for Mencius the sprout (*duan*) of the virtue of humanity. The natural feelings of commiseration, shame, deference, and approval and disapproval are the sprouts that if developed and nourished will result in the four cardinal virtues of *ren*, *yi*, *li*, and *zhi*. The four inborn sprouts, though necessary for one's moral development, are not sufficient. There are three other requirements. First, we must employ the heart-mind (*xin*) to reflect on what actions are right. As Mencius puts it: "The mind is in charge of thinking. By thinking, it gets things right; by not thinking, it does not get things right. These are what Heaven [*tian*] has given us" (6A15, my trans.). Second, we must take pleasure in doing what is right, which will fuel moral growth. Angus Graham explains this "flood-like energy" of moral growth by saying:

The moral energy which inspires us to do good without effort develops as we train ourselves in the habit of right action; but it grows inside us in its own time.... Its growth is independent of our will; it starves when we are forcing ourselves to do right against inclination, grows when we do right with full satisfaction. (Graham, *Studies in Chinese Philosophy and Philosophical Literature*, 31. See also Ivanhoe, *Confucian Moral Self-Cultivation*, 20)

That we cannot force our morality to grow is illustrated by the parable of the farmer who killed his shoots while trying to force them to grow by pulling on them (2A2). And finally, we must have the right social and political context with the right exemplary models for moral cultivation. As Ivanhoe puts it:

An environment devoid of basic necessities and comforts, good examples, and proper encouragement will usually prove impossible to overcome.

---

[9] Philip J. Ivanhoe, *Confucian Moral Self-Cultivation*, 2nd ed. (Indianapolis: Hackett Publishing, 2000).

[10] See *The Chinese Classics, Vol. II, The Works of Mencius*, 3rd ed., trans. James Legge (Hong Kong: Hong Kong University Press, 1960).

Under such unhealthy conditions, most people will fail to develop their natural moral sensibilities. Their moral sprouts will become stunted and, overgrown with less noble tendencies, they may even become difficult to discern. (Ivanhoe, *Confucian Moral Self-Cultivation*, 22)

In contrast to the Mencian view that there are four inborn roots of virtue, Xunzi holds that man's moral sensibilities do not exist in nature but rather result entirely from education and socialization. Natural to man are desires and appetites that are indifferent to virtues and vices and so need to be re-formed before he can acquire the proper virtues. Instead of the Mencian agricultural metaphor, Xunzi uses craftsmanship to convey the artificial ways by which morality is acquired.[11] Whereas Mencius maintains that morality is the development of our heaven-endowed nature,[12] Xunzi separates heaven from morality so that heaven is responsible for the way things are while man is responsible for the way things ought to be.[13] Consequently, Xunzi relied on learning from the tradition and teachings that have been handed down from the sages. As Ivanhoe puts it, "According to Xunzi, we cannot steer by our own internal light, for this light is not yet lit. The illumination of morality is something we

[11] Xunzi says: "A piece of wood as straight as a plumb line may (with soaking and shaping) be bent into a circle as true as any drawn with a compass, and once the wood has dried it will not straighten out again. The process of bending has made it that way. Thus, if (crooked) wood is placed against a straightening board, it can be made straight; and if the gentleman studies widely and each day examines himself, his wisdom will become clear and his conduct without fault" (Ivanhoe, *Confucian Moral Self-Cultivation*, 36).

[12] Ivanhoe says: "Like many early Chinese thinkers, he believed that to develop oneself according to one's true nature is to fulfill a design inscribed by Heaven upon our human hearts. To follow the natural then is to obey Heaven, and to develop oneself is to serve Heaven" (Ivanhoe, *Confucian Moral Self-Cultivation*, 17–18).

[13] Therefore, what might seem to be simply a disagreement about ethics is also, significantly, a disagreement about what we would call a metaphysics of nature with Mencius invoking something much more like a teleological conception of nature. Graham says of Xunzi, "Whatever is learned cannot be nature; our nature is all that comes about of itself without being learned, deliberated, worked for" (Graham, *Studies in Chinese Philosophy and Philosophical Literature*, 56). Again: "Heaven is morally neutral and responsible for everything which comes about of itself without human intervention. Man creates morality and manipulates for moral ends the resources (including his own natural endowment) which Heaven has put at his disposal" (ibid., 56).

must acquire; it is something handed down from the sages" (Ivanhoe, *Confucian Moral Self-Cultivation*, 37).[14]

In contrast to these two explicit views about whether human nature propels us toward virtue or not, Confucius has no explicit account of human nature. As Ivanhoe points out, to the extent that Confucius stresses the place of learning and tradition in our moral cultivation, his view of the nature with which we are born is more like Xunzi's.[15] Insofar as Confucius talks about the joy of cultivating oneself, he is closer to Mencius (Ivanhoe, *Confucian Moral Self-Cultivation*, 2). In any event, because he has no explicit theory of human nature, let alone one that is teleological, Confucius is different from Aristotle, who maintains that a rational soul makes a human being what he is and dictates his proper function. Both Mencius and Xunzi do make appeals to human nature (*xing*), and both, like Confucius, appeal to something like a "self." This is relevant in light of those who wish to claim that there is no self, and no nature that underlies a self, in Confucius.

---

[14] See also Ivanhoe's "Human Nature and Moral Understanding in Xunzi," *International Philosophical Quarterly* 34 (1994): 167–75.

[15] Myles Burnyeat's "Aristotle on Learning to Be Good," in *Essays on Aristotle's Ethics*, ed. Amélie O. Rorty (Berkeley: University of California Press, 1980), 69–92, offers an interpretation of Aristotle that stresses a good upbringing and habituation over the Socratic intellectualism that holds that virtue is knowledge. Burnyeat says: "Being a human being he has the physiologically based appetites as well. The object of these is, of course, pleasure, ... but they can be modified and trained to become desires for the proper enjoyment of bodily pleasures; this, we saw, is what is involved in acquiring the virtue of temperance" (Burnyeat, "Aristotle on Learning to Be Good," 82).

Again, he says, "Pursuit of pleasure is an inborn part of our animal nature; concern for the noble depends on a good upbringing, while the good, here specified as the advantageous, is the object of mature reflection" (Burnyeat, "Aristotle on Learning to Be Good," 86).

From such an interpretation, one might say that Aristotle's view is more like Xunzi's than Mencius' because they both stress the importance of cultivation over what is inborn. I think that Burnyeat is right to say that human beings have appetites that need to be habituated to become virtuous for Aristotle. However, his account falls short by ignoring the metaphysical basis of Aristotle's ethics. Ultimately, it is Aristotle's soul doctrine that determines what the human virtues are. This *telos* cannot be derived solely from a focus on our appetites and habituation. (See Chapter 1, note 33, for the unity of Aristotle's ethics and metaphysics.) Because of the metaphysical basis of Aristotle's ethics, he is much closer to Mencius than to Xunzi.

Fingarette, for instance, in "The Problem of the Self in the *Analects*," recognizes that the Confucian self is distinct from others, "self-observing," "self-regulating," willing, and wanting (Fingarette, 133).[16] Fingarette, however, goes on to point out that "Confucius' usage reveals no explicit doctrines of a metaphysical or psychological kind about the details of structure of will, or the processes internal to the individual's control of the will." Fingarette adds, "There is, for example, no reification of a Faculty of Will, no inner machinery or equilibrium of psychic forces, no inner theater in which an inner drama takes place, no inner community with ruler and ruled." In short, there is an absence of "an elaborated doctrine of an 'inner psychic life'" (Fingarette, 133). Fingarette goes on to talk about the task of becoming selfless in the *Analects* and claims that Confucius is not concerned with the topic of self-cultivation. Fingarette says that "Confucius teaches, as central to his way, that we must have *no* self and *not* impose our personal will" (Fingarette, 134). Here, then, despite indicating the presence of resources in the *Analects* for developing a positive Confucian view of the self and its implications for self-cultivation, Fingarette downplays these resources and attributes a "selfless" interpretation to Confucius instead.

Many commentators disagree with Fingarette that the Confucian self aspires to selflessness. Some of the dissenters bear traces of the "selfless" interpretation in their own accounts. Roger Ames, for instance, denies that Confucius is not concerned with self-cultivation. Ames argues that the task of the good person in "Reflections on the Confucian Self: A Response to Fingarette"[17] is the cultivation of a unique relational self.[18] Fingarette responds that Ames' solution still

---

[16] Herbert Fingarette, "The Problem of the Self in the *Analects*," *Philosophy East and West* 29 (1979): 129–40.

[17] Roger Ames, "Reflections on the Confucian Self: A Response to Fingarette," in *RR&R*.

[18] Roger Ames, TFFS, 198. Kwang-Sae Lee, in "Some Confucianist Reflections on the Concept of Autonomous Individual," *Journal of Chinese Philosophy* 21 (1994): 45–59, like Ames, also attempts to resuscitate the notions of *ren* and self-cultivation from Fingarette's neglect. Lee agrees with Fingarette and Ames, and numerous other commentators, that there is no such thing as an autonomous individual for Confucius. Also agreeing with Ames' and Graham's reading that human nature is a

implies that the Confucian ideal is the cultivation of selflessness (Fingarette, "Comment and Response," 196). This is because Ames' view is that the moral self is ultimately unique because it is good at playing its roles in a community. But this means that what is fundamentally humanly real for Ames, as for Fingarette, is "the social nexus" (Fingarette, "Comment and Response," 199) (or the "focus-field" for Ames) from which a self derives its determination. Like Fingarette and Ames, Henry Rosemont, in "Rights-Bearing Individuals" speaks of how one is the totality of roles in relation to others (Rosemont, 90). As such, he says: "I do not achieve my own identity, am not solely responsible for becoming who I am.... Much of who I am is determined by the others with whom I interact.... Personhood, identity ... is basically conferred on us."[19] Like Ames, for Rosemont the self is exhausted by its roles. It is a self that is so dependent on its relations that it is a nexus of relationships. These relations are made accessible and intelligible with reference to more or less standardized roles. The only difference between one self and another is the sum of the roles one plays. Independently of these roles, there is no self (Rosemont, 90).

These authors eschew any suggestion of a more substantial self in part because they realize rightly that to attribute such a view to Confucius is to attribute a metaphysical position to him – however inchoate. Their conviction that there is no tincture of metaphysics in Confucius underwrites their belief that there can be no more substantial self in Confucius – nothing irreducible to roles and relations.

---

product of particular conditions rather than a "preestablished normative standard to which one aspires" (Lee, "Some Confucianist Reflections," 57), Lee maintains that it is nonetheless the individual who is responsible for his own character through "self-awareness," "self-reliance," "self-reflection," and "self-censure" (Lee, "Some Confucianist Reflections," 58). As to how a *product* of particular conditions can nonetheless perform the kind of "self-creation" (Lee, "Some Confucianist Reflections," 57) that Lee mentions is left unanswered. Lee's assertion that traditions are open-ended, far from explaining the possibility of self-cultivation in the latter sense, begs the question of how one who is totally steeped in a tradition is capable of opening it up – especially if such a creation is not to be arbitrary. Fingarette is at least more consistent than Lee when he rejects the notion of personal responsibility along with there being a self or self-cultivation (Fingarette, "Comment and Response," in Bockover, *RR&R*, 200).

[19] Henry Rosemont, "Rights-Bearing Individuals and Role-Bearing Persons," in Bockover, *RR&R*, 91.

However, what these authors fail to realize is that they are already subscribing to a certain metaphysical view of the self, however inchoate, by maintaining that the self is reducible to roles and relations. But I shall argue that there are aspects of the Confucian self that are irreducible to its roles or relations, and I shall accept the inference that there is a tincture of metaphysics – or at least proto-metaphysics – in Confucius. I shall link this to the presence of specific faculties requisite to the cultivation of the Confucian virtues.

The initial stark contrast between Aristotle and Confucius on the presence or absence of a human essence or nature will need refinement in light of the inferred requisites of Confucian virtue. That will hold whether or not the cultivation of these virtues is the inculcation of a sort of selflessness.

As Fingarette has pointed out in "The Problem of the Self in the *Analects*," the terms that are used in the *Analects* to refer to the self and willing are "*chi, shen, yu,* and *chih*" (Fingarette, "The Problem of the Self in the *Analects*," 131). According to Fingarette, *chi* is used about 25 times and is used for self-reference and also as a contrast to others. For example, at 6.30, Confucius says, "Desiring to establish themselves, authoritative persons establish others, wishing to promote themselves, they promote others" (my trans.). Also, at 1.8, he says, "Do not befriend one who does not measure up to oneself" (my trans.). Both situations show uses of *chi* in a self-reference that is in contrast to others.

According to Fingarette, *shen* is used about 17 times in the *Analects*. Fingarette claims that *shen* is used to refer to the self as an object rather than as a subject (Fingarette, 132). As such, the self as *shen* is something that is opened to examination and regulation. For example, at 1.4, Master Zeng said:

Daily I examine my person on three counts. In my undertakings on behalf of other people, have I failed to do my utmost (*zhong*)? In my interactions with colleagues and friends, have I failed to make good on my word (*xin*)? In what has passed on to me, have I failed to carry it into practice?

In another passage, Confucius said:

If one is proper in his person (*shen*), he could bring forth action without commanding. But if one is not proper in his person (*shen*), even if he were to command, there will not be obedience. (13.6, my trans.)

This passage shows that in addition to being observable to oneself, *shen* is something that is visible to others' observation, too. As Xinzhong Yao puts it:

Shen refers to the self understood as the whole of one's existence and especially as the unity between one's mind and body. *Shen* represents the self as person or agent or reality, which reveals the holistic view of the human person in the Confucian tradition. The character *shen* originally means the stretching [of the body], and then is borrowed to mean the whole existence of a person, both his mind and his body. (Yao, "Self-Construction and Identity," 181.)

Yao refers to 15.9, where Confucius talks about how both the *shi* and the authoritative person (*ren ren*) will sacrifice themselves (*shen*) rather than compromise their authoritative conduct.

Next, Fingarette points out that *yu* is used about 40 times in Confucius to refer to wish or desire (Fingarette, "The Problem of the Self in the *Analects*," 132). As he puts it, "Persons are conceived as beings of whom it can characteristically be said that they want this or that every actual wanting being ascribed to some individual person as subject" (Fingarette, 132). Finally, *chih* is used about 17 times and is frequently translated as "will." It has the meaning of determination or aim. The difference between *yu* and *chih* according to Fingarette, is that *chih* is more intense and persistent whereas *yu* is neutral or unspecified in these respects (Fingarette, 132–33). Fingarette proceeds to draw certain general conclusions about Confucius' "real and ideal" views of human nature. In short, Fingarette claims that Confucius' self is "sharply distinct from others," is "self-observing," "self-regulating," wanting and willing (Fingarette, 133). In each case, Fingarette continues, it is the particular self that controls each of these activities. Nevertheless, Fingarette proceeds to downplay such positive aspects of the self in arguing that Confucius is not concerned with self-cultivation but rather with becoming selfless. I shall examine the flaws of Fingarette's views later but now wish to elaborate on a comparable feature of Aristotle's view, his notion of the concrete individual, of which the rational soul is but a part.

Aristotle stresses in *Metaphysics* Z 11 that we cannot eliminate matter from concrete things that are of a particular form in particular matter even though we can conceptually separate the form as a known essence. As he puts it, "Indeed there will be matter in some sense in everything which is not essence or form considered independently, but a particular thing" (*Met.* 1036b35–1037a3). So even though he allows that we can conceptualize the form or soul of a human being independently of her body (*Met.* 1042a29, 1035a25–b2, 1043b1–3), he insists that the definition of a human being consists of both soul and body. As Aristotle puts it, "It is clear that the soul is the primary substance, and the body matter; and "man" or "animal" is the combination of both taken universally (*hos katholou*) (*Met.* 1037a5–7). In fact, he insists on including the matter in the species definitions of all concrete individuals (*Met.* 1036b22–32, 1037a1–2). Bearing this in mind brings Aristotle's view closer to Confucius' view of a whole human being even though Confucius does not distinguish material and formal factors in that whole. For Aristotle, one can, abstractly, consider the soul alone, but concretely, human beings cannot be defined without taking into account their bodies and happenstance of time and place, relations and "*habitus*," and so on.

I shall argue that Aristotle's understanding of concrete human beings – particularly in its practical aspects – is intriguingly close to Confucius' understanding. Nevertheless, it seems that the contrast between their starting points, briefed at the outset, still holds. That is because Aristotle's rational soul dictates the goal or perfection of a human being at least in outline, whereas Confucius does not rely on such a soul or human nature to set the standards. Rather, for Confucius, the standards for human beings lie in an already realized past tradition, the Zhou *li* (a historically specific set of ritual proprieties that prescribes the proper behavior toward one's family, superiors, subordinates, and others in the society). In short, the human goal for Aristotle is already written into each individual soul, whereas for Confucius it lies outside the self in the roles the self is to adopt and adapt. This contrast, too, is not as sharp as it may seem, for both thinkers not only aim at a life of virtue but rely on a process of habituation to arrive at being virtuous.

Confucius requires an individual to study the *Songs* to learn what to say and to study the rites (*li*, propriety) to learn how to take a stand (16.13, 17.10). In short, learning how to say the right things and to take a stand, basic elements of appropriate behavior and action that have been handed down from the Zhou *li*, establishes one's character (see 3.14 and 15.25 for Confucius' veneration of past traditions, and 5.18 for how *li* is used in the development of the *junzi*'s virtues of *yi* (appropriateness), modesty, and *xin* (making good on one's words)). Not only is the study of past traditions good for cultivating one's character, such training also enhances one's practical and theoretical skills. For example, at 17.9, Confucius says, "Reciting the *Songs* can arouse your sensibilities, strengthen your powers of observation, enhance your ability to get on with others and sharpen your critical skills." These qualities, as he goes on to say, have practical and theoretical consequences. He continues: "Close at hand it enables you to serve your father, and away at court it enables you to serve your lord. It instills in you a broad vocabulary for making distinctions in the world around you" (17.9). That the whole process of habituation takes commitment of effort and time is evident when Confucius says:

From fifteen, my heart-and-mind was set upon learning; from thirty I took my stance; from forty I was no longer doubtful; from fifty I realized the propensities of *tian* (*tianming*); from sixty my ear was attuned; from seventy I could give my heart-and-mind free rein without overstepping the boundaries. (2.4)

Because Aristotle analyzes the human whole as form and matter, he describes habituation as the training of the nonrational soul by the rational soul and the body by the whole soul. In each case, the potential or material factor is to yield to the formal. Aristotle's view is that the human soul is divisible into rational and nonrational parts. The rational part in turn divides into the speculative part (which is perfected in being directed at eternal objects – *theôria*) and the deliberative part (which is perfected in the proper actions concerning changeable objects – *phronêsis*). The nonrational part in turn divides into the controllable faculties of desires, such as appetites and emotions (perfected by having the moral virtues), and the largely uncontrollable vegetative parts. Habituation involves the shaping of the matter by the form, the informing of potency by act. In the case of appetites, desires, and emotions, the deliberative soul provides the form and actuality. Our appetites for sex, food, and drink are properly habituated when we have temperance – the moral virtue concerning appetites of touch and taste. Acting with temperance means that we pursue these appetites to just the right amount, at the right times and places (and, where relevant, with the right person or persons). Similarly, with respect to our emotions, we have the moral virtue of mildness when we are not excessive or defective in anger. This means that we get angry to the right degree, at the right time, in the right situation, and at the right persons. To fail to express anger or to be overly angry when not called for are both vices.[20]

Aristotle's view of what perfects the individual is dictated by his view of the nature of the individual, and he argues that a study of the soul and its functions can provide enough insight into distinctively human functions that we can know something of human well-being from the examination of human being. Still, one needs to live in a certain kind of *polis* in order to have the right conditions to specify and actualize this "*telos.*" Aristotle tells us that the political association aims at the best of all goals or ends (*Politics* 1252a1ff) and that political science aims to "acquire" and "preserve" the good for a people and cities (1094b6–12). It is life in a *polis* that allows one to acquire and preserve her good. Furthermore, Aristotle says that we need certain resources to do fine actions. These are external goods such as friends, wealth, and political power (1099b1–2). We are naturally political so that we need enough not only for ourselves, but also for our parents, children, spouses, friends, and fellow citizens (1097b8–11). By providing these resources, the *polis* makes possible not just life but the good life.

The *polis* also makes possible the visibility of exemplary models. Most people need exemplary models to attain the relevant virtues. The exemplary individual (*phronimos* or *spoudaios*) does not merely exhibit for nontheoretical persons the virtues that theoretical people can know in full detail in advance. The *phronimos* specifies the human

---

[20] Notice that for Aristotle each part of the soul has its overall proper object, which delimits the right *logos*, which perfects them. Because the human goal overall is the excellent functioning of the rational soul (with *theôria* being superior to *phronêsis* because of the superiority of its objects), all other faculties are adjusted to serve this part. Hence they are functioning well or poorly depending on how they further rational activity.

telos and makes it pertinent to a given context. Because the excellent (*spoudaios*) person judges correctly about what is true, fine, and pleasant, he is the "standard and measure of what is fine and pleasant" (1113a35; see 1113a25–35 and 1109a25). In short, it is only when one lives in the company of such *phronimoi* that one will come to habituate what is truly fine and pleasant for human beings.

Similarly, Confucius repeatedly stresses the pivotal role of exemplary persons. Moreover, he maintains that exemplary persons depend on the presence of other exemplary persons for their own development. As he puts it about Zijian, "He is truly an exemplary person (*junzi*). If [the province] Lu had no other exemplary persons, where could he have gotten his character from?" (5.3). Confucius goes even further, claiming that the exemplary person's behavior can impact the whole of society. This is evident in Confucius' discussion of the ordering of names and how the exemplary person's use of names coincides with his actions to enhance the actions of others. More specifically, Confucius tells us that the improper use of names will adversely affect the use of language, the following of ritual propriety and playing music, and, finally, will prevent the proper application of laws and punishments and the ability of people to know how to act (13.3). Because the exemplary person can be relied upon to use names properly and hence language, and ultimately act upon what is said, the aforementioned adversities will be prevented and social flourishing accomplished.[21] Not only are exemplary persons the cause of other exemplary persons and the key to the proper functioning of society, Confucius also maintains that they affect others' proper actions in a natural way by being inspirational rather than coercive. For instance, arguing against the need for killing in proper government, Confucius says: "The excellence (*de*) of the exemplary person (*junzi*) is the wind, while that of the petty person is the grass. As the wind blows, the grass is sure to bend" (12.19; see also 13.6, 13.13). Aristotle concurs with all

---

[21] See Chapter 3 for an account of how the ordering of names for Confucius is not merely a political or aesthetic phenomenon that is solely governed by convention, as some commentators, such as David Hall and Roger Ames, and Chad Hansen, have argued. Rather, I argue that name rectification for Confucius is also concerned with "objectivity" because it is bound up with the objective knowledge of nature as well as with heaven's mandate of the right way of life.

these points.[22] The cultivation of virtue is heavily dependent on the presence of other exemplary individuals and upon living in a well-ordered society that is effectively governed.[23]

Even though Confucius and Aristotle hold similar views about the need for a good society and for exemplary individuals, as well as the need for habituation to acquire virtue, their different presuppositions about the person present different challenges for thought and action. I shall argue that Aristotle's individualistic metaphysics provides inadequate grounds for the relations and situations his ethics requires. Confucius' reticence on the metaphysics of self, on the other hand, threatens to make his ritualism particularistic or irrelevant.

As we have seen, Aristotle argues that the individual soul has a nature that presages its good. He goes on to discuss the political and social requirements that contribute to her development. Despite the significance of others for one's habituation, Aristotle's metaphysics prioritizes the individual substance. His account of a concrete human substance analyzes it into form and matter: this soul and this body. Nowhere does he give an adequate metaphysical account of relations, crucial though they are to the teaching of the *Nicomachean Ethics*. Even when Aristotle discusses friendship, he bases the love of friends on the love of what is good for oneself. As he puts it, "In loving their friend they love what is good for themselves" (*NE* 1157b33). Aristotle does provide an important hint when he says that one "is related to his friend as he is to himself, since the friend is another himself" (*NE* 1166a31). This implies that there are relations to others no less substantial than, and perhaps of the same type as, relation to oneself. There are even respects in which friendship relations are prior. As Aristotle puts it: "We are able to observe our neighbors more than ourselves, and to observe their actions more than our own. Hence a good person finds pleasure in the actions of excellent people who are his friends, since these actions have both the naturally pleasant features, (i.e., they are good, and they are his own")" (*NE* 1169b34–1170a2). Aristotle insists that one can befriend only another human

---

[22] However, Aristotle would not go so far as to say that the mere presence of the virtuous will convert the vicious.

[23] This issue will be dealt with in greater detail in Chapter 6.

being; that is, one who has (or is) a rational soul. One rational person can wish for the good for another rational person, and for her own sake. But the good is the excellent functioning of the individual; the relationship is "incidental."

Such a focus on the individual substance is also evident in Aristotle's *Categories*, where he gives ontological primacy to the individual substance and makes relations dependent upon and incidental to such independent and individual primary substances. It is no wonder that contemporary commentators are constantly arguing about whether Aristotle is guilty of ethical egoism; that is the view that an individual seeks to maximize his own good so that even his virtuous acts toward others are for the sake of his own moral cultivation.[24] Aristotle is not an ethical egoist because he crowns justice as the highest and most complete virtue in relation to others. As he puts it:

> Justice is the only virtue that seems to be another person's good, because it is related to another; for it does what benefits another, either the ruler or the fellow member of the community. (1130a4–6)[25]

Furthermore, he characterizes his exemplary individual (*phronimos*) as one who always acts at the right time, in the right way, about the right thing, and so on. This accomplishes what is good for another both in virtue of building the right sort of community and in providing a model for others.

While the *Ethics* seeks such a good that is at one and the same time good for the person and for others (*aretê* as the essence of individual happiness and the heart of the good *polis*), Aristotle categorically privileges the individual substance over relations in his metaphysics. This does not imply that Aristotle is ethically an egoist, or even ontologically an individualist in the modern sense of the term. Still, the fact that Aristotle's ethical egoism is a topic of lively debates shows that there is a tension in his view concerning the individual's relation to others. My observation is that this tension is rooted in his metaphysics, which privileges the individual over relations. Aristotle's

---

[24] See Chapter 1, note 16, for a discussion of Aristotle and egoism. Also see Chapter 7 for why Aristotle's view of friendship is not egoistic.

[25] For a discussion of the contrast between particular and general justice, see Chapter 1, note 16.

metaphysics fails to elucidate real relations, reciprocities of habituation that his ethics requires.

Confucius seems to emphasize relations. His subordination of the individual to the *li* is sometimes interpreted by commentators as his favoring a selfless view. Ritual propriety for Confucius dictates to an individual how she should behave toward her family, friends, superiors, and others in society. To discipline oneself in such a way that one does everything according to the traditional *li* seems to reduce one to being simply a player of various roles: son, father, minister, or husband. In such a society, the focus is not on an individual per se. What is emphasized are the social relations: one is first and foremost a father and/or a son, a husband and/or a minister, and the pertinent roles dictate one's appropriate behavior while relating to children, parents, wife, and so on.

Confucius goes so far as to assert that just playing one's roles will bring about effective government. For government to be effective, "The ruler must rule, the minister minister, the father father, and the son son" (12.11, in response to Duke Jing of Qi). Even when one is not actively employed in government, one's harmonious familial relations (e.g., the father–son relation in 12.11) contribute to governing the society according to Confucius. For example, when someone asked Confucius why he is not employed in governing, he replied by reporting the *Book of Documents'* claim that: "It is all in filial conduct (*xiao*)! Just being filial to your parents and befriending your brothers is carrying out the work of government" (2.21).

The family takes priority over an individual's desires, career, and existence. The centrality of filial piety is clear when Confucius praises how Meng Zhuangzi "refrained from reforming his father's ministers and his father's policies" (19.18). Real filial piety consists in refraining from reforming a father's way (*dao*) for three years after a father's death (1.11). Whether the father has hit upon the correct *dao* is irrelevant. Rather, the point is to follow the father's *dao* and policies simply because of reverence for him. The individual must put his or her own desires and thoughts inside – even to the point of setting aside thoughts of what is better. One strives to play a role of a good son instead of asserting what he (as an individual) thinks of a situation. In fact, one's piety toward his family even takes precedence over loyalty to the state. For instance, the governor of She told Confucius about the "true person" (13.18) in his village who reported his own father's theft of a sheep. Confucius responded by saying that the true person in his own village does the opposite: as a son, he covers up the truth for his father. Instead of uttering what he observes to be the truth, that the father has committed a crime, the son speaks in reverence toward the father.[26] Notice that there is no conflict between reverence for the father and reverence for the state in this case for Confucius because he maintains that the right action is reverence toward the father. Reverence toward a father takes precedence over the state. The son acts neither for the good of the society nor for his own good, but for his father.

There is a sense, however, in which the son's acting for the father is acting for the good of the society as well as his own good, for one could argue that, in Confucius' system, filiality is the individual's integrity because there is no soul or essence behind him to dictate what is good for him. Although the family takes precedence, filiality extends beyond the family to the good of the state. This entails that one considers the other, namely one's father (or family), first, instead of the individual's own integrity, abstracting from filiality, of course. Nonetheless, these Confucian goods are entirely particular (to the Zhou *li*). Aristotle's view is that good actions are consistent with what is good for the individual's soul. Therefore, because all human beings are specifically or formally the same, good actions are objectively good for all. It is because of Aristotle's soul doctrine, which prescribes goods or virtues for each part, that the virtues are objective and the same for all human beings. Hence, Aristotle would consistently maintain that acts such as lies and theft are wrong even when they have been committed by one's own father.

It seems an oversimplification to say that there is neither self nor choice[27] in Confucius' view just because he focuses on one's

---

[26] The irony here is that Aristotle, whose ontology is individualist, invokes a wealth of real relations in the *Nicomachean Ethics*; Confucius, who seems so relationistic, winds up making real relations (with all the adjustments they require) incidental to behaving toward a type or role. Such type or role behavior is something that one could accomplish as a sheer individual because there is not much flexibility regarding what one could do, say, in a father–son relation.

[27] In *Confucius: The Secular as Sacred* (New York: Harper and Row, 1972), in a chapter titled "A Way without a Crossroads," Herbert Fingarette points out that Confucius does not use the language of choice and responsibility because these are bound up

roles and relations to others. As I pointed out earlier, a number of Confucian commentators have argued for a dissolution of the Confucian self into its roles and relations. Fingarette, in "The Problem of the Self in the *Analects*," says that "Confucius teaches, as central to his way, that we must have *no* self and *not* impose our personal will" (Fingarette, 134) in spite of his recognition that one could deduce a human nature from what Confucius says about human beings in the *Analects*. Fingarette goes on to explain that the individual is merely a vehicle for the realization of the *dao*, which is like a concept (Fingarette, 136) in that the *dao* is completely independent of any particular individual despite the fact that it requires an individual for its realization. In fact, Fingarette talks as if all that is required from the individual is the willing of the *dao*, and the individual does not determine why or toward what end the will is exercised. As Fingarette puts it, "But the more deeply one explores the *junzi*'s will, the more the personal dimensions are revealed as purely formal – the individual is the unique space-time bodily locus of that will; it is that which controls but it is nonsignificant regarding why, specifically, or in what specific direction, the control shall be exercised." Contrasting the egoist with the *junzi*, Fingarette continues: "To understand the content of the *junzi*'s will is to understand the *dao*, not the *junzi* as a particular person. The ego is present in the egoist's will. The *dao* is present in the *junzi*'s will." Fingarette's view of the selfless *junzi* is concisely captured in the following remark: "Since the *junzi*'s will is thus ideally the medium by which, and through which, the *dao* is allowed and enabled to work and to be actualized, the 'I' of the *junzi*, as purely personal, has become, as it were,

---

with "the idea of the ontologically ultimate power of the individual to select from genuine alternatives to create his own spiritual destiny" (Fingarette, *Confucius*, 18). Again, he says: "The problem of genuine choice among real alternatives never occurred to Confucius, or at least never clearly occurred to him as a fundamental moral task. Confucius merely announces the way he sees the matter, putting it tactfully by saying it is the custom in *Li*. There is nothing to suggest a decisional problem; everything suggests that there is a defect of knowledge, a simple error of moral judgment" (Fingarette, *Confucius*, 23; see also 34). See Teemu H. Ruskola's "Moral Choice in the *Analects*: A Way without a Crossroads?" *Journal of Chinese Philosophy* 19 (1992): 285–96, for an interpretation of how such a way does not permit a choice of the ends but nonetheless permits a choice of the means.

transparent. It is a generative space-time locus of will *without personal content*" (Fingarette, 136, my emphasis). Fingarette's view of the *junzi* then, is one that is so at one with the *dao* that she always wills what is called for by the *li* for one in her role (Fingarette, 135). One does not need a self because what is appropriate for one is always dictated by one's role and that is what one always seeks to do.

One might argue that Fingarette seems inconsistent in maintaining that the *junzi* embodies only the *dao*, which is highly general (likened by him to a concept), and yet is able to will the appropriate virtues in the appropriate situations. Granted, one can generalize situations in such a way that one says, for example, in situations where courage is called for, exercise courage. However, how could the possession of such generalities, "without" any "personal content" such as specific past experiences, tell one that this is an instance of a situation that calls for courage or that is an instance of a situation that calls for *shu* (putting oneself in another's place)? How is one to summon forth the proper will in the proper situation? Just being a "generative space-time locus of will" without knowledge of particulars makes any willing arbitrary, if possible at all. Ivanhoe recognizes that one cannot carry out the *dao* simply by adhering to loyalty (*zhong*) toward the *li*. Rather, Ivanhoe maintains that for Confucius *shu* is required to make the requisite judgment, and one needs enough experience and personal content before one can appropriately amend the *li*.[28] As Ivanhoe puts it:

One was not to require strict ritual compliance from others, regardless of the consequences. And one was not to be satisfied with oneself in merely discharging one's duties in a perfunctory manner. One is to cultivate and use one's judgment to determine what is proper on a case-by-case basis. With enough experience and practice, one could learn when it was appropriate to amend, bend, or suspend the *li*. Sometimes one should not require strict compliance from others, and sometimes one should go beyond what was strictly required for oneself. One made such judgments by employing the imaginative act of putting oneself in the other person's place and determining what one should do by seeing how one would like to be treated. This is *shu*, the second strand of Confucius' "one thread." (Ivanhoe, "Reweaving the 'One Thread' of the *Analects*," 28)

[28] Ivanhoe, "Reweaving the 'One Thread' of the *Analects*," 17–33.

Numerous commentators have argued against Fingarette's over-emphasis of Confucius' view of *li* at the expense of other concepts that aid in one's judgment of particular situations. While Ivanhoe points to Fingarette's emphasis on *zhong* (which is directed toward the *li*) at the expense of *shu* in Confucius, other commentators point to his overemphasis of *li* at the expense of *yi* (appropriateness). These thinkers wonder how Fingarette can assert that the *junzi* always wills what is appropriate for his or her role while also claiming that the will's purposes are not significant. Surely, to be able to will what is appropriate (*yi*) for one's role is precisely to be able to will the right action for the right reason. As Benjamin Schwartz reminds us, "The prescriptions of *li* do not always clarify what is right (*yi*) in the infinite variety of life situations, and 'righteousness' is just as essential an attribute of *ren* as is a submissiveness to *li*" (Schwartz, *The World of Thought in Ancient China*, 80).[29] Similarly, Hall and Ames call for attention to *yi* in particular situations as follows:

Because of the non-fixed, multivalent nature of the person-in-context, the person's construal of *yi* cannot be solely a matter of applying some externally derived norm. On the contrary, this realizing person cannot surrender to some set of determining principles, but must rather exercise his own judgment creatively in response to the uniqueness of his situation. (Hall and Ames, *TTC*, 95)[30]

Against Fingarette's lack of attention to *yi*, Hall and Ames say:

The concept of *yi* not only insures the personal investment of meaning in tradition, but it prevents agreement with any interpretation of Confucius which, like Fingarette's, would suggest that tradition could contain a single set of meanings articulated in accordance with a relatively unchanging set of ritual actions. Originating ritual actions through *yi* is the model for subsequent *yi* acts. (Hall and Ames, *TTC*, 109; see 107–9)

These interpreters are right to call for *shu* and *yi*. If so, the self must be the source or locus of more functions than Fingarette listed. We now require a self with the capacity to judge and choose actions; the self must be able to cultivate dispositions to act with *shu* and *yi* and must acquire and apply a robust set of personal experiences of acting appropriately and virtuously in various situations. These capacities

---

[29] Schwartz, *The World of Thought in Ancient China.*   [30] Hall and Ames, *TTC*.

are comparable to, but thicker than, Fingarette's characterization of the Confucian self as being distinct from others, "self-observing," "self-regulating," willing, and wanting (Fingarette, "The Problem of the Self in the *Analects*," 133).

Such a list of qualities and functions is not tantamount to a metaphysical picture, but is it not the metaphysical backdrop of self-cultivation in Confucius? Most commentators, such as Fingarette, Ames, and Xinzhong Yao, think that they need to deny such a metaphysical view. Fingarette denies a metaphysics of the self for Confucius because he thinks that the *junzi*'s will is ultimately grounded on the *dao*, which is completely general and has no reference to the particular will that executes it. As Fingerette puts it:

The *dao* says that any person in my present position should do thus and so – my proper name is not built into the *dao*, or the *li*. In all aspects of the *dao* there is an inherent generality, an absence of essential reference to a unique individual. . . . The *dao* is not only intelligible independently of such reference, its moral authority is surely independent of reference to me as the unique existent that I am. (Fingarette, "The Problem of the Self in the *Analects*," 135)

Yao denies a metaphysical view of the self, even as a starting point, because he thinks that to admit a metaphysics of the self is to be committed to some static, unchangeable substance. He believes this prevents one from engaging in social relations and from cultivating oneself into one with *ren* or a sage. As Yao puts it:

The Confucian concept of the self is not a metaphysical nor an epistemological nor a psychological concept . . . it is an ethical concept and its significance for Confucian doctrine lies in a process of cultivating one's moral character that can be completed only in one's engagement in social and righteous causes. (Yao, "Self-Construction and Identity," 186)

Yao is too hasty, I think, to divorce metaphysics and ethics. Aristotle's view, in particular, keeps them together.[31] Still, Ames rejects any teleological model, such as Aristotle's, where self-cultivation is understood as a progression from potentiality to actuality because

---

[31] See my "Senses of Being in Aristotle's *Nicomachean Ethics*" for a discussion of how Aristotle's ethics is based on his metaphysics. Also see Chapter 1, note 33 for Irwin's argument for the same point.

Ames sees any model that specifies a definite goal as restricting the flexibility and range of creative self-cultivation (Ames, *TFFS*, 201).

Aristotle's metaphysics, I claim alone, precludes neither the cultivation of virtues nor the need for social relations in such cultivation. Aristotle's metaphysics of self is restrictive only in excluding, decisively, viciousness, baseness, and injustice. When it comes to what is good, there is plenty of room in Aristotle's account (which, to be true to Aristotle's own principles, we must distinguish from his personal opinions) for individual and social differences. The goal is to become intellectually and morally virtuous. One is not to cultivate oneself to be supergluttonous like pigs or superinsensitive like stones. For Aristotle, the *telos* is the human "way." As such, it is known as a universal and thus is highly general. But it does have determinate content. The *dao* may be present in the *junzi*'s will, but the *li* specifies what is good and what is to be done. The *telos* is in the *phronimos*' will. This needs specification and elaboration in a *polis*, but it has content enough to provide the means to criticize customs and practices. To understand the content of the *phronimos*' will is to understand the *telos*, not the *phronimos* as a particular person. But the *telos* is the same for all humans; the *li* is not.

Appeal to a *li* that is shared by whole villages or dynasties (13.18, 3.14) rescues Confucius from individual moral relativism. Everyone within a village or dynasty would have the same *li*, which dictates right conduct. However, appeal to *li* may not rescue Confucius from cultural relativism. Given the possibility of multiple customs, it might seem more like a kind of pluralism. In her discussion of Wayne C. Booth, Martha C. Nussbaum distinguishes between pluralism as contextualism and pluralism as multiple specification.[32] This distinction might help. Pluralism as contextualism is a view where what is good is relative to one's circumstances or context so that what is good for someone in a particular context need not be good for another in another context. Confucius seems to subscribe to this kind of pluralism in his response to the governor of She regarding the son's report of the father's theft. Because of their different contexts, what is right for She's village may not be right for Confucius' village.

---

[32] Martha C. Nussbaum, *Love's Knowledge: Essays on Philosophy and Literature* (New York: Oxford University Press, 1990), 230–44.

Pluralism as multiple specification, on the other hand, appeals to a general principle that can be specified in many ways. An instance of this is Confucius' substitution of the silk cap for the hemp cap in observing *li* because it is more economical. Such pluralism would maintain that both the silk and hemp caps are acceptable for observing *li*, suggesting there are multiple ways of following the *li*. Finally, the relation between *li* and *ren* probably might be understood as a sort of multiple specification pluralism, where the simple principle of *ren* is specified variously by different local customs.[33]

Having argued that Confucian ethics needs *li* but also *shu* and *yi*, and that it is pluralistic but not viciously relativistic, it remains to ask if Confucius needs a metaphysics of the self to account for our ability to act with *shu* and *yi*, or if the self as a sum of roles or a focus of relations is sufficient to account for such acts. Fingarette and others who subscribe to the selfless view or the view that we are determined by our roles can respond to the requirements of acting with *shu* and *yi* as follows. Depending on one's roles in various situations, one can imagine that the role will dictate that he put himself in another's place or that he use his own judgment to assess the most appropriate action for the situation (where each of these actions can tap into how other exemplars of the roles have acted in similar situations in the past). As Fingarette puts it, "The *li*, for example, is expressible in

---

[33] In "*Jen* and *Li* in the *Analects*," *Philosophy East and West* 43 (1993): 457–79, reprinted (with slight modifications) in Bryan W. Van Norden, ed., *Confucius and the Analects: New Essays* (Oxford University Press, 2002), 53–72, Kwong-loi Shun tackles the difficulty of whether *li* is subordinate to *ren* or vice versa. Instead of seeing the *li* as a means to *ren* (he calls this the instrumentalist interpretation) or seeing *ren* as being constituted by *li* (he calls this the definitionalist interpretation), Shun recommends a third alternative based on an analogy between *ren* and *li* and the relation between mastery of a concept and mastery of a linguistic practice. Shun explains that "mastery of [a] linguistic practice is constitutive of mastery of the concept," yet such a constitutive relation between the linguistic practice and concept does not mean that the concept is defined by the linguistic practice as long as there are other linguistic practices (within other communities) that share this concept (Shun, "*Jen* and *Li* in the *Analects*," 469). Because "mastery of the concept 'transcends' mastery of the linguistic practice," Shun holds that this concept can be used as a standard to assess or revise the linguistic practice (ibid.). In short, the concept of *ren* can be used to assess and revise the *li* practices that train one to become *ren*, where *ren* can be constituted in various ways. If Shun is right, the Confucian position is like pluralism as multiple specification because it allows the ethical principle of *ren* to be specified in many ways.

terms of guidelines for conduct of persons of certain kinds of status and role – the emperor, the father, the minister, the son, the friend – finding themselves in certain kinds of situations, and having to deal with other persons identified by reference to their own kinds of status and role" (Fingarette, "The Problem of the Self in the *Analects*," 135). A teacher, for instance, is one who should act with *shu* and *yi* when dealing with students who cannot complete their assignments as a result of an illness or a death in the family. In this and other similar cases, Fingarette and others who reduce the self to his roles could maintain, and quite legitimately, that one's roles suffice to prescribe both *yi* and *shu*. This is because they are part of what is called for from certain roles in certain situations, as handed down by tradition so that what is appropriate is also handed down in the *li*. These remarks do nothing to cancel the need for an account of self as that which is capable of *zhong* for *li*, of *shu* for others, or of *yi* in the circumstances. They do not forestall the usefulness of an account that shows how the self cultivates itself (whether we call that developed state "selfless" or not) by inculcating virtue (*de*) rather than vice.

Moreover, there are certain acts that Confucius discusses that seem to require stronger references to a self. These are acts where Confucius stresses one's ownership in their execution. Confucius' main focus in these cases seems to be the individual agent's personal commitment to the action. That Confucius stresses the importance of personal investment in performing actions rather than simply following the *li* blindly is obvious in passages where he puts down the mindless ways in which rituals are performed and virtues carried out. Against the sentiment that rituals are simply a fixed set of motions one undertakes, Confucius says:

In referring time and again to observing ritual propriety (*li*), how could I just be talking about gifts of jade and silk? And in referring time and again to making music (*yue*), how could I just be talking about bells and drums? (17.11)

This shows that ritual ceremonies and music do not simply consist in the motions and materials for him. Rather, one's attitude must fully accord with the situation in order to be appropriate (see 17.6). This entails that one is to participate in such events with one's whole being. As Confucius puts it, the expression "sacrifice as though present" is taken to mean "sacrifice to the spirits as though the spirits are present" but "If *I* (*wu*) myself do not participate in the sacrifice, it is as though *I* have not sacrificed at all" (3.12, my italics). Similarly, Confucius condemns the "village worthy" as the thief of virtue because even though he abides by the conventional standard of morality, his acts are motions that accord with his role without his personal commitment (17.13; see 13.5 for how learning is for the sake of cultivating one's own initiative). Mere role playing then is not sufficient for Confucius. What distinguishes one who fills her roles well and one who does not stems from a personal investment that is impossible without presupposing a self capable of personal investment and ownership, capable of filling out (and not just occupying or "playing") a role, and capable of adding creatively to the tradition. For example, when asked what *ren* is, Confucius responded by saying, "Through self-discipline and observing ritual propriety (*li*), one becomes authoritative in one's conduct. If for the space of a day one were able to accomplish this, the whole empire would defer to this authoritative model. Becoming authoritative in one's conduct is self-originating – how could it originate with others?" (12.1)[34]

This needs a more substantial self than the bearer-of-roles view prescribes. "I" (*wu*) is required to own his acts and be aware that he is owning his acts. Playing a role tells one what a father does (along with, perhaps, a fatherly attitude) or what a brother does, but it does not tell him that he himself needs to take responsibility for them. That this kind of personal responsibility is ignored by commentators who propose a selfless view or a self-as-social-roles view is evident when Fingarette points out the incompatibility of such views and personal responsibility. He says:

The Confucian viewpoint, seeing "person" as a complex abstraction from the concrete social nexus, does not require or even permit use of our concept of

[34] See Tu Weiming's "Creative Tension between *Jen* and *li*," *Philosophy East and West* 18 (1968): 29–40, where he stresses *ren* as choice. Tu explains how *ren* means that one chooses by saying: "*Ren* points to the equally important fact that he is more than the intersection of social forces. He feels himself summoned to choose, to actualize a potential selfhood which is more than the sum of genes, plus glands, plus class. Man cannot live without *li*, but when *li* becomes wholly determinative, he is no longer really man" (Tu, "Creative Tension between *Jen* and *Li*," 37).

personal responsibility for an act or consequence thereof. (Fingarette, "Comment and Response," 200)

What is required, then, is a self that is an agent – a locus of choice and responsibility – and not just a teacher and/or a father, and so on. This is a self that can examine if he is acting rightly. The reasons and purposes for acting for such a self are not to be dismissed (as Fingarette has done). Rather, these are the features that make his action good. It is true that this deeper sense of responsibility (and the self that comes in tow) implies a more stable and universal source of moral norm. Shouldering this sort of responsibility (Fingarette sees this) demands more of me than that I answer challenges with "that is simply our way" or "that is the way of our village." I shall return to this implication later.

In sum, the Confucian self, in addition to being distinct though not separate from others, has the following characteristics: (i) She is aware of herself as an agent – that is, she owns her acts; (ii) she is aware that she is in some measure something more than her roles; (iii) she can examine herself as to the degree of her commitment or authentic involvement in an action; (iv) she has reasons or purposes; (v) she chooses her action and her level of commitment in carrying out the action; (vi) she has a set of personal experiences; (vii) she is able to cultivate the dispositions to act virtuously; and (viii) she has certain wants and makes resolutions concerning those wants. Note that (i) does not imply that she is autonomous; (ii) does not imply that she is self-sufficient; (iii) does not imply that she is a private conscience; (iv) does not imply that she is a rational will; (v) does not imply that she is existentially self-made; (vi) does not imply that she is a pure experient; (vii) does not imply that she is perfectable or self-perfectable; and (viii) does not imply that she is a bundle of desires, a by-product of the glands, or a slave to the passions. Such a view of the self is not an Aristotelian metaphysics of soul. Nevertheless, it does describe a more robust "self" than is allowed by Fingarette, Yao, Ames, and others. And it is not incompatible with Aristotle's approach, even if it does not require it.

A second look at cases standard in the Confucian literature shows that this more substantial self was there all along. When Confucius mentions that filial piety consists in refraining from reforming a father's way for three years after a father's death, that talk of refrain or restraint presupposes that there is some figment of a self to be restrained beyond that of a son whose role is to adhere to the father's wishes – for what of the years following the mourning? Another situation where a more robust self is called for is one where there is a conflict in one's roles so that one is required to choose between two roles or accord one priority. Heiner Roetz reported a couple of cases around the fifth and sixth centuries B.C.E. where Shizhu of Chu was "trapped in the conflict between the obligations to family and state," while Qing Bing of Zhao was "caught in the collision of loyalty and friendship" (Roetz, *Confucian Ethics of the Axial Age*, 99).[35] In the case of Shizhu, working as an official for the King Zhao, he caught his father, who had committed murder. Being filial toward his father, Shizhu released him. But his obligation toward the state led him to request his own execution from the king. Cases like this are not resolvable within one role or the other. Instead, one needs a self with some degree of independence from those roles to decide which should take priority. When Confucius disagreed with the governor of She regarding the correctness of reporting one's own father's theft, he may have needed no act of choice. He simply followed his village's way. But any person who is raised with both options – indeed anyone who is to exercise the stronger sense of responsibility I described earlier – does need to choose. Such a choice, if it is not arbitrary, presupposes that one is more than one's roles. It also requires an appeal to a moral norm that is at once universal and open to creative determination. I have suggested that the Aristotelian *telos* as a generic map of the human "way" is a resource Confucius should consider.

At this point, one may ask, "Why Aristotle and not Mencius?" Mencius belongs to the Confucian tradition and, like Aristotle, offers what looks very much like a teleological view of the human way. Because this is an issue with which I have dealt in greater detail in Chapter 4, I shall briefly sketch my position here.

Mencius' view of morality is grounded in a human nature that is sanctioned by heaven. Heaven has inscribed in the human heart the four moral sprouts so that the development of human nature consists in nurturing these sprouts and becoming fully moral. To do this is to

---

[35] Roetz, *Confucian Ethics of the Axial Age*, ch. 8.

serve heaven. So far, this seems similar to Aristotle's teleological doctrine, which identifies the natural human function with moral (and intellectual) good. It must be said that Aristotle's account is far more developed and explicit. However, the two part company in their accounts of morality's ultimate ground, heaven for Mencius and God for Aristotle. Whereas Aristotle has an elaborate metaphysics of how God is related to the rest of the world and human activity by being the principle and cause of everything, Mencius lacks a similar account of how heaven actually affects the rest of the universe – though he asserts that it does. Without an account of how heaven is really related to human beings and to the rest of the universe, one has no more reason to adhere to Mencius' view of heaven's role in man's morality than Xunzi's view that heaven and nature are morally neutral.[36] My suggestion has been that a reconstructed Aristotle can be a quite useful resource for considering the human way in itself and as understood in the Confucian tradition.

I noted at the outset the presence of a doctrine of soul or essence in Aristotle and its absence in Confucius. Aristotle's subtle under-standing of soul's relation to body as form to matter lets him do justice to concrete human being and to the moral norms implied in purposive soul. This understanding might help fill a gap in the Confucian tradition.[37] However, the insistent individualism of Aristotle's metaphysics fails to account for the thick relations his own ethics requires. A genuine encounter with Confucian tradition would help to bring out this need. Confucius' many reminders about the centrality of relationships (especially family relations), roles, and ritualized practices provide valuable resources here. On the other hand, the Confucian self, if entirely relationalistic, could not function as a locus of choice and agency; if fully ritualistic, it could not function as a source of moral norms that might help assess existing social

[36] Also, without an explicit account of heaven's relation to the human way, Mencius' view is also open to the charge Robert Eno makes about the rhetorical role of heaven in the early Ruist texts. See Chapter 4, note 20.

[37] Once again, when speaking of the tradition, additional subtleties are required; I should need, for example, to discuss the implicit teleology of the Mencian "sprouts" of virtue in relation to Aristotle. But the point remains that I have extolled the advantages of an Aristotelian sort of metaphysics for the virtue-centered morality by both masters, and the Confucian tradition as a whole lacks this.

11

proprieties. The truth about the moral life therefore just might require further and fruitful dialogue between these two great traditions that have so much of importance to say about principle and custom, habit and nature, individual and society. It is to issues of individual and society that I turn in the remaining two chapters of this book.

In the final chapters, I ask which of the two masters – widely reputed to be aristocrats – is the most aristocratic, and in the comparison find ways to make virtue-oriented politics less aristocratic. I ask which of these traditions – widely reputed to be focused on virtues to the exclusion of duties or rights – most extends the life of virtue to the greatest number of people, and in this comparison find ways in which both traditions can be stretched to a recognition of human rights.

6

Virtue-Oriented Politics

Confucius and Aristotle

On the face of it, Aristotle's view of politics seems quite different from Confucius'. Aristotle defines the *polis* and the citizen and analyzes them according to a teleological understanding of nature. Confucius lacks not only explicit definitions but also any explicit theories about nature and teleology. Aristotle sharply distinguishes the political rule of statesmen from the household rule of fathers. Confucius assimilates political rule into household rule; political government is simply the father–son relationship writ large. Aristotle offers an analysis of different regimes, an ideal constitution, and the best constitution in actuality. Confucius never offers a theoretical analysis of possible or actual constitutions and concentrates, for the most part, on the benevolent rule of a sage-king. They also differ with respect to the role that laws should play in the governance of a state and the role that the masses could and should play in deliberating on affairs of the state.[1] Aristotle favors the use of laws and praises a regime in which the masses participate in public deliberations; Confucius is skeptical about both the rule of law and the masses' role in political deliberations. Aristotle claims that virtue is

---

[1] I use the word "state" when discussing Aristotle's *polis* and Confucius' state in the same sentence. This term is employed more loosely than either author's use of the concept. Thus used, it simply means the unit that is constituted by the ruler(s) and the people (whether they are citizens or not) and the qualities that accompany their lives. I provide a detailed explanation of how Aristotle could explain his concept of a *polis* to Confucius in Chapter 2.

achieved only by the few. But Confucius articulates a life of virtue accessible to all or most.

Yet, there are similarities. Confucius and Aristotle agree that people must play different roles and functions in a state. Both men maintain that the aim of government is to make people virtuous. They agree that virtuous men make the best rulers. Accordingly, education is of central concern in governance. The two philosophers also think that justice consists in acting for the common advantage rather than for one's self-interest.

I shall examine the differences and similarities between Aristotle's and Confucius' views of politics and then consider the strengths and weaknesses of each thinker's positions, hoping to shed light on the resources each offers for rectifying the other's shortcomings. I will then show that their shared vision of the ultimate goal of government – the promotion of moral virtue – if we take it to heart today, can transform our contemporary discourse about human rights.

Aristotle maintains that the union of man and woman and the family are for the sake of satisfying their animal needs. Villages stabilize family relations but also constitute a new sort of unity that gives voice to needs that go beyond what recurs on a daily basis (*Pol.* I, 2). The union of villages in a way that reaches self-sufficiency is the culmination of the previous human associations and also yields a new form of unity: the *polis*. Whereas the family and village are natural associations that exist "for the sake of mere life," the *polis* exists "for the sake of a good life" (1252b28–30).[2] It completes and surpasses the work of family and villages, so it, too, exists by nature because it is the culmination of associations that exist by nature:

Because it is the completion of associations existing by nature, every polis exists by nature, having itself the same quality as the earlier associations from which it grew. It is the end or consummation to which those associations move, and the "nature" of things consists in their end or consummation; for what each thing is when its growth is completed we call the nature of that thing, whether it be a man or a horse or a family. (1252b31–1253a)

[2] All references to the *Politics* are taken from *The Politics of Aristotle*, trans. E. Barker (New York: Oxford University Press, 1958). Bekker page numbers are from the Loeb edition of the *Politics*, trans. H. Rackham (London: Harvard University Press, 1932).

Aristotle also maintains that the *polis* is prior in nature to the family and to the individual even though these are prior in time. This is because the *polis* is a whole of which the individual and the family are parts. Aristotle claims that the individual and the family are essentially what they are only when they can perform their functions. But without the self-sufficiency that the *polis* makes possible, the individual and the family cannot perform their functions. Just as a hand that no longer belongs to a whole body cannot function as a hand, an individual that does not belong to a *polis* also cannot function as an individual. As Fred D. Miller, Jr., puts it: "It is very clear that for Aristotle political life is deeply rooted in human nature. For life in the *polis* is a necessary means for the attainment of human natural ends, so that one cannot exist as a human being without it" (Miller, "Aristotle's Political Naturalism," 196).[3] He is either a beast or a God (1253a29). Aristotle assumes that everything has a function natural to it; its end is to perform its function well (see *NE* I, 7). For the human being, this is achievable only in a *polis*. Hence the *polis*, like the fulfilled individual, is part of nature.[4]

---

[3] Fred D. Miller, Jr., "Aristotle's Political Naturalism," *Apeiron* 22 (1989): 195–218.

[4] See Miller's "Aristotle's Political Naturalism," 201, 206, and 211, for discussions of how his thesis that human beings are by nature political is based on Aristotle's teleology of "metaphysical naturalism."

    Some commentators puzzle over how Aristotle can maintain the *polis* as a natural association and yet talk about the role of the statesman in its construction. David Keyt, in "Three Fundamental Theorems in Aristotle's Politics," *Phronêsis* 32 (1987): 54–79, argues that there is a real contradiction. See Miller, "Aristotle's Political Naturalism," and Joseph Chan, "Does Aristotle's Political Theory Rest on a 'Blunder'?" *History of Political Thought* 13 (1992): 189–202, for arguments against Keyt's position.

    The influence of Aristotle's teleological understanding of nature on his *Politics* is evident in a number of his analyses beyond his discussion on the *polis*. For example, he detects in all compounds a ruling element and a ruled element and maintains that in general it is natural and better for the higher or superior element to rule the lower or the inferior element. This is exemplified in the rule of the soul over the body, the rule of the master over the slave, and the rule of the man over the woman (*Pol.* I, 5; see also *Pol.* VII, 14, for the hierarchy of the parts of the soul). As Aristotle puts it, "All men who differ from others as much as the body differs from the soul, or an animal from a man ... all such are by nature slaves, and it is better for them, on the very same principle ... to be ruled by a master" (1254b17–21). Aristotle's view that there are free men and slaves by nature enables him not only to justify the rule of masters over slaves but also to dismiss the view that permanent sovereignty over everyone is the highest good. He says, "In a society of peers it is right and just that office should go on the principle of rotation, which is demanded by the ideas of

Confucius offers no theoretical analysis of the state and political rule, nor has he a teleological view of nature that informs his view of the state and the way people are governed. One can perceive an inchoate view of nature and teleology in Confucius because he is quite clear that there is an excellence that all are to attain, that this is fulfilling for the human being, and that a certain sort of culture is required for its cultivation. Specifically, the highest human virtue is humaneness,[5] *ren*, which some translate as benevolence and others render as authoritative conduct or human-heartedness. It means progressively extending one's natural love for one's own family members in a less intense form to others in the community.[6] But although *ren* is the virtue that Confucius encourages everyone to attain, his view does not amount to a full-blown view of nature from which he systematically works out an account of the state and the ruler–ruled relations.[7] Still, there is an implicit teleology of roles: for Confucius, the state is essentially a bigger family that requires that the same reverence between sons and fathers occur between

equality and parity" (1325b7–9), and "The world would be a curious place if it did not include some elements meant to be free, as well as some that are meant to be subject to control; and if that is its nature, any attempt to establish control should be confined to the elements meant for control, and not extended to all" (1324b36–39). Arguing that youth is naturally endowed with vigor while age comes with wisdom also enables Aristotle to argue that the youth should make up the military force of the state while the mature should make up the deliberative part of the state. He says, "[T]he order of nature gives vigor to youth and wisdom to years; and it is policy to follow that order in distributing powers among the two age-groups of the state" (1329a15–16; see also *Pol.* VII, 14).

[5] See Chapter 1 for my discussion of three senses of *ren* in the *Analects*.

[6] The five relations – between rulers and ruled, parents and children, spouses, brothers, and friends – embody the traditional roles for Confucius. For the significance of these five relations to the cultivation of the individual, see Tu Weiming's "An Inquiry on the Five Relationships in Confucian Humanism," in *The Psycho-Cultural Dynamics of the Confucian Family*, ed. Walter H. Slote (Seoul: International Cultural Society of Korea, 1986), and Ambrose Y. C. King's "The Individual and Group in Confucianism: A Relational Perspective," in *Individualism and Holism: Studies in Confucian and Taoist Values*, ed. Donald Munro (Ann Arbor: University of Michigan Press, 1985).

[7] This is clear from the lack of any systematic account of nature in the *Analects* and the explicit assertion from one of his disciples, Zigong, to the effect that Confucius never talks about our nature and the nature of heaven (5.13). For a detailed contrast between what determines the human good in each of these thinkers, teleological metaphysics for Aristotle and ritual propriety (*li*) for Confucius, see Chapter 1.

ministers and rulers and between the people and government officials.

Aristotle defines political rule in terms of the citizen, where a citizen is one who is authorized to share in the deliberative or judicial office of a state. The state is a collection of such persons sufficient in number to achieve a self-sufficient existence (1275b18–22). This definition seems to exclude all those among the ruled who are not actively engaged in governance.[8] Confucius does not draw a sharp line between the rulers and the ruled, nor does he exclude the ruled when he speaks about the state. Thus he responded to a query regarding his not being employed in an official position as follows: "It is all in filial conduct (*xiao*)! Just being filial to your parents and befriending your brothers is carrying out the work of government" (2.21).[9] Similarly, in response to a question about how one is to govern effectively, Confucius says that the ruler, minister, father, and son should fulfill their respective roles (12.11). Aristotle agrees that

---

[8] As Peter Simpson, in *A Philosophical Commentary on the Politics of Aristotle* (Chapel Hill: The University of North Carolina Press, 1998), says, "Aristotle's definition of city (a multitude of those who share in deliberation and judgment) effectively identifies the city with those who are in control of the city and hence with the regime" (Simpson, 138). Richard G. Mulgan, in *Aristotle's Political Theory* (Oxford: Oxford Clarendon Press, 1977), says, "Because he defines citizenship in terms of participation in deliberative and judicial office, the citizen body in any constitution will be coextensive with the supreme body" (Mulgan, 61). In discussing the topic of political distribution in Aristotle, Martha Nussbaum, in Nature, Function, and Capability: Aristotle on Political Distribution, *Oxford Studies in Ancient Philosophy*, supplementary volume (Oxford: Oxford University Press, 1988), 144–84, notes that there is a "whole–part" conception that predominates Aristotle's discussion in *Politics* VII, 9–10, which "is used to justify the exclusion of manual labourers and farmers from membership in the city." The reason for their exclusion is that "manual labourers and farmers cannot achieve goodness, because their lives lack leisure, and leisure is necessary for virtue" (Nussbaum, "Nature, Function, and Capability," 156). Nussbaum maintains that *Politics* VII is a "more primitive stage in Aristotle's thinking on these issues"; *Politics* II and III represent his mature view (Nussbaum, "Nature, Function, and Capability," 160). For a critique of Nussbaum's position, see David Charles' "Perfectionism in Aristotle's Political Theory: Reply to Martha Nussbaum" in the same volume.

[9] For discussions of how filial piety forms the core of all human relationships in Confucius, see King's "The Individual and Group in Confucianism," especially 58; Francis L. K. Hsu's "Confucianism and Its Culturally Determined Manifestation," in Slote, *The Psycho-cultural Dynamics of the Confucian Family*, especially 33; and David K. Jordan's "Folk Filial Piety in Taiwan: The Twenty-four Filial Exemplars," in Slote, *The Psycho-cultural Dynamics of the Confucian Family*, 82–94.

all should fulfill their roles, but he excludes family relationships from political life.[10]

The state for Confucius is affected by everyone's actions, not only those of officers. Confucius speaks eloquently for the view that a virtuous leader inspires virtue in the people. A vicious ruler, on the other hand, would inspire vices (13.6, 12.18, 12.16). Confucius also believes that the effectiveness of a ruler is bound up with the way he interacts with his family. Being filial toward his elders and faithful to his friends will enable the ruler to earn the respect and loyalty of his people (2.20) and lead his people to aspire to the same humaneness (*ren*) he possesses (8.2, 1.2).

Aristotle would agree that a virtuous man with practical wisdom (*phronêsis*) who behaves well toward his family and friends would also make a good leader. If he lives in an ideal state, he may also be happy (*Pol.* III, 4). But Aristotle would disagree with Confucius' extension of family rule and love to political rule and friendship or love between fellow citizens. Even though Aristotle compares the rule of the head of the household to monarchical rule, monarchy is not a realistic ideal because it is appropriate only for a certain kind of people with a very special sort of monarch (*Pol.* I, 7; III, 17). Given Aristotle's remarks on virtuous monarchy, it might seem that he would agree with Confucius' extension of the virtues of household rule to the state, but such a comparison quickly falls apart. I shall consider three points of contrast: differences in the aim, in the role of self-interest, and in the kind of amity (*philia*) that is appropriate in the public and private spheres.

According to Aristotle, household management concerns itself with the goods needed for daily life. Political rule concerns itself with the good life for the citizens and what is self-sufficient for the whole *polis*. Because a household is never self-sufficient, the principles adequate to the rule of a household are never completely adequate for ruling a state.

---

[10] As Jean Elshtain puts it: "Women, slaves, and children did not partake in the full realization of goodness and rationality that defined co-equal participants in the perfect association. There was an 'essential' difference between the greater (free, male) and lesser (unfree, female) persons." See her "Aristotle, the Public–Private Split, and the Case of the Suffragists," in *The Family in Political Thought*, ed. Jean-Bethke Elshtain (Amherst: University of Massachusetts Press, 1982), 52.

Household management rules over wife, children, and slaves. But political rule, for Aristotle, is exercised over free men who are equal (*Pol.* I, 7). In the good *polis*, the citizen rules and is ruled in turn. But the head of a household ought never to be ruled by his slaves or by his wife and children. Household management aims to benefit the ruled family, including the father's own interest (*Pol.* III, 6). But Aristotle holds that rule in the *polis* is never just when the rulers consider their own personal interest, so the master's self-interested rule over his slave falls outside of political rule. Aristotle disagrees with Confucius' idea that love of our fellow citizens is simply a more diffuse form of love for our family members. He agrees that there is a difference in intensity between the love of family members and fellow citizens. But he would insist that there is also a difference in kind because the basis of the amity (*philia*) and the relations involved are different.[11]

Amity between family members is natural and based on a common life. Thus the friendship between a man and a woman is natural because they share a household for the sake of childbearing (1162a17–24). Parents have a natural love for their children because they caused these children's existence and the children are in a sense a part of themselves (1161a16–17, 1161b27–29). Parents share a life because they are responsible for nurturing and educating their children (1162a6–9). Brothers love each other because they have the same parents and share the same upbringing (1161b30–1162a3). Again there is a life in common. Friendships between citizens, tribesmen, voyagers, and the like such as friendships between hosts and guests (1161b13–16), are based on some kind of agreement rather than on nature or a common life. Sharing parents, upbringing, and education makes brothers closer to each other than hosts and guests who have agreed to share some utility or pleasure for a time. Similarly, shared parental responsibilities and day-to-day living bring spouses closer to each other than citizens who gather to deliberate about and act on behalf of the general conditions of their lives.

---

[11] See Bernard Yack, *The Problems of a Political Animal* (Berkeley: University of California Press, 1993), for a good discussion of the differences between citizens and family members (Yack, 53), as well as the differences between political friendship and the amity that characterize familial relations (Yack, 54–55).

The other reason for the difference in kind between the amity that binds family members and that which binds citizens is the need for equal virtue in the latter case. Citizens must act in harmony regarding the big questions about the good life. They need to be more or less of one mind about what is good and agree about the right kinds of actions to be taken in pursuit of their common goals (1167a33–1167b4) as well as having a certain laxness about the level of detail at which common efforts should be demanded in the state. These requirements can only be met if the citizens are similar in virtue. Familial relations, on the other hand, are between unequals. Parents must inculcate the virtues in their children, so they must be superior in virtue. Aristotle also thinks that the virtues of a man are different and superior to those of a woman. Furthermore, men and women complement each other by performing different functions (1162a21–24).

Another way of looking at the distinction between Aristotle's and Confucius' views of familial love and love of fellow citizens is that whereas Confucius thinks that our political relations are just extensions of our love for our relatives, Aristotle thinks that friendships differ by virtue of relation, virtue, or usefulness (1165a27–33). More specifically, Aristotle thinks that we owe our relatives, say our parents, the kind of honor that is appropriate to them and not every kind of honor, say that which is appropriate to a wise person or to a general. Family members and relatives are also the ones to be invited to weddings and funerals. And, more than anyone, we owe our parents support because we owe them our existence (1165a14–27). Aristotle also thinks that we should honor the old "by standing up, [and] giving up seats and so on" (1165a28). He claims that we should share everything in common with brothers and speak freely (1165a29–30). With fellow tribesmen and citizens, he thinks that we should accord them the honor that is appropriate to their virtues or usefulness. Given these different ways in which we are to honor familial relations and fellow citizens, it follows that one is not just an extension of the other, differing from the other in degree. Aristotle believes that these two are different kinds of friendships such that being good at the one does not translate to being good at the other, so he would not agree with Confucius' view that one who is filial toward her parents will also have the virtues to be a good ruler (*Analects* 8.2). In reference to the family, Confucius and Aristotle are quite close; in reference to political rule, they are not. In short, household management is essentially different from political rule for Aristotle.

Perhaps it is overly simple to regard Confucian political rule as a direct parallel to family rule and to regard political amity as the same in kind as family love. One might point to Confucius' distinction between the virtue of *ren* (humaneness) and the virtue of *yi* (appropriateness).[12] *Ren* does extend one's love for relatives to others in the society. But *yi* is concerned with the appropriate way of conducting oneself, so plainly *yi* will vary from situation to situation. *Yi*, moreover, pertains especially to matters of benefit and burden or profit and loss (16.10, 14.12, 7.16). So just as Aristotle recognizes a different way of bonding with fellow citizens and honoring them, *yi* would enable one to relate to others appropriately and accord them due honor or profit, because *yi*, like justice, implies recognizing others according to their merit or desert. Even so, *yi* does not imply a difference in kind sharp enough to satisfy Aristotle. Confucius would still claim that it is by *ren* that one can appropriately accord others their due. Knowing how to love one's relatives and others appropriately is what allows one to give all their due – familially or in the public sphere. Aristotle would of course disagree. If *yi* depends on *ren*, and *ren* is predicated on extending familial love to others, then an appeal to *yi* will not adequately underwrite the difference Aristotle wants to draw to our attention between family and political relations.

Aristotle would argue that too strong an analogy between family feeling and political life obscures important differences and leads to confusion about justice because what is just according to Aristotle varies with different relationships (1160a1, 1162a30–34):

It is not the same for parents towards children as for one brother towards another, and not the same for companions as for fellow-citizens, and similarly with the other types of friendship. Similarly, what is unjust towards each of these is also different, and becomes more unjust as it is practiced on closer friends. It is more shocking, e.g., to rob a companion of money than a fellow-citizen, to fail to help a brother than a stranger, and to strike one's father than anyone else. What is just also naturally increases with friendship, since it involves the same people and extends over an equal area. (1160a1–8)

---

[12] I discuss three senses of *yi* in Chapter 1.

Aristotle stresses that there are different types of justice in different kinds of relations, particularly between equals or between unequals (1158b12–17, 1160a1–8, 1162a30–35, 1162a34–b4). One is always a debtor to one's father and can never disavow him. But the father, as a superior, can disown his son (1163b20). Confucius would agree. But he would say the same of politics! For Aristotle, "political justice" is not applicable in familial relations. Political justice for Aristotle is always "among associates in a life aiming at self-sufficiency, who are free and either proportionately or numerically equal" (1134a26–27). Only here can there be action by citizens for the sake of a good and self-sufficient life, guided by the common interest (1279a31–32, 1283b40–1284a3).[13]

Aristotle sees different kinds of justice for different groups of people. But the core idea of justice for him is political. It involves citizens who live in some kind of relation of equality and is not a natural extension of other kinds of justice. On the contrary, the *polis* comes before villages, families, and individuals because political justice has priority over all other forms of justice (1253a19–1253b). Indeed, the other forms of justice are rightly called "just" insofar as they resemble political justice (1134a27–29).

Aristotle offers a generous analysis of different regimes, proposes an ideal constitution, and describes the best constitution for practical purposes. He recognizes that different types of constitutions befit different groups of people and might best lead them to good rule and virtue. Confucius never offers descriptions, theoretical analyses, or evaluations of different constitutions. He concentrates, for the most part, on the benevolent rule of a sage king. He does compare

---

[13] As Mulgan, in *Aristotle's Political Theory*, puts it, "[Aristotle] equates the common interest with absolute justice, by which he probably means justice in the wider or 'universal' sense, that is complete social virtue" (Mulgan, 61). See also Ernest Barker, *The Politics of Aristotle*, note V, 113, for the same point. Bernard Yack rightly equates Aristotle's political justice with his discussion of general justice, or complete virtue, in the *Nicomachean Ethics*. As Yack puts it, "Justice, he suggests, is the 'political virtue' that seeks the common advantage, the virtue from which 'all the other virtues necessarily follow' (*Pol.* 1283a38), a description that corresponds to his similar characterization of general justice as the 'complete virtue' that involves the exercise of all the other moral virtues (*NE* 1129b26)" (Yack, *The Problems of a Political Animal*, 159). These authors also reiterate the fact that regimes are only just for Aristotle if they pursue the common advantage of their state.

cultures – Zhou and Shang – as befits his emphasis on culture over law or regime.[14] But, in politics, Confucius takes for granted the feudal system prevalent during his time. He assumes a hierarchy of king, minister, lords, and common people. The people work the land and pay taxes to the government. The government looks out for the economic well-being and safety of the people. It is responsible not only for the administration of law and punishment of criminals (14.19, 13.3, 12.11, 12.7) but also for the observance of ritual proprieties (*li*). Confucius does not much consider other political systems except to call them barbaric. Aristotle is also known to call certain regimes barbaric, such as when discussing the ways that the Persians use to preserve tyrannical rule: either by eliminating outstanding men or by preventing associations that might foster friendship or mutual confidence (1313a34–b17). But, in general, Aristotle is very much aware that the Athenian constitution is not the only form of political association. He derives the available types of constitutions from divisions based on wealth and poverty and the economic occupation (farmer, mechanic, tradesman) of the dominant group. There are good and bad types, where good rule has a view toward the common interest and bad rule has a view toward the personal interest of the ruler(s) (*Pol.* III, 7). Whether kingship, aristocracy, or polity is more appropriate depends on the makeup of the society:

The society appropriate to kingship is one of the sorts which naturally tends to produce some particular stock, or family, pre-eminent in its capacity for political leadership. The society appropriate to aristocracy is one which naturally tends to produce a body of persons capable of being ruled, in a manner suitable to free men, by those who are men of leading in their capacity for political rule. The society appropriate to government of the constitutional type [i.e., the "polity"] is one in which there naturally exists a body of persons possessing military capacity, who can rule and be ruled under a system of law which distributes offices among the wealthy in proportion to merit. (1288a7–15)

---

[14] The Western Zhou (1122–771 B.C.E.) succeeded the Shang (1700–1122 B.C.E., the first dynasty with written records). The Eastern Zhou succeeded the Western Zhou and lasted until 221 B.C.E. By Confucius' time (551–479 B.C.E.), the states with allegiance to the Zhou dynasty had been warring for more than two centuries. Because of the escalating violence and cultural changes of the Eastern Zhou dynasty, Confucius looks back to the Western Zhou as an ideal.

Even though Aristotle holds that aristocracy and an exceptional sort of monarchy are more ideal, a constitution based on the rule of the middle class (also called a "polity") is the most practical (*Pol.* IV, 11). He claims, nonetheless, that "in relation to particular circumstances" "there is nothing to prevent another sort from being more suitable in the given case; and indeed this may often happen" (1296b10–13; see also *Pol.* IV, 12, for specific discussions of what constitution befits what sort of people). So, in addition to recognizing a best form of constitution, Aristotle also recognizes that different groups of people under different circumstances require different types of constitutions and rule.

Confucius and Aristotle also differ in their attitudes toward the rule of law. Aristotle advocates it. But Confucius is skeptical about it:

Lead the people with administrative injunctions (*zheng*) and keep them orderly with penal law (*xing*), and they will avoid punishments but will be without a sense of shame. Lead them with excellence (*de*) and keep them orderly through observing ritual propriety (*li*) and they will develop a sense of shame, and moreover, will order themselves. (*Analects* 2.3)

Confucius is also against killing and violence when dealing with people who do not obey the government. Ji Kangzi asked Confucius about governing effectively (*zheng*), saying, "What if I kill those who have abandoned the way (*dao*) to attract those who are on it?" "If you govern effectively," Confucius replied, "what need is there for killing? If you want to be truly adept (*shan*), the people will also be adept. The excellence (*de*) of the exemplary person (*junzi*) is the wind, while that of the petty person is the grass. As the wind blows, the grass is sure to bend" (*Analects* 12.19; see also 13.11). Confucius' view is that the most effective form of government is founded on an exemplary ruler whose actions are so virtuous (excellent, *de*) that the people will naturally be inspired to virtue. Penal law might keep the people in line when they are being watched, but that will not be internalized – as shame is in the virtuous even when they are not being watched. People may appear to be excellent (*de*), abiding by all the laws, and yet be inwardly bankrupt, with no sense of *ren*, or *yi*. They might carry out the letter of the law without living by the spirit of the law. This is why Confucius says, "The village worthy's excellence (*de*) is excellence under false pretense" (*Analects* 17.13, my trans.).

But Confucius goes further. The governor of She, in conversation with Confucius, said: "In our village there is someone called 'True person.' When his father took a sheep on the sly, he reported him to the authorities." Confucius replied: "Those who are true in my village conduct themselves differently. A father covers for his son, and a son covers for his father. And being true lies in this" (*Analects* 13.18). Reporting a theft is of course what the law demands. But, for Confucius, the father–son relationship should take precedence. By blindly following the law, the "true person" of She is not doing what is right. Penal law alone not only is not sufficient for cultivating virtue but may even run counter to filial piety; an overreliance on law risks training people to focus on external conformity.

Confucius' skepticism about penal law is coupled with his esteem for the unwritten ritual proprieties handed down from the Zhou. Even though the norms of *li* were not written down in Confucius' time, they were captured in the traditional practices of filial piety, reverence for the elders, and the rituals and ceremonies surrounding ancestor worship, mourning, and the like. The glory of the Zhou may be vanished, but fragments of the proper way survive. In response to the question, "With whom did Confucius study?," Zigong replied:

The way (*dao*) of Kings Wen and Wu has not collapsed utterly – it lives in the people. Those of superior character (*xian*) have grasped the greater part, while those of lesser quality have grasped a bit of it. Everyone has something of Wen and Wu's way in him. Who then does the Master not learn from? Again, how could there be a single constant teacher for him? (*Analects* 19.22)

The *Songs* are also a source of the *li*; thus Confucius encourages his students to study the *Songs*, saying:

Reciting the *Songs* can arouse your sensibilities, strengthen your powers of observation, enhance your ability to *relate to* others, and sharpen your critical skills. Close at hand it enables you to serve your father, and away at court it enables you to serve your lord. It instills in you a broad vocabulary for making distinctions in the world around you. (*Analects* 17.9, italics denote my trans.; see also 16.13)[15]

---

[15] *The Book of Songs* contains about 300 poems (see *Analects* 3.5), some of which originated from the Shang dynasty but most of which are from the Zhou. Together with *The Book of Changes*, *The Book of History*, *The Book of Rites*, and the *Spring and Autumn* (chronicle of events, 722–481 B.C.E.), *The Book of Songs* is one of the five

Li, then, prescribes proper behavior for every role in society: ruler, minister, duke, father, son, and all the rest. Obviously, its prescriptions do not address every detail of behavior. There is room and need for individual adjustments and family amendments. Still, a definite manner of action and attitude seems to be inculcated by the proprieties. I do not find in the *li* quite so much flexibility or so much room for individual "creativity" as have recent commentators such as Tony Cua and Roger Ames. Confucius stresses the importance of following the Zhou *li*, as well as his role as a transmitter rather than an innovator of tradition. Whatever creativity we find in Confucius is limited, then, by the existing norms and tradition. For instance, he speaks of substitution of a silk cap for a hemp cap because it is more economical. But the practice of wearing a certain type of cap for ceremonial purposes is not one that is open to individual creativity. One can imagine Confucius balking at an individual's substitution of a baseball cap for such ceremonies. Thus I favor a more conservative interpretation of the Confucian *li*.[16] To cultivate both *ren* and *yi* will allow one to act harmoniously in a society where others adhere to a similar mode of behavior and belief. Cultivated from a young age, *li* is more effective than mere laws that may be evaded:

Through self-discipline and observing ritual propriety (*li*) one becomes *humane* in one's conduct. If for the space of a day one were able to accomplish this, the whole empire would defer to this *humane* model. (12.1, italics denote my trans.)

Confucius tells Yan Hui, a disciple, that one must not look at, listen to, speak about, or do anything that might violate ritual propriety (*Analects* 12.1). Indeed, observance of *li* will have a positive effect on the people:

If their superiors cherished the observance of ritual propriety (*li*), none among the common people would dare be disrespectful (*Analects* 13.4); and,

---

canonical texts. As James Legge puts it, "'The five *Ching*' are the five canonical works, containing the truth upon the highest subjects from the sages of China, and which should be received as law by all generations" (Legge, *Confucius: Confucian Analects, The Great Learning and The Doctrine of the Mean*, 1). See *Shih Ching* (*The Book of Songs*), trans. Arthur Waley (New York: Grove Press, 1960).
[16] I defend this interpretation in Chapters 3 and 4.

if those in high station cherish the observance of ritual propriety (*li*), the common people will be easy to deal with (*Analects* 14.41).

Li is the crown of the other virtues, such as *ren* and *zhi* (knowledge):

When the knowledgeable can apply their knowledge [*zhi*] through humaneness [*ren*], and can govern with dignity but cannot inspire through ritual propriety [*li*], they are not yet adept [*shan*] at it. (15.33, my trans.)

Li is the content of cultivation. It is what structures the social hierarchy and harmonizes the parties to it into a virtuous functioning whole. *Li* can and law cannot accomplish this, according to Confucius.

Aristotle certainly makes serious use of custom and habit in his ethical and political thought. But he argues for a more positive view of law.[17] For example, monarchy is more enduring if constitutional (i.e., ruled by law). There are types of democracies and oligarchies where the rule of law is better than rule by citizens who lack leisure for political activity:

When the farming class and the class possessed of moderate means are the sovereign power in the constitution, they conduct the government under the rule of law. Able to live by their work, but unable to enjoy any leisure, they make the law supreme, and confine the meetings of the assembly to a minimum. (1292b25–29)

On the other hand, in a democracy where a large increase in population and wealth enables the majority to have means and leisure sufficient to partake of political activities, the people rather than the laws are sovereign.[18]

Aristotle allows for the rule of a virtuous leader. But he argues that such individuals are rare. Politics therefore cannot count on them.

---

[17] Plato's disillusionment with the more intuitive personalist approach may help explain this.

[18] Aristotle applies the same kind of reasoning to the various forms of oligarchy. For instance, in a moderate oligarchy where the majority of the citizens have property but in moderate amounts, the generality have what we would call constitutional rights. But because they have neither so much wealth as to excuse them from all business nor so little that they need to be supported by the state, the rule of law works better for them than rule by their own assemblies. Other forms of oligarchy also have the rule of law but for a different reason. In their case, it is a lack of power over the majority that makes them resort to the rule of law. Only the most extreme form of oligarchy, where few persons own larger properties and thus possess the time and the power, can exercise its own rule (1293a30–34).

Recognition of human failings and of the tendency for strong monarchies to turn into tyrannies leads him to counsel forms of the rule of law for a variety of situations. Confucius contrasts the rule of law with the inspirational rule of an exemplary individual and the power of *li* in the cultivation of virtue. But Aristotle readily combines the rule of law with custom and habituation. He sees a complementarity because laws can help inculcate virtuous habits. And law for its part needs virtue for its formulation and implementation. As Bernard Yack says, the laws "have their origins in practical reason. In a passage that comes close to suggesting a general definition of law, Aristotle suggests that law is 'a rule of reason from some practical reason [*phronêsis*] and intellect [*nous*]' (*NE* 1180a21)." Yack also points out that Aristotle does not rank written laws higher than unwritten laws.[19]

In constitutions based on the rule of law, Aristotle maintains that just laws should be sovereign (1282b1–6). Still, the generality of laws prevents them from making usefully exact pronouncements about particular cases. Here a human mind is needed:

> Rightly constituted laws should be the final sovereign; and personal rule, whether it be exercised by a single person or a body of persons, should be sovereign only in matters on which law is unable, owing to the difficulty of framing general rules for all contingencies, to make an exact pronouncement. (1282b1–16)

Aristotle does write of law as more sovereign than the rule of man (1287b5–8). But the contrast with Confucius should not be overstated, for Aristotle is speaking not just of formal rules here but also very much the counterpart of the normative patterns of *li*, as becomes clear when we consider the role that Aristotle assigns to habit and *ethos* in the cultivation of virtue. As Bernard Yack puts it: "Law's capacity to shape moral dispositions through the inculcation of certain habits is ... one of its greatest contributions to political life. Unwritten laws perform this function better than written laws do, since the habits they shape are more spontaneous and less alien to the individual. They are thus 'more supreme' in the way that they shape moral character, and they deal with 'more supreme matters' in that they are concerned primarily with the most important political

---

[19] Yack, *The Problems of a Political Animal*, 179.

goal: moral education" (Yack, *The Problems of a Political Animal*, 181, 204). Again, Yack says, "Moral dispositions rather than political institutions define the Aristotelian rule of law" (ibid., 201).

A similarity between Confucius and Aristotle concerns the diversity of the people who live in the state. Aristotle's discussion of this topic takes the form of his discussion of unity in the *polis*. He maintains that there should be the right degree of unity in the *polis* to keep it as a *polis*. Too much unity will make it too much like a household. A self-sufficient *polis* needs different and complementary capacities (*Pol.* II, 2). Unlike a military alliance, which may be strengthened by a large number of similar people, a *polis* "must be made up of elements which differ in kind" (1261a23–24). This leads Aristotle to the corollary that even when some are better than others at ruling, nonetheless, "through the natural equality of all the citizens" (1261b31), it is better that citizens take turns to rule:

This means that some rule, and others are ruled, in turn, as if they had become, for the time being, different sorts of persons. We may add that even those who are rulers for the time being differ from one another, some holding one kind of office and some another. (1261b32–36)

So, even with offices, diversity and complementarity are central. While recognizing that too little unity will cause problems for a political association because the people may then lack a common goal, and may even be acting at odds with each other, too much unity will also destroy a *polis* (*Pol.* II, 5): "It is as if you were to turn harmony into mere unison, or to reduce a theme to a single beat" (1263b). The need for different elements in a state that still harmonize with each other is also crucial for Confucius. But he pursues a harmonious functioning of persons in their roles – rulers and subjects, ministers and dukes, parents and children. As he puts it, "Exemplary persons seek harmony, not sameness; petty persons are the opposite" (13.23). As to effective government: "The ruler must rule, the minister minister, the father must be a father, and the son a son" (12.11; see the *Doctrine of the Mean* [hereafter *DM*] 1.5, 15.1–3). Because Confucius holds that harmonious home relations extend to the state, he is broadly concerned that everyone fulfill his or her particular role. As with Aristotle, he makes the point in terms of music, but also ritual, which is tied together with music in his view: "One stands to be improved by the enjoyment found in attuning oneself to the rhythms of ritual propriety [*li*] and music [*yue*]" (16.5), and "It is said in the *Book of Songs*, 'Happy union with wife and children is like the music of lutes and harps. When there is concord among brethren, the harmony is delightful and enduring" (*DM* 15.2). *Li* articulates roles; *yue* (music) harmonizes them.

Still, Aristotle and Confucius differ in their willingness to allow for a variety of arrangements that are politically and morally legitimate. As we have seen, Confucius does not concern himself with political associations beyond his own ideal, which rings changes on the Zhou model (3.14). But Aristotle allows for human varieties that he thinks call for varieties of regimes. Aristotle's discussion of five types of democracies and four types of oligarchies is an instance of such varieties. (*Pol.* IV, 4–5). There could be a democracy where the poor counts as much as the rich, or another where only those with property can participate but the property qualification is so low that the many can qualify, yet another where birth determines one's share in office, and another where birth does not count. Then there are those where the law is the final sovereign and others where the people rather than the law are the final sovereign. Apart from these characteristics of the ruler, the occupation of the ruler and ruled will contribute to the democracy by making it, say, a democracy that is primarily agricultural or trade-oriented (that also places the law as sovereign due to people's lack of leisure to actively engage in political legislation). Aristotle's willingness to admit all of these factors stems in part from his principle of self-sufficiency, where he realizes that many different functions and different people with different skills go into making a self-sufficient *polis*. He is not focusing on only one kind of function or rule like Confucius does. Rather, Aristotle recognizes that just as different people within his ideal *polis* need to do different jobs in order to have a self-sufficient *polis*, likewise there could be different constitutions with emphases on different occupations and functions, which in turn give their constitutions the characteristics they have. He conceives of as many flavors of constitution as there are ways of distributing offices among the members of the *polis*. Not all of these are morally legitimate, but many are. Aristotle's allowance that different legitimate constitutions are appropriate for different people reflects no moral relativism on his part but rather a recognition that the pedagogy of virtue demands different starting points for people with different histories, characters, customs, strengths, and interests.

Aristotle's admission that several regime types have moral legitimacy – even the second best is good enough for practical purposes – makes for a different attitude toward the populace than we find in Confucius. For one thing, the excellences of different classes differ in kind; Aristotle does not demand that the same kind of virtue be sought in every class. There are special excellences for ruling and obeying, for mechanics and merchants, and so on. Moreover, Aristotle's admission makes for a different attitude toward practical wisdom. Certainly everyone should strive to cultivate moral virtue and practical wisdom. But Aristotle does not hang the political fortunes of every sort of state upon a virtuous ruler or citizenry. He welcomes regime types based on the rule of law, where self-sufficiency and the good life can be achieved in the absence of ideal rulers or even an exemplary populace. Virtue is required in the formation and implementation of law. But neither the exemplary excellence of a single leader nor the complete excellence of all or most citizens is required for the life of an acceptable regime.

Confucius' extolled Zhou feudal system does require the discovery of a wise sage-king and will not survive or thrive without the practical wisdom of such a statesman sage. This might seem to imply that the mass of people need no virtue of their own and need only follow this paragon. But that would be too hasty an inference. Confucius' analogy between family relations (especially those between fathers and sons) and government relations (especially between the ruler and ruled) proposes in effect that the mass of people in his ideal state (the men, at least) would have the same kind of virtue as the ruler. His virtues are not just a paradigm for them. They are also an emblem of the practices that permeate this ideal or idealized society. Confucius does lean on the special excellences demanded of distinct roles. But moral virtue is very much a singular notion for him. Political virtue and family virtue are essentially the same. Good fathers share in and exhibit essentially the same kind of virtue as sage-kings.[20] So the

---

[20] And children and wives can exhibit essentially the same kind of virtue as political subjects. I set aside the blatant paternalism of the Confucian way for the purposes of this volume. A rectified Confucianism, such as I recommend elsewhere and

permeation is not just top-down but through and through in an ideal state. But the sage-king is the initial cause of such an ideal, just as good fathers are the cause of good children.

In Aristotle's ideal constitution, only the ruler – or the citizen in his temporary role of ruler – can exercise genuine practical wisdom on a public plane. Nor can one exercise the ultimate of virtue in a constitution of the wrong type. In Confucius' view, however, it seems that the good private person is also the good citizen and the virtuous man. This is clear when Confucius responded to the question of why he is not in government by saying: "It is all in filial conduct (*xiao*)! Just being filial to your parents and befriending your brothers is carrying out the work of government" (2.21). Whereas Aristotle more sharply distinguishes the virtues of the citizen from the virtues of the good man, and separates both from any excellences that might pertain to his family relationships, Confucius blends them. Perhaps in a way Confucius allows more people to attain genuine moral virtue, the same kind of virtue as the ruler or *junzi*. They act in their private capacity, as Aristotle would see it, where Aristotle would look for participation. But their seemingly familial and communal virtues are of social and political significance in Confucius' view. For Confucius, the virtues of the *junzi* are accessible even within one's family.

But Confucius recognizes only one ideal and accordingly encourages one to seek rule only when the system is not corrupt. Otherwise one must withdraw. As he puts it:

Be steadfast to the death in service to the efficacious way [*shandao*]. Do not enter a state in crisis, and do not tarry in one that is in revolt. Be known when the way prevails in the world, but remain hidden away when it does not. It is a disgrace to remain poor and without rank when the way prevails in the state; it is a disgrace to be wealthy and of noble rank when it does not. (*Analects* 8.13; see also 15.7)

So even though Confucius allows more people to attain the same kinds of virtues as the *junzi* or moral leaders, he urges them to refrain from exercising their virtues in the public sphere when the state is not in wholesome condition. Aristotle, on the other hand, has fewer

toward which I gesture at the conclusion of this chapter, can avoid the paternalism but would still – if it is to be Confucian at all – have it that political virtues and familial virtues are essentially the same in kind.

people achieve the virtues of a true ruler, but his practical proposals for less than ideal situations and viable constitutions can legitimately be worked on by less than ideal rulers.

Having discussed some key similarities and differences in the virtue-oriented politics of Confucius and Aristotle, let me next sketch more briefly the shortcomings of each and how the other might offer resources to rectify those shortcomings. More briefly still, I shall say something about the implications of the points that have been gleaned from this comparison for our contemporary discourse of rights.

First, Aristotle's account of the nature of the state and its end enables him to justify his view that the *polis* exists for the sake of achieving a good life. Confucius would agree with Aristotle that achieving the life of virtue is of the utmost concern to the ruler and the state. Yet he simply declares it and never provides an argument to that effect. Here Aristotle's discussion of the nature of the *polis* and the nature of the human soul and its ends could help. If human beings are so constituted that certain activities are better than others, one can show that the ultimate aim in life is to live in such a way that these higher parts are cultivated and these higher goals sought. Confucians do not have the resources to persuade someone who does not already believe that the best way of living is to cultivate the Zhou *li*. Indeed, without some such grounding in a theory of human nature and the human good, a would-be follower of Confucius does not actually even understand the ground of his own master's normative pronouncements. I have argued in Chapter 5 that there are, tacitly or incipiently, such resources in Confucian tradition, but they are largely undeveloped.

On the other hand, Confucius' account of ritual propriety (*li*) could help supplement Aristotle's all too brief account of unwritten laws. Aristotle needs, but does not supply, an extended account of *ethos* as the conditioning context for action and habituation. Such an account could have led to a more inclusive view of moral cultivation. Because unwritten laws, such as Confucius' *li*, are all-pervasive in culture, Aristotle could have developed an account where moral cultivation is not restricted to the well born but is accessible to common folk as well. This account could act as a bridge between the fortunate citizens and the unfortunate noncitizens so that Aristotle need not discriminate against noncitizens in respect of virtue. Following Confucius, Aristotelians would be able to see that *li* can pervade our everyday lives and serve as the vehicle for cultivating the virtues.[21] (For example, one would not need to be born into an aristocratic family in order to have the opportunity to cultivate moral excellence.) A move in this sort of direction could make the life of virtue accessible to laborers, tradesmen, farmers, mechanics, and even women. The goal here would be to extend Aristotle's vision of moral virtue into the family and daily life – while maintaining a distinction between household and political contexts more robust than Confucius intended.

Third, Aristotle's analysis of law could help Confucians understand that the rule of law need not be antithetical to the rule of custom or the cultivation of moral virtue. Adherence to the law need not amount to mere external conformity, at least not in the context of certain sorts of regimes. It might be possible to persuade Confucians not only that a sage-king could make good laws that would work hand in hand with normative rituals but that an assembly of incompletely but moderately virtuous persons could articulate out of custom a set of laws or lawlike rules to guide the masses toward the way of virtue.[22] The rule of law need not deprive people of their sense of shame, nor adjourn the rule of virtue.

Fourth, Aristotle's understanding of the variety of constitutions and their causes might help Confucians to understand that there are legitimate forms of rule other than that of a sage-king. Because Confucius agrees that a state is made up of people who do different jobs and play different roles, Aristotelians might persuade Confucians that states could vary depending on what roles there are, which are dominant, and the number of people who play them. That analysis paves the way to a recognition of the moral acceptability of regimes other than the single highest ideal. As long as the people can live in such a way that they observe *li* attuned to their circumstances and the cultivation of moral virtues, they need not be dismissed as

---

[21] See Chapter 4 for a more elaborate discussion of this matter.
[22] Such "cooperation" between the king and his associates is not alien to the Confucian tradition. I discuss this in Chapter 3. See also *Analects* 13.3 for a more positive attitude toward laws.

barbarians. Both Aristotle and Confucius take moral education to be the principal means and among the chief ends of political rule. This is manifest in Aristotle's view that the *polis* exists not merely for the sake of life but for the good life and in Confucius' insistence on having a virtuous leader to inspire virtue in the people. Confucius thinks that moral education can and ought always to rise from family virtue. Aristotle recognizes – more realistically, I think – that moral education, like any other, must begin from where people and their culture actually are. The key here is a recognition that political and social circumstances are pedagogical conditions.

One large lesson that both traditions can learn, from the sheer fact of the existence of the other philosophical school as an exotic tradition of virtue and also from the fortunes of virtue traditions in the long history of civilization, is the difficulty of achieving virtue. Both Aristotle and Confucius already knew that virtue is a precarious achievement in the individual and in society, but I suspect that this point would stand out even more were they alive today to survey historical developments. What does the fact of this precariousness of virtue imply for the theory and practice of virtue, Confucian and Aristotelian? Let me tease out just a few implications, beginning by revisiting the four points of comparison just concluded.

I argued that Aristotle's account of nature and its teleology better enables him to justify his way to a virtue-oriented politics in contrast with the Confucian way, whose strategies of validation are all rhetorical. Once a direct appeal to the Zhou *li* is rendered inept by time and distance, the appeal becomes an invocation of Master Kong himself as an authoritative sage or religious founder, what Aristotle would call a "godlike man" (1253a29). Admittedly, Aristotle has a similar problem when Aristotelian science, logic, and metaphysics are rejected. He has the problem because even if Aristotelian ideas in these areas are still viable, most people believe they are not. In either case, they have lost their persuasive power. In the face of these troubles, an argument to the effect that a virtue-oriented politics is compatible with at least some form of rights theory might help to make it persuasive again, at least to people concerned with excellence and appropriateness in human affairs.

I claimed that Aristotle's understanding of the variety of constitutions and their causes might help Confucians to understand that beyond the rule of a sage-king there are other legitimate forms of rule. And I argued that one or another of these forms may be more pedagogically appropriate in a given circumstance, although acceptance of this fact may require a more catholic experience than was available to Confucius. Still, a Confucian – especially a contemporary one – might be brought to accept this broader zone of tolerance. Confucians, no less than Aristotelians, ought to recognize the moral legitimacy of certain alternative political arrangements and therefore to tolerate or even welcome them. The language we use to discuss and endorse this tolerance is the language of pluralism of rights. We say that a variety of forms of political rule have the moral right to exist. Now it is widely supposed that virtue traditions are inimical to modern ideas of rights because most extant rights theories, and certainly the dominant ones, are based on notions of autonomy and possessive individualism that are alien to both Confucian and Aristotelian traditions.[23] I wish to float the

[23] As David Hall and Roger Ames, in *The Democracy of the Dead*, put it, "A fundamental problem with rights-based understandings of democracy is that they have few mechanisms to prevent individuals from becoming alienated from communities because the rights serving as the fundamental signs and rewards of a just society are so often enjoyed in private. Such rights do not prevent individuals from joining together in communities or social unions, but neither do they enjoin or stimulate community building" (Hall and Ames, *The Democracy of the Dead*, 108). Leo Strauss, in *Natural Right and History* (Chicago: University of Chicago Press, 1953), and Alasdair C. MacIntyre, in *After Virtue*, argue against any rights talk in Aristotle. Fred D. Miller, Jr., in *Nature, Justice, and Rights in Aristotle's Politics* (New York: Oxford University Press, 1995), on the other hand, finds that Aristotle is already using " 'rights' locutions" and hence finds in Aristotle the concept of rights (Miller, *Nature, Justice, and Rights in Aristotle's Politics*, 111). John M. Cooper, in "Justice and Rights in Aristotle's Politics," *The Review of Metaphysics* 49 (1996): 859–72, supports Miller's thesis for the most part, and as long as one distances Aristotle's concerns from the modern and contemporary theorists' valuation of "subjective freedom." Richard Kraut, in "Are there Natural Rights in Aristotle?" *The Review of Metaphysics*, 49 (1996): 755–74, is willing to admit similarities between Aristotle's concepts of justice and the concepts of rights held by philosophers with "full scale theories of natural rights" (ibid., 774). But he is doubtful that the similarities are strong enough to say definitively that Aristotle has a concept of rights. Kraut's position stems from his view (with which I am sympathetic) that Aristotle makes very little use of rights talk (ibid., 773). Vivienne Brown, in " 'Rights' in Aristotle's *Politics* and *Nicomachean Ethics*?" *The Review of Metaphysics*, 55 (2001): 269–95, is not convinced by Miller's thesis because she thinks that he has not shown what he claimed, namely that "political rights of a Hohfeldian kind are employed in Aristotle's *Politics* and *Nicomachean Ethics*" (V. Brown, 271). It is beyond the scope of this chapter for me to argue about Miller's thesis. That we can

programmatic suggestion that Aristotelian and Confucian traditions, precisely to the extent that they have listened to each other, will be more open to an acknowledgment of some very important moral rights.[24]

The opening occurs just in the moment of mutual recognition, where each identifies an exotic tradition of virtue in the midst of radical cultural differences. It is the recognition of a tradition that, while different enough to argue with (indeed so different it is sometimes difficult to know where to begin), nevertheless deserves respect and is somehow *entitled* to explore its own vision of political virtue. Exactly at this point of mutual recognition in the thick of radical cultural difference, there is an experience that translates readily into the language of rights.[25] It may or may not be possible for each tradition to appreciate that it ought to accept alternative personal visions of virtue, which is one with recognizing rights of individuals. That is an additional issue because whether the primary locus of rights for these types of virtue traditions is the society, the family, the tradition, or the individual is not to be presumed but is part of what needs to be argued out between them. I hasten to add that for any virtue tradition the limit of this recognition is the ability to see that these alternatives are alternative visions *of virtue*. It does not seem to me to be part of any virtue tradition to acknowledge that the pursuit of any ends other than virtue (pleasure, power, wealth, expediency) has a right to be, although virtue theories can, of course, find a place – a subordinate place – for these externals. But as long as it can be recognized as a pursuit of excellence of character and custom – no matter how otherwise radical the cultural differences – it ought to be able to be and to flourish. It is my conviction that an acknowledgment of rights of this sort can grow directly from the

---

develop out of Aristotle's politics support for the promotion of moral rights is the purpose of my discourse in this chapter.

[24] See my "A Confucian Approach to Human Rights," *History of Philosophy Quarterly* 21 (2004): 337–56, where I argue that a virtue theorist should accept and promote the rights of every human being to the necessary conditions of virtue.

[25] This does not at all imply complete political or social autonomy, or a right to be left alone. After all, part of what I am claiming here is that an argument can and should ensue in which each tradition should try to persuade the other that it has advantageous features to offer and in which it might come to recognize shortcomings in itself that might not appear outside of a confrontation with an alien tradition.

experience of mutual recognition that occurs when Aristotelians and Confucians recognize one another as speaking for alternative traditions of virtue.

I also argued earlier that Aristotle's analysis of law could help Confucians understand that the rule of law need not be antithetical to the rule of custom or the cultivation of moral virtue. Indeed, if most people most of the time need good laws in order to make room and even breathing space for virtuous citizens and institutions, and even the exercise of virtues, then in the name of virtue people ought to claim that they have a right to a legal system in which good laws can be made and enforced. With a politics that takes its orientation from virtue, laws and rules are not the point. They are means and supplements to virtue.[26] But if a system of law is in general a necessary means to virtue, then for the sake of excellent character and harmonious relationships, people ought to claim as their due a system in which good laws can be formulated. This might take any number of forms, depending on the culture. Nevertheless, it is something owed to people because it is needed for most people to attain virtue and because people should claim the conditions of virtue as their due. Such a claim is, in a plain sense, a rights claim.

I have also argued that Confucius' account of ritual propriety (*li*) could supplement Aristotle's all too brief account of unwritten law because he does not supply as fully as he might the necessary account of *ethos* and the means of its cultivation. Confucians are peculiarly sensitive to what Aristotelians would call *ethos* and beyond this have an acute sense of the way in which more ceremonious rituals focus and intensify our customs and our moral practice. Aristotelians can learn from this. Both traditions could then appreciate that the normative customs that pervade our everyday lives ought to act as vehicles for the cultivation of virtue in ways that would make the life of virtue accessible to the most ordinary of people, including the most menial of workers. Part of this involves, as I suggested, a Confucian recognition that the life of virtue extends into family relationships and in fact has its roots there. But it goes further. Both Aristotle and Confucius recommend that a society should care

---

[26] Remember that virtue, too, is a means to an end (the good life; i.e., the life in accordance with virtue).

for the least advantaged of its members. Both seem to base this recommendation on the generosity and magnificence of people of means. In other words, they stress the side of the virtuous actor rather than the beneficiary. But there is another, complementary basis and emphasis. Those in need ought to be helped because the needy have a right to assistance when there is the real possibility of it. This sort of right is not at all antithetical to a virtue-oriented politics once this politics admits that the primary moral rights are rights to the conditions of virtue. Assistance can be justified on the grounds that the pursuit of virtue is impossible unless at least the minimum needs of animal life are met. It is neither a matter of *noblesse oblige* nor a holdover from some fictitious state of nature that underwrites individual entitlements. Moral rights can be – and ought to be – claimed in the name of virtue. This is a justification that, if it confirms a somewhat narrower array of rights, confirms them for a moral reason: the cultivation of virtue.

My thesis, then, is that the most basic moral rights are rights to the necessary conditions of virtue. This is the way to human rights that a virtue-oriented politics recommends. The argument is simple. If one ought to be virtuous, then one ought to have the means of developing and exercising virtue. When there are means available, they should be made available on just these grounds. This appeal to the grounds of virtue implies (I argue elsewhere) subsistence rights, rights to education, and, though it is a more subtle point, certain rights to political access. It will not and it should not imply all the rights standardly listed by liberal rights theorists or the political manifestos of the day. A distinctive approach to rights springs from a virtue-oriented politics, with the power of developing a way of its own and the promise of critique of the regnant views about rights. I believe that the dialogue between Confucius and Aristotle – fascinating and instructive in itself – is even more notable as an important springboard for the development of this distinctive way to moral rights.

In this chapter, I have shown something of what Aristotle and Confucius can learn from each other in the political realm and what a virtue-oriented politics that draws on Confucian and Aristotelian resources can offer to our contemporary discourse on rights. Even though I have spoken about the differences between familial and political amity in Aristotle and Confucius in the course of this chapter, I have yet to explore the metaphysical basis for their differences. As in previous chapters, such a metaphysics will prove to be a strength in Aristotle's account that can be used to remedy the lack of grounds for appeal in Confucius' account. At the same time, comparing Confucius' and Aristotle's views on amity also reveals a weakness in Aristotle's account that can be remedied by the strength in Confucius' view of human relationships. Getting clear about the strengths and weaknesses in their respective views of friendship, then, sheds light on the deep structure of human relationships that manifests itself, Aristotle and Confucius agree, in the highest of virtues.

7

Making Friends with Confucius and Aristotle

Confucius and Aristotle agree that friendship is central to the ethical life. Aristotle says that friendship is a virtue or involves virtue. Confucius says that the right kinds of friendship lead one to virtue.[1] Both believe that genuine friends exhibit certain virtues and help each other to cultivate them. They agree that friendship is pleasant as well as useful, though friendships based solely on pleasure or utility are deficient. Aristotle and Confucius concur that cultivation and expression of virtue is the main point of friendship and its service to human life.

The differences between Aristotelian and Confucian friendship flow from their metaphysics. As I have shown in earlier chapters, Aristotle's explicit metaphysics has no counterpart in original Confucianism. I will show how Aristotle's metaphysics leads him to divide friendship into three types and to order them hierarchically toward a focal sense that is most final, complete, and self-sufficient. Confucius makes no explicit distinction between kinds of friendship, though we can find examples in Confucius' *Analects* that fall roughly under the three Aristotelian types. This is not merely a failure to be explicit but is a symptom of metaphysical leanings that shape his own views about human beings and their relationships, knowledge, and actions.

Commentators agree that Confucius is more concerned with practice than theory, but they disagree about whether theorizing

---

[1] *Analects* 15.10, 1.8, 9.25, 8.2.

would be a useful supplement, an innocuous addition, or a serious detraction from the Confucian way. I argue that Aristotle's metaphysics can provide Confucius with a rationale for his claims about the priority of the friendship of virtue over the other types. On the other hand, Confucius' practical emphasis on human relationships presents its own theoretical challenge. I shall argue that Aristotle needs a more robust metaphysics of relations to deal adequately with friendship, especially the friendship of virtue.

The English term "friendship" is narrower than the Greek "*philia*," which refers to any number of emotionally toned forms of human bonding. Aristotle's *philia* includes parental, sibling, governing, spousal, and companion relationships. The Chinese term that is most akin to "friend" is *peng you*. Confucius has little to say about *peng you*[2] and mainly focuses on the familial and political relations in which these are embedded. Confucius speaks typically of the same five relationships as Aristotle's *philia*. He has no covering term for them, not even the term "relationship."[3] He merely refers to them as "the five" ways (*dao*). Aristotle's *philia* is a covering term for these relationships; its sense is not limited to *peng you* as one out of the five. "Friendship" in this chapter is meant to refer to human relationships with the same breadth as Aristotle's *philia* or Confucius' "five ways."

Friendship and community go together. For Aristotle, friendship in communities includes political and familial friendships. Such

---

[2] Sometimes comments in the *Analects* concern *peng you* more broadly, sometimes *peng* (fellow travelers or students of the same teacher) more specifically, or *you* (here, something more like a mentor, though the term can also mean "friend" more broadly). All of these are translated as "friend" or "friends" in English. This is misleading. For example, Confucius is faulted for saying that one should not take as a friend someone who is less virtuous than oneself. However, the remark is not about *peng you* generally but only about *you* in the more specific sense. Therefore, the gist of *Analects* 1.8 and 9.25 is that one should not relate to another as a mentor unless she is more virtuous. That is an entirely unobjectionable point. Oddly, though Roger Ames recognizes this distinction (Hall and Ames, *Thinking from the Han*, 257–69), it does not affect his translation (Ames and Rosemont, *The Analects of Confucius: A Philosophical Translation*, 230), which makes it seem, once again, as if Confucius were counseling that *in general* we should not befriend people unless they are moral superiors.

[3] The lack of a covering term for the "five" need not mean that this concept is not recognized by Confucius. Rather, it could mean that it is so pervasive that no covering term is needed.

friendships are possible when some sort of community is given,[4] and genuine community is possible only on the basis of a corresponding sort of friendship. Aristotle and Confucius agree that friendship involves commonality and sharing. What is common to friends will vary with the kind of community between them. For instance, a king's beneficence to his people consists of his care for them, while a parent's beneficence consists not only in his nurturing and educating them but also in his being their cause (*NE* 1162a6–7; see also 1161b18–19, 1161b27–30). Like Aristotle, Confucius recognizes not only friendships between equals but also friendships between unequals; i.e., people who are superior or inferior to their friends (19.3). Unlike the friendships of superiority between ruler and subjects or parents and children, the friendships among siblings or companions are more equal in sharing "the same feelings and character" (*NE* 1161a10–30).[5] All friendships are based on the

---

[4] *NE* 1161a33–37, 1162a9.

[5] Recent commentators have explored the connection between equal and unequal friendships, focusing especially on the relationship between filial obligations and virtue friendship. This is a topic that is important to Confucians because filial piety is a virtue that is intimately connected with the development of humaneness (*ren*, the highest Confucian virtue, where one extends his love for his family to others in the society). For instance, Nicholas Dixon, in "The Friendship Model of Filial Obligations," *Journal of Applied Philosophy* 12 (1995): 77–87, argues for an understanding of filial obligations that is based on the friendship model instead of institutional expectations or the repayment model. He claims that his friendship model is able to preserve and stress the voluntary and loving characteristics of parent–child relationships, contrary to Joseph Kupfer's assertions regarding the differences between parent–child and peer friendships (i.e., the lack of autonomy on the part of the child and the lack of independence on the part of both, upon which the voluntariness of the relationship is based). Dixon says, "Central to the friendship model is that the extent of filial obligations is determined by the extent of our friendly relations with our parents. Exactly the same holds in the case of peer friendships, where deeper friendships generate more extensive duties of friendship" (Dixon, "The Friendship Model of Filial Obligations," 83). Elizabeth Belfiore, in "Family Friendship in Aristotle's Ethics," *Ancient Philosophy* 21 (2001): 113–32, like Dixon, does not think that differences between the parent–child and peer friendships, such as the lack of equality and reciprocity (Belfiore, 128), should prevent significant links between family and complete friendship. In fact, even though she does not discuss the Confucian concept of filial piety, her claim is very akin to it in that she maintains that family friendship "is the origin of complete friendship. ... We first love and act as friends toward family members" (Belfiore, 114). James Schall, in "Friendship and Political Philosophy," *The Review of Metaphysics* 50 (1996): 121–41, would agree with Belfiore's finding the origin of complete friendship in family friendship, for he says: "Moreover, as Aristotle had

sharing of something good or pleasant, or at least something that seems so. What friends share, what goods they have in common, determines the kind of community that is constituted by their relationship.

Another point upon which both thinkers seem to agree concerns the issue of loyalty between friends and the question of when friendships should be dissolved. Aristotle maintains that one should stop loving a friend who becomes vicious because only what is good is lovable. However, he does not think that one should dissolve the friendship as soon as his friend becomes bad. Instead, Aristotle thinks that one should try to rescue his friend first and only leave him if he is incurably vicious. Another situation where Aristotle thinks one might stop befriending someone occurs when one friend becomes more virtuous while the other remains the same. Because they no longer enjoy the same things, they will no longer want to live together and remain friends. Nevertheless, Aristotle thinks that one must not act as if the friendship has never existed. He thinks that one should remember the friendship with the other and not treat the other as a total stranger as long as the other has not become totally vicious.

Confucius urges that one should try to lead his friends along the path of goodness (*shan*), but if they refuse to follow, then one ought to dissolve the friendship instead of disgracing oneself (12.23, 4.26). Confucius also agrees with Aristotle that friends should be similar in virtue, for he says, "Do not have as a friend anyone who is not as good as you are" (1.8, 9.25). Consequently, Confucius agrees with Aristotle that we will move on to new friendships. But he also maintains, like

intimated in the first book of the *Politics*, the condition of the household is the cornerstone of the structure of the *polis*. ... Perhaps it can be argued that the condition of friendship in the household is, in a sense, more important than the discussions of friendship in the *polis*" (Schall, 139). I think that Aristotle would agree with the claim that temporally, and for us, complete friendship originates in family friendship. However, I doubt that he would agree with Schall's claim that family friendships are more important than friendships in the *polis*. Just as Aristotle prioritizes the *polis* over the village and family, complete friendship in the *polis* takes precedence and is the focus of the others. See Chapter 6 for the reasons Aristotle distances his *polis* from the family. For Aristotle, these differences between the *polis* and the family account for most of the differences between his and Confucius' politics.

Aristotle, that old friends are to be accorded special treatment and not treated like total strangers. For example, he says, "Where exemplary persons ... do not neglect their old friends, the people will not be indifferent to each other" (8.2). He praises one of his student's respectful treatment of old friends (5.17) as an exemplification of being very good in his relations with others (see also 19.3).

It is clear from the foregoing that both thinkers notice that friendship can and should benefit both friends; both enjoin us to pursue certain sorts of friendships and dissolve others; and both direct us to the friendship of virtue as the sort to be pursued above all. The fact that both Aristotle and Confucius agree that we can be selective in our friendships (outside the family) also shows that friendship is a matter of choice rather than feelings that easily come and go.[6]

For example, Aristotle distinguishes between loving as a feeling and friendship as a state that requires a decision. As such, the reciprocity and capacity for choice that are needed for friendship entail that only human beings can be friends. Loving as a feeling can be expressed even toward soulless things for Aristotle (1157b29–33). Confucius, too, would agree that friendship is a choice because he tells us not to befriend someone who is not as good as oneself and warns us about the types of friends that are and are not beneficial to us. He says:

Having three kinds of friends will be a source of personal improvement; having three other kinds of friends will be a source of personal injury. One stands to be improved by friends who are true, who make good on their word, and who are broadly informed; one stands to be injured by friends who are ingratiating, who feign compliance, and who are glib talkers. (16.4)

Consequently, it is up to us to select the friends with whom we spend time and the types of activities that such friendships share.

However, it is again evident from the two texts that these authors differ with respect to the ways they think about friendship as being a choice. Aristotle's thinking about this matter is influenced by his view about the soul as a source of decision, whereas Confucius' thinking is

---

[6] See note 5, this chapter, for how some Aristotelian commentators disagree about the presence of choice in family friendships. See Chapter 6 for the differences between family friendships and friendships between citizens for Aristotle and Confucius.

not similarly informed. Nevertheless, there is nothing in Aristotle's analysis about the presence of a soul being the prerequisite for decision that is incompatible with what Confucius wants to maintain. On the contrary, like the stress that Confucius wishes to put on the friendship between good people, Confucius' injunction to befriend certain people while avoiding others may be strengthened or clarified by Aristotle's more metaphysical explanations, as I will show shortly.

Aristotle distinguishes, in *NE* 8, between friendships for utility, pleasure, and virtue. There is also contemplative friendship, which I will discuss. Aristotle claims that there are three types of objects that are lovable. They are the useful, the pleasant, and the good. It is the difference in object that causes the difference in the kind of friendship.

For Aristotle, friends for utility love each other only for their usefulness. They do not really enjoy each other but are together for some ulterior purpose; nor do they love each other for who the other is.[7] Because this kind of friendship turns most upon externalities, it is the lowest. Friends for pleasure are better because they enjoy the same activities and so enjoy being together insofar as they share the activities. Despite being superior to utility friendships, both of these friendships are incomplete because they are coincidental upon something external to their own substance and character, whether upon what the friends can provide or upon their easily changeable desires and interests.

The highest type of friendship is for virtue. The virtues of good people allow them to spend their lives pursuing a good for others that is also good for themselves. Because this effect is mutual in virtuous friendship, it is both useful and pleasant. Because virtuous people enjoy each other for who they are – and because their character is firm – their friendship is stable. Because they are virtuous in themselves, whom they love and the good they love are one and the same.

Confucius does not theorize about the different types of friendship or even distinguish them as types. Still, he provides examples

---

[7] For example, one may befriend the other for a ride to school, while the other may befriend one for class notes.

that fall roughly into the three Aristotelian types. Confucius also elevates friendship between virtuous people. He remarks on the usefulness of friends and the pleasure they bring.[8]

More resemblance exists between their views about virtuous friendship. The highest Confucian virtue is humaneness (*ren*). One who possesses *ren* extends his love for his family to others and tries to establish others.[9] Confucius encourages people who are already virtuous[10] and those striving for virtue[11] to befriend virtuous people. Befriending the virtuous helps the acquisition and retention of virtues. Thus, the friendship between good people is useful because they reinforce each other's virtues. Confucius' exemplary individual with *ren* also takes pleasure in virtuous friends[12] and enjoys their stable character.[13] For Confucius as for Aristotle, virtuous friendship is useful and pleasant. Although the master Confucian virtue *ren* is not identical to Aristotelian *dikaiosunê* or *phronêsis*, Aristotle and Confucius agree that virtuous friendship is the most important and is more useful and pleasant than the others.

Although he invokes and refers to three qualities of friendship, Confucius does not distinguish them sharply as types. Confucius has no theory that provides a basis for a distinction of types in a difference of objects. Nor does he lay out criteria and conditions of friendship such as loving the other for who he is, reciprocity, mutual awareness, and stability, all of which play a pivotal role in Aristotle's view. Nevertheless, these criteria and conditions are not in principle incompatible with what Confucius maintains. In fact, they may help him to justify beliefs about virtue and friendship that he exhorts us to adopt but for which he never offers a rationale.

---

[8] See *Analects* 1.1, where he discusses the joy that comes from visiting with friends. He also endorses the sentiment of Zengxi, who says in a delightful passage, "At the end of spring, with the spring clothes having already been finished, I would like, in the company of five or six young men and six or seven children, to cleanse ourselves in the Yi River, to revel in the cool breezes at the Altar for Rain, and then return home singing" (11.26).

[9] *Analects* 1.2, 6.30, 12.22, 13.19. Humane people "establish others in seeking to establish themselves and promote others in seeking to get there themselves" (6.30). Confucius says that, "Filial and fraternal responsibility ... is the basis of humaneness" (1.2). Hence, proper family relationships are the root of all virtue.

[10] *Analects* 1.8, 9.25.   [11] *Analects* 15.10, 16.4, 16.5.   [12] *Analects* 16.5.

[13] *Analects* 6.23, 6.20.

Aristotle's ethics flows from an understanding of purposive nature thriving in actualization, Confucius' from a sense of concord in relations and balance among ingredients. Aristotle's agents operate from deliberation among options based on reasonable judgment, Confucius' from an almost aesthetic sense of what is fitting and fine, based on a sensibility cultivated in ceremony and ritual that is virtually heedless of crises and strong alternatives.[14] Confucius provides no metaphysical supplement to his ethical reflections, and therefore readers must ferret out for themselves the metaphysical implications of Confucian observations and pronouncements. Still, in a rough and preliminary way, we can say that Aristotle's metaphysics is substantialist and (in one sense of the term) individualist, while Confucius' is processive and relationalistic.

There is a reason in metaphysics for Aristotle's distinction and ranking of the types of friendship. This is the same reason he ranks the life of *theôria* higher than the life of *phronêsis*. The reason is Aristotle's three senses of substance, only one of which is focal, paramount, and the basis of and final cause for the others.[15] The three senses of substance or form are: (i) the concrete substance, which consists of this form and this matter indissolubly together; (ii) the species form, which contains a reference to matter taken generally and is known as a universal of the formula "this *kind* of form together with this *kind* of matter"; and (iii) the pure form, which is the final cause considered by itself,[16] also known as a universal because it is essentially the same in every instance. Aristotle's soul doctrine also tracks these three senses. If we were pure minds, we would not have

---

[14] *Analects* 8.8, 16.13, 20.3.

[15] I have argued for these distinctions and correlations more elaborately in "Senses of Being in Aristotle's *Nicomachean Ethics*," in *The Crossroads of Norm and Nature: Essays on Aristotle's* Ethics *and* Metaphysics, 51–77, but want to sketch the view here as an aid to interpretation. See also Julie K. Ward's "Focal Reference in Aristotle's Account of Φιλία: *Eudemian Ethics* VII 2," *Apeiron* 28 (1995): 183–205, especially 202–3, where she offers three reasons for the primacy of virtue friendship. Even though Ward appeals to Aristotle's analysis of primary substance in the *Metaphysics* also to argue for the primacy of virtue friendship, her account is unlike mine in that she does not discuss the different senses of substance (i.e., concrete, species form, and pure form) and how their relations to primary substance can explain how the other kinds of friendship relate to virtue friendship.

[16] Or formal cause; they are the same in every natural whole.

the appetites, desires, and emotions that spring from our composite nature. The nonrational part of the soul corresponds to the concrete sense of substance; i.e., this form plus this matter. Because matter is variable, the emotions admit qualitative differences and so we may be more or less virtuous or vicious. Friendships for utility and pleasure are ways in which an individual caters to his individual needs and pleasures.[17] Because the nonrational part of the soul concerns individual needs and pleasures, it is also the part that concerns friendships for utility and pleasure. And because the nonrational part corresponds to the concrete substance or composite, the composite also corresponds to these two types of friendship.[18]

Just as primary substance is the most complete sense of substance, the friendship of virtue is the most complete sense of friendship. But there are two parts to rational soul and two further senses of substance in Aristotle's metaphysics. Each corresponds to a life of excellence, practical and theoretical. Thus, there are really two types of virtue friendship: practical and contemplative.[19]

---

[17] An individual's needs and pleasures are to be distinguished from the utility and pleasure that the virtuous person pursues. Whereas the former are good to an individual because of his particular desires and circumstances (e.g., his building a third house just for himself), the latter are unconditionally good (e.g., the virtuous act of housing the homeless is unconditionally useful and pleasant). Andrew Payne, in "Character and the Forms of Friendship in Aristotle," *Apeiron* 33 (2000): 53–74, recognizes this distinction when he says, "To summarize, Aristotle sees the difference between the good and pleasant unconditionally and the good and pleasant to someone as marking the difference between what is good and pleasant to the virtuous due to their interest in virtuous activity, and what is used and enjoyed by particular people because of their needs, physical debilities, or defects of character" (Payne, 68). The distinction between pleasures and utilities that are good to someone and those that are unconditionally good is also exemplified by Aristotle's discourse on self-love. See, for instance, Charles Kahn's "Aristotle and Altruism," *Mind* 90 (1981): 20–40. Kahn contrasts two kinds of self-love, that of the "morally inferior men who identify themselves with, and hence seek to gratify, 'their appetites and in general their emotions or passions (*pathê*) and the irrational element of the psychê'" and "the admirable self-love of good men," who seek "the excellence and pleasure of the good life," which is the activity of the true self (i.e., *nous*), which is responsible for rational deliberations and speculations (Kahn, 30–31). By focusing on the nonrational part of the soul that corresponds to the concrete substance, I am also focusing on the utility and pleasure to an individual himself rather than the utility and pleasure that are unconditionally good.

[18] Albeit in different respects.

[19] Kahn, in "Aristotle and Altruism," recognizes these two parts of the rational soul and their corresponding excellence. He says, "Insofar as my friend's life exhibits

For Aristotle, the rational part of the soul is divided into the deliberative part, perfected in the virtue of practical wisdom, and the speculative part, perfected in contemplative wisdom. The deliberative part corresponds to the Aristotelian species form.[20]

The deliberative soul corresponds to the species form because the deliberative part is responsible for undertaking an action that is either good or bad, which is determined by its form or essence. Because what is good follows from something's form or function, there is a good for action that is the same for all human beings because they share a specific form or function. This point is more subtle than many people make it out to be. Because actions deal with things that are changeable, the corresponding sense of substance must take account of this changeable aspect but must do so in a general way. The sense of substance that can account for both the specific sameness (the good for all human beings) and the variable aspect taken generally is the species form, which consists of the form and matter taken universally. Morally virtuous friends are not concerned merely with their own needs and pleasures but with a good that is the specifically human good made relative to their particular abilities and circumstances. The good for human beings in general is determined by their species form, which is the basis for virtue friendships. Without this there would be either a collection of particular goods[21] or solely a divine good that seems rather too much for a human being.[22]

Finally, consider the speculative part, whose excellent functioning makes up the highest good. Unlike deliberation, which is concerned with actions, speculation is concerned with contemplating first principles and causes that are immaterial and unchanging. Whereas the deliberative part is inseparable from matter and motion, the speculative part is separable from matter and motion, as are its objects. Indeed the ultimate object of *nous* is itself. The speculative part with its virtue corresponds to the pure form among Aristotle's

the activity of the same rational principle which is active in me, his rationality and hence the moral and intellectual excellence of his life do in fact belong to me, since they are the proper work of a principle which is mine as much as his" (Kahn, 39).

[20] Recall that this is the form considered in relation to its matter taken generally.

[21] That is, if there were only concrete substances without a universal.

[22] That is, if there were only a pure unenmattered form.

senses of being. Clearly, the relevant type of friendship is some sort of friendship of virtue – not the practical sort but rather "contemplative friendship," the sort Aristotle means when he says that one can think better with friends of the right sort.[23]

Charles Kahn explains the hierarchy in Aristotle's three kinds of friendship by focusing on two different kinds of self-love (Kahn, "Aristotle and Altruism," 30, and see note 17, this chapter). Even though Kahn does not explicitly distinguish the second kind of self-love (i.e., the "admirable self-love of good men") into two types that will correspond to my division of virtue friendship into two types, namely practical and contemplative, there is evidence that Kahn's second kind of self-love is divisible into two types that will correspond to my two virtue friendships. For example, Kahn maintains that the true self is the "impersonal" or "superpersonal principles of reason (*nous*)" (Kahn, "Aristotle and Altruism," 38) that are common to all human beings. The good man's self-love is his commitment to the excellent functioning of this principle (i.e., virtue), which is the same in everyone. Hence, one can take the same pleasure in another's 'happiness as in one's own. Nevertheless, Kahn also recognizes that there is a sense in which one is not identical with one's friend for Aristotle. Specifically, despite the sameness of *nous* in everyone, Kahn says that "the mode and circumstances of its activity are inevitably different for each of us ... [and] the concrete problems on which, and the conditions in which, reason is exercised will differ from person to person" (Kahn, "Aristotle and Altruism," 39). More explicitly, even though friends who are morally virtuous share the same *nous* that is responsible for rational deliberation, the situations within which they exercise their deliberations are different and hence they are not identical with each other. On the other hand, friends who share the virtue of speculation are identical because their lives exhibit "the activity of the same rational principle" (Kahn, "Aristotle and Altruism," 39).[24] As such, Kahn's analysis of

---

[23] *NE* 1170b13.

[24] Dennis McKerlie, in "Friendship, Self-love, and Concern for Others in Aristotle's Ethics," *Ancient Philosophy* 11 (1991): 85–101, would agree, for he says: "The good man's concern for himself depends on his awareness of the goodness of his thoughts and perceptions. The same is true of his concern for his friend. The friend's life also consists in the activities of thinking and perceiving. Since the

true self-love that manifests itself in the superiority of speculation over moral activities is similar to my analysis of the superiority of the theoretical life over practical life, which in my view can be explained by the superiority of the third over the second sense of substance in Aristotle.[25]

Although Aristotle makes room for contemplative friendship – indeed his teaching requires it – we may still ask why he considers it the highest friendship. We need only look to his criteria for the primacy of substance to see that the form alone is higher because form is prior to matter and prior therefore to the composite and even to the species form. Primary substance must be individual, knowable, definable, prior in time, and be cause rather than effect (*Met.* 1028a29–b1). Hence the primary activity must be self-sufficient, continuous, and final so that it is a cause that is never an effect and an end that is never a means to any further end. The concrete individual substance is perishable and so does not satisfy the conditions of

---

friend is good these activities will contain goodness" (McKerlies, 95). The goodness of *nous*' activity, then, is the basis for one's self-love and one's love for his friend in contemplative friendships.

[25] It is interesting to note that Andrew Payne would disagree with Kahn's characterization of the first kind of self-love as the selfish kind, in contrast to the second kind, which Kahn characterizes as admirable. Payne does not think that utility friends are necessarily more selfish than virtue friends because he maintains that the latter are just as self-interested as the former. Payne thinks that the main difference between utility and virtue friendships is that utility friends "focus on what is good for someone rather than on what is good unconditionally" (Payne, "Character and the Forms of Friendship in Aristotle," 70). I think that Kahn is correct in asserting that utility friends are more selfish than virtue friends. This is because utility friends are more centered on what is good for themselves, unlike virtue friends, who focus on the unconditional good or virtue (i.e., what is good for everyone). Because this unconditional good, especially the activity of contemplation, is not restricted to specific individuals and circumstances – in fact, according to Kahn's analysis, it is identical to the active intellect itself, which is totally impersonal – loving this *nous* is indeed unselfish because this principle is totally independent of us and is "one and the same for all human beings" (Kahn, 37). See my earlier discussion in this chapter for why genuine self-love is unselfish for Aristotle. See also Robert Sokolowski's "Friendship and Moral Action in Aristotle," *The Journal of Value Inquiry* 35 (2001): 355–69, where he says: "If we are to be capable of true friendship, we must be able to take a distance to our own, and not let our interests predominate. A person who puts his own interests forward in an unjust manner will not be capable of the more refined benevolence that friendship requires. He will be capable of friendships of utility and pleasure, but not of noble friendship" (Sokolowski, 358).

priority, definability, or knowability (though it is prior in time of generation). Second substance or species form satisfies the criteria of definability and knowability but fails to satisfy the criteria of individuality and self-sufficiency, finality, and temporal and causal priority. Only the substantial form itself satisfies all the criteria because it is unencumbered by matter or even general reference to matter.

This ontological hierarchy among composite, species form, and substantial form is the basis of the hierarchy among the four types of friendship. The superior friendship is more self-sufficient, continuous, and final. Even though friendships for utility and pleasure are based on the concrete substance, pleasure friendships are superior to utility friendships because a friend for pleasure loves the other for who he is to a certain degree (i.e., his being as a person) rather than for what he can supply her (e.g., the accidental goods that are coincidental to him). This is consistent with the fact that there are better and worse ways of satisfying our individual appetites and emotions. One who pursues virtue friendships is better than those who pursue pleasure friendships because what the former loves is not just a concrete individual or substance but how the friend represents the pursuit of what is good for all human beings and hence the love of human good. This is even more stable than the love of the concrete individual, just as the latter is more stable than the love of some accidental goods. This is why contemplative friendship is even better than virtue friendship. One can contemplate the truth more continuously, and the truth at issue is more final and self-sufficient. Similarly, *nous* is also more knowable. Of course, only *nous* knows this. Therefore, it is most self-sufficient, being at once the object and the substance responsible for the activity. This provides us, incidentally, with a better understanding of how Aristotle justifies friendship on the basis of self-love. The human self at its core is *nous*. As shown earlier, this alone fulfills Aristotle's criteria for primary substance. Because *nous* satisfies these criteria, it is the best part of us and hence is most lovable. The fact that Aristotle's self-love is primarily and essentially love of and by *noêsis* shows why it is not egoistic. Aristotelian self-love is not egoistic because *nous* is not the locus of desire and craving, caprice and fantasy. Moreover, one contemplative *nous* is just like another, both in what it is – its unchanging activity – and in what it knows. Aristotle's statement that a friend is another self can refer to the fact that a human friend is another composite whole with a similar body and desires; it can refer to the fact that the other is a member of the same species who shares universal properties; it can refer to the fact that when one is contemplating one is not just abstractly the same as the other but actually shares the identical activity with the identical objects.[26]

There is no systematic, metaphysically grounded account of friendship in Confucius. He does not recommend a notion of primary substance nor consider theory to be superior to practice. Confucius constantly stresses being able to put into practice what one knows. He says that he worries about failing to practice what he has learned and failing to execute what he understands to be appropriate (*yi*) (7.3). He says, "If people can recite all of the three hundred *Songs* and yet when given official responsibility, fail to perform effectively, or when sent to distant quarters, are unable to act on their own

---

[26] There are fascinating twists of Aristotelian thought in what can be called the paradoxes of noetic friendship. For example, it might seem as if (1) noetic friendship is impossible because when *nous* is contemplating, it is itself thinking itself by itself. Therefore, it is wholly self-involved and not able to befriend the other, so noetic friendship is impossible. But (1′) *nous* can know another *nous* as another itself and could not do otherwise. Therefore, *nous* loves the other as it loves itself if it loves at all. (2) Love is bound up with incompleteness, want, and dependency even if they do not define it. *Nous* is complete and self-sufficient. Therefore *nous* cannot love. (2′) *Nous* can recognize itself and therefore can recognize itself in the activities of embodied beings. *Nous*, as the best part of the rational soul, is the form of the human body. Therefore, *nous* can love when it recognizes itself in the activities of a human body because there and perhaps there alone it recognizes itself in something *other*. (3) One would not wish that a friend become divine, according to Aristotle. *Nous* is best and most divine. Therefore, one would not wish that his friend identify with his *nous*. As a consequence, one would not wish what is best for one's friend. Moreover, because Aristotle says that one is *nous* most of all, one would not wish that his friend be most himself, lest a relationship with him be impossible. But (3′) identity is the strongest form of relationship. Because *nous* is always formally identical with *nous*, when two people achieve contemplative friendship, far from being separate they are in this sense identical. The appearance of paradox in these and other instances is a consequence of failing to follow the shifts of meaning in Aristotle's *pros hen* equivocation. We are not *nous* without qualification but only in a respect. In a sense, we are composite beings, and in another sense we are substantial forms. In a sense, *noêsis* is capable of friendship, and in another sense it achieves something (a sort of identity) better than friendship. Qua friend, *nous* is the form of a particular body; qua *archê nous* is agent intellect – thought thinking itself. I am grateful to Wes DeMarco for urging me to get clearer about these apparent paradoxes regarding *nous* and friendship.

initiative, then even though they have mastered so many of them, what good are they to them?" (13.5). Confucius emphasizes the practical applications of learning and regards impracticality as evidence of worthlessness – quite different from Aristotle, who celebrates *theôria* precisely because of its uselessness.

Confucius would also reject the use of certain qualities, such as self-sufficiency and finality, as standards or criteria for the superiority of contemplation and contemplative friendship. Confucius does not subscribe to many of the criteria that mark out the senses of substance and friendship. Accordingly, he would neither agree with Aristotle that contemplation of self-sufficient and unchanging objects is the highest of human activities nor agree that friends sharing such activities are superior to friends sharing moral virtue.

Confucius, like Aristotle, prizes the stability and constancy of good character.[27] Unlike Aristotle, he does not prize the ideal of final and unchanging knowledge of first principles and causes. Instead, Confucius stresses constant progress in knowledge and improvement in wisdom.[28] It is not that Confucius treasures instability or values uncertainty. Rather, learning never ceases, and even the stability of character is a constant commitment to improvement. There is no ultimate success: one is always on the way.[29]

This disagreement about the certainty and stability of knowledge also leads to a disagreement about the wise man's fallibility. Because Aristotle holds that *nous* grasps eternal truths, the one with *sophia* will grasp the truth infallibly and the *phronimos* will invariably act rightly and exercise the virtues so that he will always take pleasure in the

---

[27] *Analects* 6.23.

[28] Confucius contrasts people who seek knowledge and wisdom with people who pursue humane practice by comparing the unceasing flow of a river with the endurance of a mountain. As he puts it: "The wise take delight in water; the humane take delight in mountains. The wise are active; the humane are still. The wise enjoy; the humane endure" (6.23). The wise are compared to the unceasing flow of water, while the humane are compared to the solidity and enduringness of the mountain.

[29] Because Confucius enjoins us to improve ourselves unceasingly, and because he also recommends befriending people who are as good as we are, it seems to follow that Confucius will endorse our continually seeking out new friends who match up with our current state of development (but see note 2, this chapter). This implication seems at odds with the standard caricature of Confucius as staid and conservative.

right objects, do what is right, and be without regrets.[30] On the contrary, Confucius maintains that even someone with the highest virtue of humanity is fallible. He says, "There have been occasions when an exemplary person fails to act in a humane way" (14.6). These thinkers' respective positions on the fallibility of the virtuous reflect their respective positions on whether one can attain ultimate knowledge or wisdom. Whereas Aristotle would say that one can attain ultimate theoretical and practical wisdom, Confucius would respond that no one is so wise that her knowledge is permanent or her virtue faultless.[31]

Confucius does not prize self-sufficiency. He repeatedly observes that we always act out roles in contexts according to some normative pattern of practice. Not only would Confucius disparage thinking for the sake of thinking, he would be dismayed by Aristotle's elevation of self-sufficiency. Human relations in the Confucian vision are not externally linked self-sufficiencies, and friendship is no mere "external good." Rather, genuine friendship is a matter of the deep interpenetration of human lives.[32] Confucius would worry that Aristotelian *autarkeia* would direct us away from useful practice, would skew our sense of ourselves and others, and would constitute a dubious touchstone for ethics or metaphysics. We have already seen that Aristotle links love of others with self-love. Confucius would agree. For neither thinker is self-love a matter of egoism – ethical or otherwise – but rather is to be understood in parallel with their observation that helping to develop the friend's character develops one's own character. Given that linkage, neither man seems worried about mixed motives. Beyond this, there are differences. Aristotle holds that the virtuous person is self-sufficient and the contemplative most self-sufficient of all. The thinker who is "well supplied with topics for study" (1166a26) will enjoy spending time with himself and loving himself because his whole soul will desire the same things,

---

[30] *NE* (9.4) 1166a27–29, (6.5) 1140b23–25, (6.9) 1142b27–28, (6.13) 1144a24–27.

[31] Confucius argues that without ongoing learning, even actions that are humane, courageous, and truthful (*xin*) would be flawed (17.8; see also 5.28 and 8.13).

[32] This interpenetration of lives is the matrix of all virtue, and its home base is the family. If one does not know how to conduct himself appropriately toward his father and brothers, he will not know how to conduct himself appropriately toward his superiors, inferiors, and equals in society.

namely the contemplative objects (1166a13–18, 22–23, 25–26). Confucius, too, believes that the virtuous man is one who loves himself though not because of his ability to be self-sufficient in practice or ultimately his contemplation of eternal objects.

Because there is no recognition of eternal objects or an unchanging activity in which these could exist and be known, nor is there a trajectory of thinking toward self-sufficiency and finality, there is no contemplative friendship in Confucius. Confucius does not seem to believe in – or at any rate is not interested in – a set of eternal verities that friends could contemplate conjointly. He neither recognizes nor endorses the systematic investigation of determinate forms, first principles, and causes that is Aristotelian science. But the most important differences between Aristotle and Confucius can, I think, be traced to the values and standards that shape each man's view of action and knowledge.

Confucius was not exactly a prophet of a new age. He did not claim to originate a system of thought but presented himself rather as a scholar of antiquities, recommending the way of life of the earlier Zhou dynasty.[33] Although he did justify his endorsement, he did not argue for it. He offered no system of moral principles or rules by which to measure and regulate conduct. The lack of argument and rules leads many in the West to deny Confucius the title of "philosopher."[34]

Much of Confucian ethics is something like what you would get if you took the parts of Aristotle about modeling and cultivation, and habit and context, and subtracted the soul doctrine and metaphysics of human nature. The craft analogy that Aristotle invoked is ubiquitous in Confucius. He has the sense that virtue is not a matter of

---

[33] *Analects* 7.28.

[34] However, more recently, a few have celebrated it and urged a Confucian turn toward an ethic of manners and style. This is marketed as an edifying philosophy that can help the West recover from the errors perpetrated by the likes of Plato and Aristotle, and Kant and Hegel. These authors recommend Confucius on the basis that his ethic of social style is the only ethic we need – and really the only ethic any society ever has. They are skeptical about philosophical argument and metaphysical appeals. But much of this book is devoted to showing that some more justifying argument and even a little metaphysics would be a great help to Confucian tradition, in itself and in fostering dialogue with other traditions of virtues and rights.

rules and applications but of trained sensibilities and skills. The difficulty is that all of the content comes from the social practices, so that criticism and development of those practices do not come easily and have no higher court of appeal.

Confucius teaches concordance. By attending to analogies between harmonious ethical relationships and congruous harmonies in other areas of life,[35] we may eventually learn modes of perception and action directed to the proper, balanced, and fitting. We are to cultivate responsiveness, taste, and a sense of ethical style by training our sensitivity to consonance and balance.[36] This is less a matter of reasoning and justification than of acquiring a taste for harmony, a sense of it, and a thirst for it.

Original Confucianism focuses on refined examples of concord in ceremonious ritual and other social observances.[37] These are used as analogies for moral bearing and conduct. It is possible, however, to run the analogies in the opposite direction, from the moral to other human practices – arts and sciences and so on – and even to the nonhuman cosmos. Then the correspondences would resonate more widely. Attention to the large-scale correspondences between the analogies among the harmonies would be the Confucian way of contemplation.[38]

Aristotelian contemplation is directed to the principles themselves – or to the Being whose being sustains the principles. This contemplative attitude does not rest with the embodiment of principles in various objects or different fields, though it might begin with them. One exception is Aristotle's *Poetics*, where organic form and its principles shimmer through the *mythos* of tragedy. Mostly the contemplative attitude appears in the special science of metaphysics, or at the far end of natural science, at the end of wonder. Perhaps Aristotle could learn from Confucius the more aesthetic sense of

---

[35] Human and nonhuman life (17.9).

[36] Confucianism is directed toward cultivating a fine sensibility that can perceive what is concordant and what is not, that will desire it, and that can acquire the skill to effect it.

[37] Although there are examples from the natural world as well.

[38] Perhaps general principles (such as *zhong*) might offer themselves for consideration. Original Confucianism has very little to say about this (see, however, *Zhongyong* 1.2). I say more about this in Chapter 4.

contemplation that rests with an enjoyment of the sensuous embodiments of principle and form.

If Confucius could acquire a taste for metaphysics and Aristotle could expand the sphere of contemplation to include the enjoyment of harmonious relationships as embodiments of ultimate principles, it just might be the start of a beautiful friendship.

Glossary of Chinese Terms

bianshi	砭石
bu zhi	不 及
cheng	誠
da ren	大 人
dao	道
de	德
duan	端
fa	發
he	和
he wai nei	合 外 内
ji	己
jin	近
jing	敬
junzi	君 子
kuo	過
li	里
li	利
li	禮
li fa	曆 法
ming	名
qiang	強
ren	人
ren	仁

ren ren	仁人
ru	如
shan	善
shan dao	善道
shen	身
Shennong bencaojing	神农本草经
shu	恕
tian	天
tian ming	天命
tian wen	天文
wai	外
wanwu	萬物
wei	未
wen	文
wu	吾
wu dao	無道
wu qiang	無疆
Wushier Bingfang	五十二病方
wuxing	五行
xian	贤
xiangke	相克
xiangsheng	相生
xiao	孝
xiao ren	小人
xin	心
xin	信
xing	行
xing	性
xue	学
yan	言
yang	阳
yi	義
yi	宜
yin	阴
yong	庸
yong	勇

yu	欲
yue	樂
zheng	正
zhengming	正名
zhi	知
zhong	中
zhong	忠
Zhongyong	中庸
Zhou	周
Zhou li	周禮
zi	自

Name Index

Ji, Kangzi, 177
Jordan, David K., 170

Kahn, Charles, 202, 204, 205
Kant, Immanuel, 21, 210
Kenny, Anthony, 40, 122
Keyt, David, 168
King, Ambrose Y.C., 169, 170
King Wen, 67, 178
King Wu, 67, 130, 178
King Zhao, 163, 127
Kraut, Richard, 30, 189
Kupfer, Joseph, 196

Lao-tzu. See *Laozi*
Laozi, 79
Lee, Kwang-Sae, 142–43
Legge, James, 41, 43, 58, 100, 101, 102, 124, 139, 179
Leighton, Stephen, 107, 109, 110
Lisowski, Peter, 90, 95
Lloyd, Geoffrey Ernest Richard, 76, 81, 88, 89, 90
Lord of Wey, 82
Losin, Peter, 107, 110
Loux, Michael, 34

MacIntyre, Alasdair, 3, 7, 9, 10, 21, 22, 24, 25, 49–50, 59, 61–62, 69–70, 189
Martin, Michael R., 37
McKerlee, Dennis, 204
Mencius, 79, 138, 139–41, 163–64
Mengzi, 138. See also *Mencius*
Mill, John Stuart, 21
Miller, Fred D., 168, 189
Mulgan, Richard G., 170, 175
Munro, Donald, 81, 169

Nakayama, Shigeru, 81
Nietzsche, Friedrich, 4, 21
Nussbaum, Martha C., 158, 170

O'Meara, Dominic J., 34
Osamu, Kanaya, 100

Payne, Andrew, 202, 205
Plato, 26, 40, 45, 79, 80, 135, 180, 210
Polansky, Ronald, 107

Qing Bing of Zhao, 163

Ranyou, 52
Reeve, C. David Charles, 30, 41, 122
Roetz, Heiner, 23, 42–43, 127, 163
Rorty, Richard, 44
Rorty, Amelie O., 31, 141
Rosemont, Henry, 25, 35, 121, 143
Ross, William David, 30
Ruskola, Teemu H., 154

Schall, James, 196, 197
Schwartz, Benjamin, 25, 40–41, 45–46, 47, 127, 156
Sherman, Nancy, 40, 41
Shizhu of Chu, 127, 163
Shun, Kwong-loi, 117, 159
Sidgwick, Henry, 30
Sim, May, 36, 40, 56, 157
Simpson, Peter, 170
Sivin, Nathan, 81, 90
Socrates, 45, 79
Sokolowski, Robert, 205
Strauss, Leo, 189

Tiles, James E., 110
Tu Weiming, 9, 21, 22, 25, 26, 45, 46–47, 101, 102, 104, 122, 128, 129–30, 131, 161, 169
Tuozzo, Thomas, 107–8

Van Norden, Bryan W., 138, 159

Waley, Arthur, 179
Walzer, M., 44
Wang, Qing-Jie, 44–45
Ward, Julie K., 201
Warner, Richard, 34
Welton, William A., 107
Whitehead, Alfred North, 23

Xunzi, 140–41

Yabuuti, Kiyosi, 88, 89, 90
Yack, Bernard, 175, 175
Yao, Xinzhong, 157, 162

Zheng (Master Zheng), 28
Zhu Xi, 4, 122

Subject Index

active intellect. *See* agent intellect
actuality, 35, 46, 126, 135, 136, 137, 148, 157. *See also* actuality, first; actuality, second; *energeia*
actuality, first, 136, 137. *See also* form, substantial; *psychê*; soul; substance
actuality, second, 137
aesthetic, 2, 4, 51, 72, 149, 201, 211
aesthetic sense, 4, 201, 211
aestheticism, 2
affect, 128. *See also* affection; emotions; *pathê*
affection (category), 51, 54
affection (feeling), 51, 54, 55, 117
agent intellect, 205, 207
aitia, 76. *See also* cause
altruism, 20
amity, 19, 116, 172, 173, 174, 192, 193. *See also* friendship
anison, 51
apodeixis, 76, 77
appetite, 29, 39, 103, 125, 140, 141, 147, 148, 202, 206
appropriateness. See *yi*
archai, 77
arête, 6, 52, 109, 151
aristocracy, 176, 177
astronomy, 73, 89, 90, 91, 97, 98
attitude, 42, 57, 66, 67, 87, 120, 160, 161, 179, 211
autarkeia, 209. *See also* self-sufficiency
autarkês, 35

authoritative conduct, 28, 50, 83, 112, 116, 117, 120, 138, 139, 145, 161, 169
authoritative measure, 73
authoritative person, 24, 25, 26, 28, 80, 85, 86, 144, 145, 161, 188. *See also* exemplary individual; *junzi*; *phronimos*; *spoudaios*
authoritative practice, 3, 5, 7, 75, 76. See also *li*
authoritative tradition, 127. See also *li*
autonomous individual, 12, 21, 142, 162
autonomy, 12, 21, 189, 190, 196
Axial Age, 23, 127, 163

being, senses of, 108, 135, 157, 201, 203
benevolence, 7, 50, 166, 169. See also *ren*
bianshi, 94
Book of Documents, 152
Book of Songs, 38, 39, 68, 82, 85, 97, 121, 146, 147, 178, 179, 207
bu zhi, 101, 102
buyi, 33, 54

calendar reform, 10, 73–74, 75, 89–91, 98. See also *zhengming*
calendar studies, 88–90
cardinal virtues, 139
care, 14, 43–45, 55, 57, 66, 191, 196
cause, 34, 35, 60, 64, 76, 77, 78, 92, 134, 135, 137, 164, 185, 196, 201, 205. See also *aitia*

219